SEVEN WAYS OF LOOKING AT RELIGION

SEVEN WAYS OF LOOKING AT RELIGION

The Major Narratives

BENJAMIN SCHEWEL

Yale

UNIVERSITY PRESS

New Haven and London

Published with assistance from the foundation established in memory of Amasa Stone Mather of the Class of 1907, Yale College.

Yale University Press books may be purchased in quantity for educational, business, or promotional use. For information, please e-mail sales.press@yale.edu (U.S. office) or sales@yaleup.co.uk (U.K. office).

Set in Janson type by IDS Infotech Ltd.
Printed in the United States of America.

Library of Congress Control Number: 2016963571
ISBN 978–0–300–21847–3 (hardcover : alk. paper)

A catalogue record for this book is available from the British Library.

This paper meets the requirements of ANSI/NISO Z39.48–1992 (Permanence of Paper).

10 9 8 7 6 5 4 3 2 1

For Keri

Contents

Acknowledgments

This is a book I always wanted to read but could never find. So I decided to write it, and it took me nearly a decade to figure out what to say. I therefore must first and foremost thank my teachers Peter Ochs, Kevin Hart, and William Desmond, without whom I would have never been able to imagine, much less complete, this book.

My research has benefited from regular conversations with numerous friends and colleagues. Many of the concepts and ideas I present in the following pages arose through my ongoing discussions with Gerald Filson and Christopher Schwartz. I must thank Farzam Arbab and Sona Farid-Arbab for helping me think about the methodological aspects of this work. I am also grateful to the Faculty of Divinity at the University of Cambridge, where I worked on this project as a visiting graduate student during the 2013–2014 academic year, and to the Institute for Advanced Studies in Culture at the University of Virginia, where I had the pleasure of revising this manuscript during the 2014–2015 academic year. In particular, I am indebted to Charles Mathewes for organizing an all-day workshop on this book at the institute and for providing thoughtful feedback on the entire manuscript.

Finally, I want to thank my parents, Michael Schewel and Priscilla Burbank, and my wife, Kerilyn Schewel, for their ongoing efforts to help me bring this book to completion. To Kerilyn in particular, let me say that none of this would have been possible without your tireless love and constant support.

Introduction

WESTERN INTELLECTUALS HAVE LONG theorized that religion would undergo a process of marginalization and decline as the forces of modernity advanced. Indeed, this framework of "secularization" is one of the few theories to have achieved "a truly paradigmatic status within the modern social sciences." Secularization theory reached its peak influence during the middle decades of the twentieth century, when global affairs seemed to corroborate its basic claims. "Like dying supernovae," three analysts explain, "every major religion on every continent seemed to be rapidly losing its influence on politics, economics, and culture." It was with these dynamics in mind that sociologist Peter Berger announced to readers of the *New York Times* in 1968 that "by the 21st century, religious believers are likely to be found only in small sects, huddled together to resist a worldwide secular culture."[1]

Yet secularization theory has fallen on hard times in the intervening years. The main cause of this disruption has been the so-called resurgence of religion in public settings throughout the world. Examples include the Six-Day War between Israel and Egypt, the Iranian Revolution, Hindu nationalism in India, Buddhist nationalism in Sri Lanka, Catholicism's role in overthrowing communism in Eastern Europe, prominent movements of religiously inspired nonviolent civil disobedience, the rise of evangelical conservatism in the United States, the appearance of

Liberation Theology in South America, and the emergence of radical Islamism, to name a few. Demographic studies have also played a part by highlighting the enduringly high levels of religious belief in both the quintessentially "modern" United States and the world at large.[2] Proliferating critiques of secularization theory have additionally disclosed the theory's many class-based and Eurocentric assumptions, as well as its deep involvement in European colonialism. As a result, scholars have rightly concluded that a "straightforward narrative of progress from the religious to the secular" is no longer viable today.[3]

Nevertheless, it is not yet clear what kind of narrative we should be telling instead. Certainly, scholars generally agree that religion has evolved from its tribal beginnings through the so-called archaic, axial, and medieval periods, up through modernity, and into the current global age. But it is by no means clear what dynamics have driven this process forward. Perhaps secularization theory was basically true and the contemporary resurgence of religion is only a last-ditch effort on the part of religious believers to halt their own demise. Or perhaps religion has been historically developing and improving, such that each stage of religious history, including the current one, is somehow better or more complex than what came before. Alternatively, maybe religion developed and improved until a certain point but has since been losing its force. Or religion might be neither developing nor declining, but rather transforming in a more neutral way. It could even be that "religion" never existed at all, but has simply been constructed in the modern West and then exported throughout the world. Well-regarded thinkers are today actively arguing for each of these perspectives.

The persistence of narrative plurality may seem strange to those who imagine that disciplined empirical research would have, by now, proven which narrative is best. Unfortunately, this has not been the case. In some places religion is declining. In others it is resurging. In others still, religion remains just as influential as it has been for centuries before, albeit now in a distinctly modern form. How, then, should we go about choosing between the various narratives that are currently being advanced?

Whatever solution we may ultimately adopt, we should begin by making sure that all the options are clearly understood. How many major narratives of religious history exist? By whom are they employed? How do they each operate? What stages of religious history do they describe? How do they characterize contemporary dynamics of religious change? What future trajectories do they envision? The goal of this book is to answer these questions.

Seven Narratives

My basic claim is that the contemporary academic discourse on religion pivots around seven narrative frameworks, which I describe as the (1) subtraction, (2) renewal, (3) transsecular, (4) postnaturalist, (5) construct, (6) perennial, and (7) developmental narratives. I will briefly explain what I mean by each term before justifying my choice of these specific narratives:

(1) The "subtraction" narrative is based on the idea that religion is a way of coping with the conditions of ignorance, powerlessness, and cultural passivity that plagued early human existence.[4] Following this rationale, as humanity's knowledge, power, and pace of cultural change advance, which is evidently happening in the modern world, we should become less and less religious. Some subtraction narratives claim that this process of religious decline is necessary and inevitable. Classical secularization theory thus fits neatly within the subtraction narrative framework. Yet other subtraction narratives argue that processes of religious decline can be slowed or halted if humanity strays from the proper course, the contemporary "resurgence" of religion being a prime example. And others still seek to reframe the growing prominence of religious actors as part of a broader process of religious decline, perhaps in a desperate attempt to halt the rising tide of secularization, or as an inconsequential trend within a global marketplace of ideas that has already become largely irreligious.

(2) The "renewal" narrative roots the problems of modernity in humanity's departure from a religious truth that was better known to inhabitants of an earlier epoch. Although different renewal narratives highlight different truths, they all agree that humanity can solve its current problems only by reengaging the relevant truth today. From this perspective, the rising public influence of religion is often interpreted as a sign of humanity's dawning desire to find its

way back to the proper religious path. Indeed, many religious movements contributing to the global resurgence of religion are explicitly fueled by such visions of renewal. Consider, in this regard, the numerous fundamentalist movements that idealize an earlier instance of religious history and seek to reinstitute its ways.[5] However, we also find more sophisticated visions of renewal among, say, Catholics who view Western modernity as a hasty reaction against the Church and orthodox Christian teaching, or Hindus who believe that modern capitalistic society has blinded us to the spiritual truths that were outlined in the Vedas long ago.

(3) Despite their differences, subtraction and renewal narratives both accept that there is an inverse relationship between modernity and religion; the more modern we are, the less (authentically) religious, and vice versa. The only difference is whether we consider this inverse relationship good or bad. The "transsecular" narrative aims to move beyond this dichotomy by demonstrating that modernization does not cause religion's marginalization and decline, but rather its transformation.[6] In other words, transsecular narratives recharacterize the same forces that subtraction and renewal narratives identify as agents of religious change.[7] In this regard, one prominent transsecular narrative argues that modernity has transformed religion by placing religious beliefs in a space of open possibility, whereby we can now choose whether or in which way to believe, while another transsecular narrative presents modernity as a globally varied phenomenon in which different cultures adopt different secular-religious configurations as they interact with transformative modern forces.[8]

(4) The "postnaturalist" narrative focuses on the relationship between science and religion and suggests that even though modern science rightfully disrupted premodern views of nature, recent developments in natural science are revitalizing the investigation of spiritual ideas. Postnaturalist narratives thus do not suggest that the Scientific Revolution was somehow problematic or naïve, but rather that naturalism—the belief that only the kind of material things that appear in the natural-scientific framework exist—has for many years hampered our exploration of spiritual reality. In this way, like subtraction narratives, postnaturalist narratives highlight the value of modern science, while, like renewal narratives,

they appreciate the merit of premodern religious ideas and criticize narrowly held secular beliefs. However, postnaturalist narratives uniquely argue that embracing modern science does not rule out religion, but rather deepens and transforms its underlying beliefs.

(5) The "construct" narrative explores how a general concept of religion—which is to say, one that sees religion as a universal phenomenon that is variously instantiated throughout history and around the world—was constructed in the modern West and then applied to non-Western and premodern peoples. Construct narratives debate whether this new view of religion was a discovery, an illusion, the mask of an expansionary political endeavor, or a mix of all three.

(6) The "perennial" narrative claims that all the world's religions exhibit common characteristics. The notion that all religions are partial expressions of a transtraditional mysticism falls clearly within the perennial narrative domain. However, not all perennial narratives advance such views, as we also find authors who, for example, highlight the universal existential structures that make humans religious. The perennial narrative framework is becoming increasingly popular today among those who describe themselves as "spiritual but not religious."[9]

(7) The "developmental" narrative advances the idea that religion has proceeded through several stages of evolution. Many researchers describe this process of cumulative evolution in a neutral manner, focusing, for example, on the growth of social complexity and cognitive capacity, while others describe religion's evolution in a more normative light by emphasizing the advancement of morality and spiritual understanding. Developmental narratives were first introduced in the West in order to locate all other religious traditions within a progressive arc that peaked in European Christianity. This kind of developmental narrative rightly fell from favor as scholars recognized the limitations of a Christo- and Eurocentric framework. However, this did not spell the end of the developmental narrative as such, since researchers have continued working to articulate broader and more open-ended developmental accounts of religion. Such narratives are becoming prominent today, as the evidence of religion's intimate

involvement in the general development of humankind becomes ever more difficult to deny.

Each of the seven chapters that follow examines one of these narrative frameworks in greater detail. The goal in each instance is to help us grasp the basic logic that each narrative employs, appreciate the diverse ways it can be utilized, and become cognizant of its basic insights and limitations. Toward this end, I have found it helpful to concentrate in each chapter on the work of three prominent authors. This approach not only helps us discern the inner core of each narrative by considering several of its iterations, but also lets us see how people who argue quite different things can employ the same narrative logic. Indeed, one of the main merits of this system of narrative categorization is its ability to make sense of what is otherwise a quite nebulous and unruly body of scholarship on religion.[10] That said, my goal is not to claim that these seven narratives encompass every way of conceptualizing religion. Nor do I want to claim that everyone who writes about religion today fits neatly within one narrative framework. My argument is rather that these seven narratives are the most prevalent and important ones in contemporary scholarship.

Other Narratives

Despite these concessions, a reader might still reasonably worry about the potential restrictiveness of my list. Why these seven narratives and not others? What about, for example, the "postsecular," or "deconstructive," or "embodiment," or "cyclical" narratives of religious history? Aren't these narrative frameworks just as prominent as the seven identified above, if not more so? Although I welcome such critical remarks, I have thus far found that every proposed addition fails to warrant inclusion. Indeed, most end up not even being *narrative* frameworks at all.

Admittedly, the growing body of "postsecular" discourse does exhibit a common narrative element. The idea is that secularization theory has failed to account for the changing place of religion in the modern world, and hence to be an adequate guide for contemporary social and political affairs. It goes without saying that I appreciate this perspective, as I use it to frame this book's argument. However, this narrative element is not equivalent to a distinct narrative framework. Indeed, the very premise of the postsecular narrative is that we do not yet know what alternative narrative framework to employ.[11] Of course, some authors use the term "postsecular" to make the closely connected claim that modern religion has not undergone marginalization and decline, but rather transformation.[12] I would argue, however, that this use of the term is imprecise, and I have alternatively developed the term "transsecular" to describe the relevant narrative claim.

Another term that fails to make the cut is "deconstructive." Using a deconstructive methodology to investigate religion does not make us narrate religious history in any particular way. Both Martin Heidegger and Talal Asad, for example, employ a deconstructive methodology but still employ quite different narrative frames. Heidegger recommends renewing pre-Socratic Greek spirituality, while Asad documents the colonialist forces that influenced the construction of the modern Western discourse on religion.[13] The former is a clear example of a renewal narrative, while the latter is a paradigmatic construct narrative.

The same criticism applies to those who claim that using embodied cognition theory to study religion gives rise to a distinct "embodiment" narrative. Embodied cognition theory is a conceptual scheme developed by cognitive scientists, psychologists, and philosophers to describe how human cognition is distributed throughout the human body and its socio-symbolic engagements with the world.[14] Many researchers have productively used this theoretical lens to investigate the ritual, symbolic, and practical dimensions of religious life.[15] Nevertheless, their research does not exhibit common narrative commitments. Consider, in this light, how some authors use embodied cognition theory to argue that humanity is gradually abandoning belief in transcendence and embracing naturalism (subtraction narrative), while others use it to critique the Enlightenment fragmentation of body and spirit and to recommend the renewal of a more holistic premodern pattern of belief (renewal narrative).[16]

The "cyclical" narrative of religious history describes systems of practice and belief that see perpetual cycles in religious history. Ostensibly, all tribal religions, as well as many forms of archaic and axial religion (e.g., Hinduism), employ this perspective.[17] It might therefore seem both logical and important to place the cyclical narrative alongside the others I have identified. However, the aim of this book is not to describe every view of religious history that has appeared throughout the ages, but rather to consider those that inform contemporary scholarship. Thus, insofar as cyclical views of religious history do not frame significant ongoing bodies of scholarly debate, they fall outside the domain of the present inquiry. That said, if we were to categorize the cyclical perspective, it would fit neatly in the perennial narrative domain, since the term "perennial" describes things that are both eternal and perpetually recurring. Cyclical views of religion simply emphasize the element of recurrence, whereas most contemporary perennial narratives tend to emphasize eternality.

Having offered these exculpatory remarks, I must clarify that I do not claim that my list of seven narratives somehow wraps things up once and for all. Indeed, I am perfectly willing to add to the list if it becomes necessary to do so. However, the point is simply to explain that problematics (e.g., the postsecular), methodologies (e.g., deconstruction), conceptual schemes (e.g., embodied cognition theory), and antiquated perspectives (e.g., cyclical narratives) are not suitable candidates.

The Question of Truth

Although the primary purpose of this book is to describe the seven narrative frameworks that shape the contemporary academic discourse on religion, I cannot avoid discussing each narrative's truth-value. I do not employ a radically constructivist perspective, whereby humans haphazardly create their worldviews from the raw materials of experience. Rather, I believe that there is an objective world, that certain claims can be proven true and others false, and that some views of religious history are therefore more valid than others.

Unfortunately, we do not yet have sufficient empirical evidence to clearly demonstrate which narrative framework is best. Indeed, part of the problem is that each narrative provides certain insights into the history of religion that others generally overlook. There is a distinct pattern of subtraction, whereby we abandon certain aspects of earlier religious epochs as our knowledge of and control over the world advance. There is also a pattern of renewal, whereby we strive to revitalize certain things that were problematically left behind. The forces of modernity do stimulate religion's transformation and not its wholesale marginalization and decline. The development of natural science has led us to reconsider the place of certain spiritual realities and forces in a scientific worldview. The concept of "religion" has been uniquely thematized in the modern West and then projected outward and backward onto non-Western cultures. Different religious communities and traditions do gravitate toward a perennial set of patterns, beliefs, and existential structures. And religion has undergone a significant process of historical development.

One way of resolving this dilemma is to approach each narrative as a competing research program that must vie against the others until consensus gradually forms around one view. From this perspective, researchers should continue arguing for the narrative framework they prefer and against all others so that the process of Darwinian-style selection can proceed more efficiently.

Another possibility is to see each narrative as a methodological heuristic that can be used to analyze distinct processes of religious change. Our goal should therefore not be to show that only one narrative is true, but rather to utilize whatever narrative best suits our particular investigation and to allow knowledge of broader historical processes to aggregate over time.

A third approach is to try integrating the insights of all seven narratives into one meta-narrative. We could proceed with this task either by subsuming under one of the existing narratives the best insights of the other six or by developing a distinct and superior eighth narrative. Either way, the belief would be that the contemporary academic discourse on religion is severely hindered by its lack of a broader, synthetic narrative paradigm.

I will discuss each of these strategies further in the concluding chapter. However, it may be useful to state from the outset that I find the third most convincing, albeit with some important caveats. Although I ultimately claim that a sufficiently broad and open-ended developmental narrative lets us see how insights from the other six narratives hang together as facets of a coherent whole, I refrain from trying to explain precisely how we move from one stage of religious history to the next. Regardless, whatever approach one ultimately adopts, a sound knowledge of the major narratives that are currently at play is an essential prerequisite.

New Directions in the Philosophy of Religion

In recent years, a number of philosophers have argued that the philosophy of religion should move closer to the broader academic study of religion. Whereas most contemporary philosophers of religion focus on examining either the rationality of religious beliefs or the existential structures of religious experience, the suggestion is that much more attention should given, for example, to examining the concept of "religion," to considering normative frameworks in which to think about religion's various operations, to bringing religious ideas into conversation with wider ethical, political-philosophical, cognitive-scientific, and metaphysical debates, and to examining the forces that have and continue to shape religious history.[18] The arguments put forth in this book fit well within this new approach to the philosophy of religion, and I hope that they will prove useful to all those who are currently engaged in such methodological debates.

CHAPTER ONE

The Subtraction Narrative

THE SUBTRACTION NARRATIVE OF religion has been highly influential during the past century and a half. Its central premise is that religion originally arose as a way of dealing with the ignorance, powerlessness, and cultural passivity that plagued early human existence. As we have acquired more knowledge, power, and cultural dynamism, however, we have rightfully become less religious. Subtraction narratives use this logic to equate modernization with the marginalization and decline of religion. Indeed, the belief is that a fully "modern" society would have hardly any religion at all.

Auguste Comte (1798–1857) developed one of the first and most influential subtraction narratives. He argued that humanity has been progressively departing from its initial tendency to believe that all things possess a humanlike spirit and moving toward a modern "positivism" that rejects supernaturalism and concentrates entirely on the immanent tasks of science, technology, and practical morality. This process has involved three intermediary stages. We first went beyond animism by positing a plurality of semitranscendent divinities. Then we collapsed these divinities into a single transcendent God. Later we treated God as a "mere abstraction, which can furnish no basis for any religious system of real efficacy, intellectual, moral, or, above all, social." And more recently we be-

gan abandoning even such restricted religious ideas in order to embrace positivistic atheism.[1]

Although many contemporary subtraction narratives employ a
similar logic, they are less certain about religion's imminent demise.
Humanity, it is often argued, will not abandon religion as quickly as
it should because most societies are not developing in the proper
way. Hence, the challenge is to figure out how to lead the masses
down the intended secularizing path, or at least to diminish the
chaos created by their enduring religiosity. The subtraction narratives of Daniel Dennett and John Dewey, which we will consider
below, both proceed in this manner. However, moving in a bolder
and more distinctive direction, Marcel Gauchet rejects Comte's vision of the future, claiming instead that religion had already ceased
to exist by the time Comte wrote. I will explain and critically evaluate these three subtraction narratives in order to clarify the content
of the subtraction narrative as a whole.

Daniel Dennett

Since "for many people, probably a majority of the people on
Earth, nothing matters more than religion," Daniel Dennett recognizes the importance of investigating religion.[2] However, he is perplexed by how so few are willing to do so by using the best
intellectual tools we have—namely, those produced by natural science. This unwillingness springs from a fear that analyzing religion
in a natural-scientific manner would make it impossible to believe
in God, or at least would unnecessarily upset religious believers.
Yet these are not legitimate reasons if our goal really is to understand religion. No one would argue against studying, say, language
as a natural phenomenon, and the contemporary explosion of
natural-scientific linguistic research demonstrates the effectiveness
of this approach. We can expect that a similarly potent advance in
our understanding of religion would emerge once we began viewing it through a natural-scientific lens.

To help us appreciate what a natural-scientific approach to religion might entail, Dennett draws analogies from a range of better-
understood phenomena. For example, might not religion have
evolved like an insatiable taste for sugar or alcohol, the unintended

consequence of genetic traits that developed for entirely different reasons? Or perhaps religion is more like the bacteria that symbiotically inhabit our bodies. The question, then, would be whether religion is a beneficial, neutral, or destructive symbiont. Religion could also be an evolutionary "good trick," like money or marriage, that societies have universally discovered to enhance their chances of survival.[3] Whatever the ultimate answer, Dennett argues that we must first develop a plausible scientific theory and then put in the hard work of experimental evaluation. Dennett hopes that his subtraction narrative will contribute to the advancement of the first task so that the scientific community can pursue the second.

Dennett begins his narrative by highlighting the tendency that exists within both animals and humans to detect more agency in the world than actually exists. This tendency is at play when dogs bark at falling snow or when night-creaks spark thoughts of lurking murderers. The evolutionary rationale for this trait is easy to discern; sometimes there actually is a mountain lion on the roof or a murderer creeping through the hall. This is a clear example of an evolutionary "better safe than sorry."

Dennett argues that belief in invisible spiritual agents arises as an unintended consequence of this trait. After a loved one dies, many mundane occurrences bring the expectation of that person's presence vividly to mind. Such experiences can be a source of both pain and comfort. Historically, one of the most effective ways to diminish the pain and to heighten the comfort is to interpret these memories as encounters with the departed person's disembodied spirit. Our loved one has not, the thought goes, disappeared from the world, but only changed his or her form, so we must continue our relationship in a non-sensible manner.

We begin sliding toward "religion" when the loved one is a parent. The parent-child relationship is one of the most important means of transmitting non-genetic information and indelibly marks the child's psyche. Faced with a parent's death, which in earlier epochs happened much sooner in the process of individual development, early peoples wanted to continue receiving parental knowledge and protection. When combined with the tendency to interpret emotion-laden memories of a departed loved one as encounters with their immaterial spirit, this desire led us to try devising means to convince the parental spirits to give their aid.[4] In this way, the earliest form of religion arose as a practically oriented cult of ancestor worship.

Dennett turns to B. F. Skinner's study of pigeon superstition to understand how complex rituals emerged around this pattern of religious belief.[5] Skinner designed an experiment in which pigeons randomly received food and observed that they soon developed an elaborate dance in their attempts to repeat the food-triggering conditions. Dennett humorously dramatizes their process of thought: "Now, let's see: the last time I got the reward, I'd just spun around once and craned my neck. Let's try it again. . . . Nope, no reward. Perhaps I didn't spin enough. . . . Nope. Perhaps I should bob once before spinning and craning. . . . YESSS! OK, now, what did I just do?"[6] The pigeons' false belief that their actions motivated food giving led them to develop a complex dance of invocation. Likewise, early humans' false belief that their actions influenced the decision of ancestral spirits to bestow knowledge and protection led them to develop complex religious rituals.

But if early tribal religion was little more than a superstitious response to a false interpretation of memories of the dead, why, then, did it flourish as ubiquitously as it did? Dennett offers three evolutionary rationales. First, tribal religions likely aided decision making in a time when people had many important decisions to make and very little information upon which to rely. Second, tribal religions seem to have universally discovered the placebo effect and deployed it as a kind of collective health care. As Dennett explains, displays of shamanic power increased participants' confidence that help was on the way, which in turn revved up their immune systems, and the regular repetition of communal ritual systematized these effects. In fact, contemporary studies show that even today, people seek shamanic healing for conditions that are particularly responsive to the placebo effect. And third, tribal religion provided a powerful stimulus to cultural learning. In lieu of external symbolic storage systems like writing, the most effective means for storing knowledge is the kind of collective reenactment seen in tribal ritual. This is perhaps the most important benefit of tribal ritual, as rapid non-genetic evolution could not have emerged without some such mechanism for cultural learning.[7]

In Dennett's view, religion moved beyond ancestor worship when a new class of religious "stewards" began working to protect sacred traditions from deviation and doubt. The main difficulty these stewards faced was the fact that belief in supernatural agents who can be influenced by human behavior forces us to make empirical claims. Whether we credit divine intervention for a good crop or for an enemy's defeat, belief in supernatural agency requires us to see its powers at work in the world. Nevertheless, because no spiritual beings exist, we never find robust evidence of divine intervention. Religious stewards are therefore led to develop increasingly abstract notions of divinity in order to protect religion from its otherwise inevitable falsification.

Without giving much more thought to the matter, Dennett explains that this abstractive process propelled religion through its polytheistic, monotheistic, and deistic periods. He then explains that deism, which conceptualizes God as the lawgiver of the world, brought us near to Dennett's own naturalistic perspective. Dennett presents the radical Enlightenment thinker Benedict Spinoza as the one who ultimately made the leap from deism to naturalism: "Benedict Spinoza, in the seventeenth century, *identified* God and Nature, arguing that scientific research was the true path of theology. For this heresy he was persecuted. There is a troubling (or, to some, enticing) janus-faced quality to Spinoza's heretical vision of *Deus sive Natura* (God, or Nature): in proposing his scientific simplification, was he personifying Nature or depersonalizing God?"[8] However, it wasn't until Charles Darwin explained how life and intelligence arose in the physical world that naturalism reached its mature form: "When we looked through Darwin's eyes at the actual processes of design of which we and all the wonders of nature are the products to date, we found that Paley was right to see these effects as the result of a lot of design work, but we found a non-miraculous account of it: a massively parallel, and hence prodigiously wasteful, process of mindless, algorithmic design-trying, in which, however, the minimal increments of design have been thriftily husbanded, copied and re-used over billions of years.... That is, indeed, a thing of beauty, as mathematicians are forever exclaiming, but it is not itself something intelligent, but wonder of wonders, something intelligible."[9]

Whether or not the masses can or will recognize naturalism's truth is an entirely different question. Dennett acknowledges that religion is very attractive for many people and will not stop being so anytime soon. He therefore recommends that the enlightened among us (whom he calls "brights") approach religion like any other intractable social vice, allowing people freedom in the private sphere but regulating their options in the public domain to protect the social good. This process of mitigating regulation should be complemented by efforts to extend scientific education, to advance our scientific understanding of religion, and to combat religion's influence through effective media campaigns. On this front, Dennett argues that those among the educated classes who no longer hold orthodox beliefs but still feel some attachment to religion should be specifically pursued, as their influence does much to sustain religion's false aura of prestige. In considering this missionary strategy, Dennett emphasizes how religious actors are working hard to proselytize the masses and to gain control of the public sphere. The contemporary resurgence of religion demonstrates how effective such efforts can be. Naturalistic thinkers who would like to see humanity become more enlightened should find in those efforts the impetus to embrace their own proselytizing imperative.

The main difficulty we face in evaluating Dennett's subtraction narrative is distinguishing his claims concerning the importance of investigating religion with a natural-scientific lens from the particular narrative of religious history he tells. I say this because accepting Dennett's methodological point seems to require us to accept his narrative perspective. But this is not the case, as Dennett advances many narrative claims through a mixture of conjecture and historical speculation.

Consider: Dennett begins by highlighting humanity's overactive tendency to detect agency in the world. He goes on to assert that all our encounters with spiritual agency arise because of this tendency and draws a tenuous connection to B. F. Skinner's controversial investigation of pigeon "superstition" in order to explain religion's emergence.[10] Next, he introduces the idea of religious "stewards" who work to protect religious practices and beliefs from falsification and explains that their interventions guide religion's subsequent evolution. Finally, he offers several suggestions about how governments and leaders of secular thought can effectively regulate and curtail the influence of religion today. I find it hard to see how this is a scientific argument. Each step would have to be examined in much greater detail, its implications rigorously tested and its limitations carefully considered, to warrant this claim. Nevertheless, Dennett makes little effort to proceed in this manner. Instead, he simply invokes the Darwinian basis of his project to drape his speculations with the mantle of "science." Mary Midgley has aptly described this maneuver as the "sort of trouble which arises when, with writers less careful than Darwin, the dramas take over." She continues: "About evolution, [the] theory itself has again and again been distorted by biases flowing from over-simple, un-balanced world-pictures." Darwinian thinkers thus become so "obsessed by a picture so colourful and striking that it numbs thought about the evidence required to support it. Standards of proof then fall headlong."[11]

We can see this distortion in Dennett's claim that "the stewardship of religious ideas creates a powerful phenomenon: belief in belief, which radically transforms the content of the underlying beliefs, making rational investigation of them difficult if not impossible."[12] The idea here is that the efforts of religious specialists to protect religious ideas from falsification are one of the primary engines of post-tribal religious evolution. This conclusion fits with Dennett's prior commitment to the neo-Darwinian theory of memetics and reinforces ideas about clerical ineptitude and misconduct that loom large in the secularized Western mind. However, it is not hard to undermine his claim by pointing out instances in which religious "stewards" have, to the contrary, systematically worked to expose their beliefs to potential falsification.

One example is Mohandas Gandhi's practice of nonviolent civil disobedience, which famously arose from his attempts to apply moral teachings from the Bible and the Bhagavad Gita to the injustices that characterized his social milieu. He did not know whether the radically nonviolent line of action he proposed would yield the intended results. Yet he risked his life and the safety of his friends, family, and co-nationals to act upon his hypothesis that these religious teachings were true. The results were impressively confirming. Thus, although Gandhi was, to use Dennett's language, a religious "specialist" who "stewarded" religious ideas, his goal was never to protect his practices and beliefs from falsification. Dennett makes no effort to engage such counterfactuals.

Having made this point, I must mention that my general problem is not with Dennett's efforts to articulate a naturalistic narrative of religious history. Indeed, it would be perfectly legitimate for him to tell such a story if he properly acknowledged what he was doing. Robert Bellah has taken steps in this direction by describing his own account of religious history as an attempt to develop the narrative that many scientifically minded moderns tell about the world.[13] In this light, instead of claiming to articulate a scientific account of religion that others can begin to empirically test, Dennett should have more honestly explained that he is simply trying to tell a plausible Darwinian account of religious history that draws insight from recent natural-scientific studies of certain religious phenomena. His failure to make this admission diminishes the value of his work.

John Dewey

John Dewey (1859–1952) is one of the most influential intellectuals the United States has produced; he made major contributions to logic, epistemology, political philosophy, philosophy of science, psychology, and education. Along with Charles Peirce and William James, he is particularly known as a founder of American pragmatism. Though his oeuvre is immense, all Dewey's work was guided by his desire to recharacterize knowledge as something that is achieved through experimental engagement with the world. As part of this concern, Dewey sought to show how experimental knowledge is just as much involved in politics, ethics, aesthetics, and religion as it is in logic and natural science.[14] He also examined the historical origins of the tendency to detach knowledge from experimental engagement with the world.[15] His subtraction narrative appears at the conjunction of these two lines of inquiry.

Dewey begins his subtraction narrative by claiming that supernatural religion appears when experiences of powerlessness and ignorance misdirect our "natural" religious impulse toward ritual and prayer. Describing this religious impulse as the sense of "awe and reverence" we feel when contemplating "the dignity of human nature" and "nature as the whole of which we are parts," Dewey explains that it nourishes confidence in the possibility of channeling reality's forces toward the realization of our noblest individual and collective ambitions and helps sustain this confidence during periods of difficulty and despair.[16] However, our religious impulse ceases to have its intended effect when we bind it to belief in supernatural agents. This is because supernaturalism leads us to try transforming our place in the world through ritual and prayer instead of through experimental activity. Abandoning supernaturalism and embracing naturalism are therefore essential today if we are to begin channeling our religious impulse in the proper direction.

Dewey begins his analysis by describing how people undertake processes of inquiry to transform some problematic aspect of their relationship with the world. Sometimes the required change is readily discerned—for example, squashing a pesky mosquito—while other times the dilemma is more complex—for example, figuring out how to stop workers from dying of malaria. Regardless, the aim of inquiry is always to resolve a disjunction between our desires and our relationship with the world. But what if the situation in question is so mysterious and complex that we have little hope of discovering a workable solution? And what if the situation is so fundamentally important to our well-being that any wrong decision would likely lead to our demise? Dewey argues that humans have historically responded to such predicaments by positing the existence of powerful supernatural beings and using ritual and prayer to try convincing them to help us. Instead of systematically studying soil contents, weather patterns, and agricultural techniques to overcome low crop yields, for example, we pray and perform harvest rituals. These acts give us the comforting illusion of doing something to resolve our difficulties but leave our place in the world unchanged.

Yet the persistent failure of ritual and prayer does not normally lead us to abandon supernaturalism outright. Instead, we try altering our religious activities and convictions until, for whatever reason, things seem to be improving. In the long term, this pattern of adjustment leads us to posit increasingly abstract, and hence more difficult to falsify, notions of divinity.

A major turning point in this process came when the Greeks articulated a rationalistic vision of divinity. Instead of striving to win the gods' favor through ritual and prayer, they posited a "realm of fixed Being which, when grasped by thought, formed a complete system of immutable and necessary truth," and claimed that perfectly understanding this system would secure a good life.[17] Herein lies the origin of what Dewey calls the "quest for certainty," which Enlightenment thinkers later took up when they claimed that modern science improves life by giving us complete knowledge of the world. The only difference was that these modern thinkers considered the "realm of fixed Being" to be a material system governed by blind mathematical laws. Dewey thus argues that Enlightenment thinkers were ironically led by supernaturalistic habits of thought to embrace naturalism.

Admittedly, many Enlightenment thinkers sought to interpret the new scientific worldview in a way that made room for religion. Cartesian dualists presented reality's spiritual and material dimensions as two wholly separate domains, while Spinoza argued that science and religion each offered a partial view of a single metaphysical order. Kant, in turn, presented science and religion as mutually exclusive ways of framing an ultimately unknowable world, while post-Kantian idealists like Fichte, Hegel, and Bradley described nature as a crystallization of a dynamically evolving spiritual reality.[18] All these theories failed, however, to reconcile science and religion because they remained within the supernaturalistic quest for certainty, assuming as they did that the goal of thought is to grasp the eternal structure of the world.

Dewey explains that we can actually reconcile science and religion by disassociating thought from the quest for certainty. To understand this claim, it will help to briefly consider how the idea of, say, a poisonous berry might have originally appeared. We probably first learned that some berries are poisonous and others are not through brute trial and error. With time, we began recognizing commonalities between certain poisonous berries—color, shape, smell, taste, and inclusion in other animals' diets—and used this knowledge to evaluate new berries we encountered. Our knowledge of poisonous berries thus arose from and found its meaning in purposeful action. Dewey claims that natural science operates in exactly the same manner, albeit in relation to a very different line of purposeful action, namely that of manipulating the basic features of the physical world. Natural scientists develop theories by reflecting upon their efforts to manipulate the physical world and then use these theories to develop more sophisticated and accurate means of manipulation. The goal of science is thus not to gain certain knowledge of reality in itself, but rather to help us navigate physical reality in a more fluent and effective manner.

Dewey sees no reason why we cannot apply this same methodological strategy to religion. The only difference is that the purpose of religious inquiry is to learn how to cultivate trust, hope, and faith in our ability to improve the world. The challenge is to figure out how to pursue such inquiry in an experimental and non-supernaturalistic manner. Although for many, religion without supernaturalism is not religion, Dewey contends that learning to cultivate faith, hope, and trust in a scientific and non-supernaturalistic manner would leave us more spiritually fulfilled than ever before.[19] Indeed, he contends that supernatural religion only persists today because we have not yet developed an adequately scientific pattern of non-supernaturalistic religious inquiry.

Dewey's apparent willingness to acknowledge the modern relevance of religious inquiry might make it hard to understand why I place him within the subtraction narrative domain. If Dewey envisions the modern transformation of religion, and not its wholesale marginalization and decline, as well as contemporary religion's reconciliation with modern science, why not describe his narrative as either transsecular or postnaturalist? There is no denying that elements of Dewey's narrative can be used for transsecular and postnaturalist purposes, but it is important to recognize that he argues that supernatural religion should decline as our knowledge of and control over the world expands. Consider the argument that animates this classically subtractive claim: Early humans did not understand why things happened or how to change them. Working from their understanding of other people, they imagined that natural events were caused by supernatural beings and could therefore be changed by convincing these supernatural beings to behave differently. However, most of us now accept that natural events are not caused by supernatural beings. Classically religious efforts to transform events through ritual and prayer are therefore built upon faulty premises. This means that supernatural religion should decline as our understanding of the world matures. In this way, while Dewey suggests that modern society should develop a non-supernaturalistic pattern of religious inquiry, his point is simply that we should learn how to cultivate qualities that have long been associated with religion in a naturalistic and scientific manner. Accordingly, although Dewey acknowledges the enduring relevance of certain aspects of traditional religious life, he so neuters and curtails their religious dimensions that the resultant product can hardly be called "religion."

I find the assumption that supernatural beliefs make us behave in a non-experimental manner problematic because there are many contradicting historical episodes. Consider the efforts of religiously inspired abolitionist groups. They did not simply pray to God to free the slaves, carry out rituals, and leave it at that. Rather, they derived challenging and far-reaching moral insights from the ethical teachings of their religious tradition, prayed for the strength, insight, opportunities, and influence to translate their ethical insights into reality and action, and systematically labored to transform public policy and discourse. Their approach to religion was simultaneously grounded in supernatural belief and committed to transformative, experimental action.

Furthermore, to draw again on the example of Gandhi, his autobiography describes how he systematically worked to enact certain spiritual principles through a continuous process of scriptural study, experimental efforts to apply his insights to social problems, and reflection on the outcomes of these efforts.[20] Although the social movement he launched ultimately failed to achieve the depth of social change he envisioned, it did yield lasting and repeatable knowledge concerning the effectiveness of spiritually oriented, nonviolent civil disobedience as a means of social change. In this way, Gandhi displayed a pattern of religious inquiry that came very close to Dewey's scientifically reconstructed ideal while also unapologetically embracing supernatural belief.

The current community-building efforts of the Bahá'í Faith offer another relevant example.[21] The Bahá'í Faith is the one of the youngest of the world's religions and expressly aims to contribute to the construction of a just, peaceful, and unified world civilization that is characterized by material and spiritual prosperity.[22] Bahá'ís currently dedicate much energy to learning about the dynamics of spiritual community building in neighborhoods and villages around the world. Rooted in local community efforts, this learning process is systematized by an evolving network of institutions and agencies. Spaces for reflection and planning are created at local, regional, national, and international levels to consolidate learning and direct guidance and support back to the grass roots. All participants, whether identifying as Bahá'í or not, see themselves as active contributors to a process of collective learning. Although this description superficially treats what is in reality a profound, complex, and rapidly evolving process, the purpose is only to provide but another example of how a more scientific pattern of religious inquiry can proceed within a framework that explicitly embraces transcendence.[23]

I would also challenge Dewey's claim that the project of cultivating faith, hope, and trust can be more effectively pursued with a worldview that rejects supernaturalism. Indeed, one consistent criticism that even supportive thinkers make of "disenchanted" worldviews is that they leave little room for higher purpose.[24] This is a very intuitive claim, as it is hard to imagine how it would be easier to cultivate faith, hope, and trust in our ability to transform the world within a framework that acknowledges only material entities and forces than within a framework that accepts belief in a benevolent God who actively helps humanity to develop and grow. Dewey's response would be that belief in God ends up sidetracking the development of noble characteristics. However, after considering several examples that contradict this claim, we can see that the question is more about the kind of supernaturalism espoused than about the general belief in a supernatural reality.

In this regard, Dewey rightly argues that the quest for certainty has long burdened the operation of religion in the West. Charles Taylor also highlighted this dynamic when he described Latin Christendom as the "scene of a total, almost obsessive identification with certain favourite schemes, driven to any wild or repellent consequences, justifying murderous schisms."[25] However, it is interesting to note that, while Dewey roots his criticisms in a non-supernaturalistic worldview, Taylor develops similar points from within a framework that explicitly acknowledges transcendence. The point here is not to say that Taylor's notions are better because he incorporates transcendence into his worldview, but rather to show that one can appreciate Dewey's analysis and critique of the Western tradition without embracing naturalism.

Marcel Gauchet

The central claim of Marcel Gauchet's subtraction narrative is that early tribal society exhibited religion's essential form and that subsequent religious transformations were not developments, but rather steps toward religion's ultimate demise. Religious history is not therefore an "evolutionary process by which vague or rudimentary religious ideas have become more precise, profound, and systematic," but rather "just so many stages of [religion's] abatement and disintegration." In other words, "when dealing with religion, what appears to be an advance is actually a retreat." By completing this process of devolution, Christianity stimulated the emergence of modern secular society, which is why Gauchet describes it as the *"religion for departing from religion."*[26]

Gauchet's narrative stems from his broader account of humanity's existential condition. We are born into a preformed social world, yet with the capacity and inclination to transform ourselves and the world. We are therefore simultaneously passive and active beings. Yet human history displays a clear directional shift from passivity to activity. As he puts it, earlier societies show a complete "submission to an order received in toto, determined before and outside our will," while modern societies show belief in a social order that originates "in the will of individuals."[27] Gauchet equates the former state of affairs with religion and the latter with secular society.

From Gauchet's perspective, then, religion constitutes a "well-defined type of society based on the priority of the principle of collective organization over the will of the individuals it brings together." A religious society is one in which the "forces of change are put completely in the service of preserving and giving unwavering assent to what exists."[28] This social configuration appears most clearly in the "tribal" phase of history, where the attempt is made to forestall all social change by grounding social reality in an eternal sacred order. There is no need for a state or social hierarchy, as the sacred order reigns unproblematically over every aspect of individual and collective life.

This social configuration had its advantages. It effectively combated social domination by establishing unrelenting equality before a sacred order, it limited social conflict by placing social responsibility above individual concerns, and it mitigated the struggle with nature by establishing a static harmony with the environment. Thus, as Gauchet remarks, it is "not without good reason" that religion "preoccupied our forefathers and dominated practically all of history."[29]

Nevertheless, tribal religion was ultimately unable to maintain the status quo; humanity's creative impulses were simply too relentless. As a result, tribal society gradually dissolved and was replaced by a new archaic configuration. The central feature of the archaic epoch was the emergence of divine kings (e.g., the pharaohs) who claimed to possess the power to restore humanity's relationship with the eternal sacred order. However, the simple fact that these kings sought to *restore* humanity's relationship with the eternal sacred order demonstrates that religion's hold on archaic society was weaker than before. Religion reigned unproblematically over tribal society; in archaic society, however, disharmony with the sacred order was a problem that needed to be solved.

This sense of disharmony was extended during the axial age, spanning roughly the period from 800 to 200 BCE, when the foundational systems of today's civilizations emerged. Marginalized prophetic figures (e.g., Buddha, Moses, Confucius, and Socrates) critiqued the divine kings by claiming to have received more accurate knowledge of how to restore humanity's relationship with the eternal sacred order. Whereas divine kings worked to restore eternal harmony from a position of worldly authority, the axial figures sought to do the same with minimal worldly influence. The eternal sacred order therefore became even more distant from social reality during the axial age. Monastics and ascetics began abandoning society in order to pursue their new visions of religious truth.

Gauchet explains how the unique Jewish-axial configuration set the stage for Christianity's emergence. The Jews rebelled against the Egyptian pharaoh by inverting the logic of divine kingship. In their view, instead of empowering a ruler to establish a sacred empire, the Jewish God liberated His chosen people from an oppressive worldly force. This vision of God allowed the Israelites to establish themselves as a fledgling nation, but also forced them to constantly face the question of why, if they were God's chosen people, they were so weak and others so strong. If their God was so much more powerful than the false divine kings, why did God not give the Jews their own divine king and a worldly empire over which he could rule? The Hebrew prophets made sense of this predicament by explaining that God used difficulties to prepare His followers for the eventual coming of a messianic divine king.

It is in this context that the figure of Christ vaulted onto the scene as an "inverted messiah." Like a divine king and axial prophet, he claimed to reconcile social and spiritual reality. However, unlike them, he did not seek to establish a new world order. Rather, he claimed to leave the world unchanged while helping humanity reconcile itself with a wholly transcendent God. Christ furthermore used his own death as a way of radicalizing the Jewish vision of purifying trial. He taught that God tested His chosen people, not to prepare them to gain control of the world, but to reconcile them with His transcendent purpose and will. Gauchet makes much of this development because he believes that it forced humanity to imagine the world as wholly separate from the eternal sacred order. This is how Christianity set the stage for secular society.

Yet the path from Christianity to secularism was not entirely straightforward. Were Christians meant to submit entirely to established political powers? Or should they strive to gain influence over worldly affairs in order to bring social reality closer to Christian ideals? Gauchet claims that this tension could not be solved within Christian thought, for it stemmed from the paradox of Christ's twofold nature and reconciling function. Christ is "the perfect union of two natures which, just as profoundly, remain completely distinct."[30] The same union will supposedly one day be realized in the world, but only on the occasion of Christ's second coming. For the time being, then, Christians must believe in a future reconciliation between God and the world that cannot be hastened by human endeavor.

The Roman Empire's collapse drew the Church into worldly affairs by presenting it with the alluring possibility of creating a "City-World, where the executive mechanisms and the wheels of authority would be subordinate to eternal aims, under the leadership of a single shepherd, who himself was closest to God." Yet this proved to be an impossible task, for one cannot establish a hierarchical socioreligious order that aims to help humanity recognize, via the salvific power of Christ, the ultimate powerlessness of all worldly socioreligious orders. So "ecclesial mediation was . . . built on something that cast doubt on the very possibility of mediation."[31] Europe's Christian kings later used this line of thought to rebel against Catholic rule and to claim that the Church should submit to secular political authority. The Protestant Reformation added impetus to this movement by claiming that God gave control of the world to human beings and that the task of religion was to prepare humanity for eternal life.

It is here, Gauchet argues, that humanity abandoned religion outright. This is not to say that religious belief disappeared after the Protestant Reformation, but rather that post-Protestant societies no longer sought to ground themselves in an eternal sacred order. Instead, they pursued human-directed projects of social change. This pattern of social life inverts the early tribal configuration, and hence, in Gauchet's view, is fundamentally irreligious. It is in this light that we should interpret his otherwise perplexing remark, made before the collapse of the Berlin Wall: "If we were to imagine an imminent miracle freeing the Polish people from Soviet oppression, we could also imagine Catholicism, due to its role in safeguarding national identity, playing a spiritually dominant part within the framework of a free government. . . . We would nevertheless still be dealing with an *atheistic society*, made up of and governed by a *believing majority*."[32] The point here is that, regardless of how important religious identities and beliefs might be in certain modern societies, their influence is no longer truly "religious." Rather, these identities and beliefs are simply used to advance irreligious projects of human-directed social change. In this way, though people may claim that they want to, for example, revitalize Christian ideals or to establish an authentically Hindu (or Buddhist or Jewish or Islamic) state, they are actually only using the remnants of religion to advance a secular order. The global resurgence of religion has less to do with religion than with the fact that people throughout the world are currently drawing on traditional identities and beliefs to make a place for themselves in an irreligious age.

When evaluating Gauchet's subtraction narrative, we must begin by assessing his claim that religion is "a *historical* phenomenon, that is, one with a definite beginning and end, falling within a specified period followed by another," because it grounds all his subsequent arguments. To gain critical perspective on this idea, consider using this same argumentative strategy when narrating, say, the history of philosophy.[33] In current intellectual debates, some philosophers argue that philosophy has been improving. Others suggest that it has been struggling to live up to ancient ideals. And still others claim that philosophy has been neither advancing nor improving, but simply swirling around the same conceptual puzzles, or perhaps just articulating and critiquing the cultural assumptions of the day. Which view is correct?

A Gauchet-like figure would intervene by saying, "Listen, ancient Greek philosophy *was* philosophy. Philosophy was the attempt of a slave-owning aristocratic elite to contemplate the eternal Forms. Subsequent socioeconomic developments have made it increasingly difficult for slave-owning aristocratic elites to exist and have also undermined our ability to believe in eternal Forms. The history of philosophy is therefore nothing more than the history of philosophy's decline, even to the point where we now inhabit an egalitarian, capitalistic society in which authentic philosophy is no longer possible at all. It therefore makes no sense to speak of 'philosophy' in the world today." Disconnected from the provocativeness of the conclusion, all our hypothetical Gautchetian is really saying is that philosophy operated one way when it first arose but now operates in a fundamentally different way. This claim only becomes sensational when we insist on equating philosophy with what the ancient Greeks did.

The same critique holds when we consider Gauchet's account of religious history. Admittedly, we cannot be religious today precisely how we could during the tribal, archaic, axial, or medieval periods. The social conditions that sustained the early patterns of religious life have changed so fundamentally that it is almost impossible to imagine returning to their ways. Yet this does not mean that religion is dead. Rather, the point is simply that religion has undergone many profound transformations and will probably continue doing so in the future. Indeed, if each phase of religious history is characterized by certain fundamental transformations that make previous patterns of religious life impossible to maintain, why should the same dynamics not animate the religious upheavals that grip the world today? This is the broader lesson that Gauchet's narrative conveys once we abandon his overly narrow definition of "religion."

These three perspectives, those of Dennett, Dewey, and Gauchet, give us a good sense of the overall shape of the subtraction narrative framework. The basic idea is that there is an inverse relationship between religion and the progressive patterns of social transformation that characterize the modern world. The more modern we are, the less religious we should be, and vice versa. Certainly, many subtraction narratives acknowledge the modern persistence of religion. Yet they generally do so by presenting modern religion as a threat to enlightened progress, a problematic shadow of what naturalistic spirituality ought to be, or something not really "religious" at all.

In noting these dynamics, we must consider how to assess the subtraction narrative's general merit. Of course, the empirical analysis of contemporary social dynamics must play an important part. In this regard, it is interesting to note that there is little evidence to suggest that religion declines as science, technology, capitalism, democracy, education, and the principles of freedom and equality spread. To the contrary, many indicators suggest that these forces often strengthen or revitalize religion's influence.[34] Additionally, the idea that the rest of the world will follow western Europe's path of secularization has been undermined by the very different modern configurations in, say, the United States, India, China,

Japan, Poland, and Russia.[35] Even in western Europe, dynamics of international migration are stimulating demographic shifts that disrupt certain established secular norms.[36]

Still, there are those who empirically defend the subtraction narrative lens. Pippa Norris and Ronald Inglehart, for example, argue that religion persists among vulnerable populations and withers among populations that enjoy economic prosperity and security.[37] Their idea is that religion arises as a way of coping with "existential threats" and declines as the scope of our existential threats diminish. This means that religion would only marginally exist in a world where everyone enjoyed Scandinavian-like stability and prosperity. That said, the authors acknowledge that it is unlikely that humanity will build such a worldly utopia any time soon. Hence, religion will continue to play an important role in contemporary life. Indeed, as long as levels of poverty, inequality, and conflict continue to spread, religion's global influence will also expand.

Without getting into the particulars of Norris and Ingelhart's empirical analyses, it is interesting to note how their subtraction narrative acknowledges that modern religion is not necessarily declining, and may even be gaining influence, since many authors highlight these same dynamics to attack the subtraction narrative framework. The question, then, is whether we ought to interpret the relevant data through a subtractive or non-subtractive framework. At present, it seems that the best we can do is to acknowledge that the empirical data plausibly support both interpretations. In making this claim, my purpose is neither to disparage empirical analysis nor to encourage subtraction narrativists to stick to their guns. Rather, I want simply to highlight the fact that framing narratives of religious history almost always say more about the world than empirical data can either falsify or confirm. This means that our decisions about which narrative framework to adopt are inevitably influenced by wider values and beliefs.

I will conclude by highlighting one of the fundamental intuitions that sustains the subtraction narrative framework. Simply put, those who espouse subtraction narratives tend to believe that secularized Western intellectual elites have the best handle on how things work and that everyone would benefit by embracing their particular worldview. Alternatively, those who do not hold the practices and beliefs of the secular elite in such high regard are much less likely to embrace subtractive perspectives. Peter Berger has described this dynamic:

> There exists an international subculture composed of people with Western-type higher education, especially in the humanities and social sciences, that is indeed secularized. This subculture is the principal "carrier" of progressive, Enlightened beliefs and values. While its members are relatively thin on the ground, they are very influential, as they control the institutions that provide the "official" definitions of reality, notably the educational system, the media of mass communication, and the higher reaches of the legal system. They are remarkably similar all over the world today, as they have been for a long time. . . .
>
> . . . I may observe in passing that the plausibility of secularization theory owes much to this international subculture.[38]

CHAPTER TWO

The Renewal Narrative

THE RENEWAL NARRATIVE FRAMEWORK argues that the decline of an earlier religious tradition caused the problems in the modern world and that we can solve these problems only by renewing this tradition today. Although renewal narratives offer different accounts of what the ideal tradition was, how it was left behind, what problems emerged as a result, and how we can revitalize it, they all employ the same narrative logic. Consider how the three narratives examined below—those of Alasdair MacIntyre, Martin Heidegger, and Muhammad Iqbal—are each oriented around totally different phenomena, the "virtue tradition" of medieval Catholicism, pre-Socratic polytheistic spirituality, and "golden age" Islam, respectively. Most religious fundamentalists employ a renewal narrative, idealizing "some perfect embodiment of the true religion in the past" and working to reinstitute its ways.[1] Indeed, even sophisticated renewal narratives can fall into backward-looking fanaticism, as evidenced by Heidegger's embrace of Nazism and Iqbal's perspectives being co-opted by the Iranian Revolution.

Subtraction and renewal narratives offer inverted accounts of the same basic premise. Both agree that modernization involves the marginalization and decline of religion, but they disagree about whether or not this is a good thing. By extension, then, they each respond to the contemporary resurgence of religion in inverted ways. Whereas subtraction narratives see the resurgence of religion as either a grave threat to humanity's well-being or a superficial fluctuation within a broader process of religious decline, renewal narratives approach it as a sign of humanity's growing desire for substantive spiritual renewal. Because of their antithetical perspectives, advocates of subtraction and renewal narratives often vociferously oppose one another, as demonstrated by Enlightenment debates concerning the role of Christianity in the European public sphere and contemporary American debates about evolution. As long as we equate modernity with religion's marginalization and decline, we will struggle to move beyond such dichotomies.

Those who espouse renewal narratives face the challenge of explaining why the modern West has advanced so remarkably despite the decline of the ideal religious orientation. In this direction, many endeavor to reframe the supposed achievements of the modern West (e.g., science, technology, capitalism, and liberal democracy) as either harmful aberrations or as consequences of a residual religious influence. Either way, renewal narratives posit that the supposed achievements of the modern West are not as validating as they seem.

Alasdair MacIntyre

Alasdair MacIntyre claims that the chaos of contemporary moral discourse stems from the fact that we have abandoned the "virtue tradition" of moral inquiry, which is to say the tradition of Greek, Jewish, Christian, and Islamic practice and thought according to which humans can realize their great inborn spiritual potential by cultivating virtuous dispositions. Enlightenment thinkers rejected the virtue tradition's account of human nature but sought to preserve its basic moral precepts within a secular and naturalistic worldview. Lacking any substantive metaphysical grounding, the Enlightenment project ultimately failed to achieve its goal and left the modern West in a state of moral conflict and decay. For this reason, MacIntyre argues that we can repair the current moral chaos only by renewing our engagement with the virtue tradition today.

MacIntyre's argument begins with a suggestive thought experiment: Imagine a world in which a repentant humanity tries to piece science back together generations after a string of catastrophes incited its willful destruction. Working from fragments, we might reconstruct the external form of a few theories, but we would have no way to objectively evaluate their content. How could we weigh the merits of, say, special relativity theory or quantum physics without a community of inquirers that actively employed advanced mathematics and optic technology and had an extensive background familiarity with the web of scientific theory? For this reason, as earnest and energetic as our efforts might be, our reconstructed "science" would be little more than the lifeless shell of the science we know today. MacIntyre considers this a good analogy for our present moral predicament. We previously inhabited a vibrant moral tradition—the virtue tradition—and organized our moral inquiry around its vision of human nature. Unfortunately, various social upheavals incited this tradition's willful destruction. We have since been trying to piece something like the old moral order back together again. But lacking collective involvement in a community of knowledge and practice that is organized around the virtue tradition's framework, we end up with nothing substantive on which to stand.[2]

To help us appreciate the depth of our current moral predicament, MacIntyre draws attention to arguments surrounding the issue of abortion.[3] A first line of thought holds that people have a right to make decisions about their bodies. Therefore, as long as the embryo exists inside a mother's body, she has the right to choose whether or not to continue gestation. Arguing from the principle that we should only do to other people what we would have them do to us, others claim that because we all value the opportunity to live, we cannot deny this opportunity to a nascent human being. And a third group argues that murdering people is wrong and that, because an embryo is a person, though less developed, abortion is also murder and should be forbidden. Without taking a position on these arguments, MacIntyre explains that each logically flows from an underlying vision of human nature: the first, from a Lockean notion of human rights; the second, from a Kantian account of the golden rule (i.e., the categorical imperative); and the third, from a neo-Thomist view of moral law and personhood. Given that we have no rational or empirical way of deciding which set of assumptions is right, we cannot resolve the debate on abortion except by assuming that our own personal perspective is correct and then trying to gain enough power to force our beliefs upon others.

MacIntyre argues that both Friedrich Nietzsche and Max Weber describe this contemporary moral (dis)order well. Appeals to moral objectivity are, in Nietzsche's view, masked attempts to bend others to our will, while society is, for Weber, "nothing but a meeting place for individual wills, each with its own set of attitudes and preferences and who understand the world solely as an arena for the achievement of their own satisfaction."[4] Both Nietzsche and Weber claim that we must recognize and accept this state of affairs in order to learn how to mitigate and transmute its most destructive consequences. MacIntyre alternatively argues that the only way to address our current moral predicament is to transform the underlying view of human nature that Nietzsche, Weber, and earlier Enlightenment thinkers espouse.

To bolster this claim, MacIntyre elaborates the concept of human nature that the virtue tradition employs and examines the historical consequences of its rejection. According to the virtue tradition, humans are born with a latent spiritual potential that can only be realized by individually and collectively cultivating virtuous dispositions. This view of human nature provides moral inquiry with a clear orientation and goal. Its job is to understand what the virtues entail, how these virtues help actualize our spiritual potential, and how we can effectively cultivate virtuous dispositions. Vigorous moral debate certainly arose within the virtue tradition, but it was more like the debate we see in natural science today, in that it admitted the possibility of being resolved by the community of inquiry. This possibility of resolution sharply contrasts the interminable conflict that plagues contemporary moral discourse.

The virtue tradition of moral inquiry fell into disarray when Enlightenment thinkers abandoned its underlying view of human nature yet tried to preserve its moral precepts within a secular and naturalistic worldview. The problem with this "Enlightenment project," as MacIntyre calls it, is that moral precepts operate in the virtue tradition like guardrails for the broader project of virtue cultivation. In other words, the point of moral precepts in the virtue tradition is not to fulfill deontological requirements, but to map the boundaries of proper spiritual growth. Without the associated idea of human nature, then, the virtue tradition's moral precepts lose their function and become abstract, contingent rules that certain people enforce because they like or are served by them.

Enlightenment thinkers recognized this difficulty and sought to respond by grounding morality in some already-possessed feature of human nature. This is the logic that underlies Adam Smith's suggestion that the pursuit of self-interest leads to a prosperous and morally upright world. Unfortunately, as McIntyre explains, all such efforts failed in the end. Modern thinkers accordingly began doubting the very possibility of grounding morality. Figures like Nietzsche and Weber clearly diagnosed this nihilistic tendency in Enlightenment thought, which is why their resultant suggestions remain so attractive and persuasive today. Nevertheless, MacIntyre rejects the idea that we can escape our contemporary moral chaos by optimizing or sublimating contemporary dynamics and argues instead that the only way forward is to reground our thinking in the framework of the virtue tradition.

We can deepen our appreciation of this suggestion by briefly examining how MacIntyre treats the concept of virtue in his analyses of instrumental activities, practices, and traditions. With instrumental activities, he argues, we aim to achieve a concrete goal that can be accomplished by various means. One can, for example, communicate across distance via smoke signals, letters, phone calls, and emails. As new and more efficient instruments are created, we inevitably leave old ones behind. Within every practice, however, one pursues an unattainable ideal that cannot be separated from a particular activity. Thus, although one can finish writing a book and use different technologies to do so (e.g., pen and paper, a computer), one cannot finish the practice of writing. Maintaining a practice in the long term therefore requires us to develop certain dispositions, like diligence and perseverance. These dispositions are what MacIntyre calls "virtues." A virtue, as he explains, "is an acquired human quality the possession and exercise of which tends to enable us to achieve those goods which are internal to practices and the lack of which effectively prevents us from achieving any such goods."[5]

Virtues also sustain a healthy interaction between individuals and a wider cultural tradition. Individuals, he explains, discern their talents, aims, and inclinations by exploring the possibilities that appear within their inherited cultural tradition. The cultural tradition, in turn, evolves as each generation of individuals carves out their slightly different paths. A vibrant tradition allows individuals to develop in a healthy manner, while well-adjusted individuals care for and serve their tradition. But what is it that enables some individuals to persevere in their quest to live a good life and to improve their tradition while others abandon these endeavors for lesser paths? Likewise, what is it that enables certain traditions to evolve in a healthy manner and to sustain just and prosperous social orders while others stagnate and do great harm to their peoples? MacIntyre's answer to both these questions is that it depends upon the extent to which individuals and traditions possess or lack the relevant virtues, in particular those of honesty, courage, truthfulness, prudence, humility, and charity.[6] And these virtues are precisely those that the virtue tradition has historically pursued. MacIntyre therefore argues that the virtue tradition provides us with the most expedient way of securing the individual and collective good.

Moreover, MacIntyre argues that the virtue tradition enables an authentically objective pattern of moral inquiry. Agreeing on the virtue tradition's underlying view of human nature lets us investigate whether certain actions cohere with certain virtues and the moral precepts that mark their limits, as well as whether certain practices help us develop virtuous dispositions.

Noting these dynamics, MacIntyre concludes that the virtue tradition is altogether superior to its Enlightenment successor. Yet he also acknowledges that we cannot develop an a priori vindication of this claim. Rather, we must participate in the endeavors of a community that operates within the virtue tradition in order to experience the merit of its framework. MacIntyre believes that the Catholic Church offers a powerful space in which such experience can take place. Nevertheless, he recognizes that modern society has

too complex a history with Catholicism for a straightforward renewal to be possible today. Indeed, the gap between Catholicism
and modern society is so well established that the only choice for
Catholics is the one early Christians embraced when, upon seeing
the Roman Empire's pervasive vice and lack of spiritual receptivity,
they abandoned the empire and gradually built up new patterns of
local community life. Thus, as MacIntyre puts it, "what matters at
this stage is the construction of local forms of community within
which civility and the intellectual and moral life can be sustained
through the new dark ages which are already upon us." He continues: "And if the tradition of the virtues was able to survive the
horrors of the last dark ages, we are not entirely without grounds
for hope. This time, however, the barbarians are not waiting beyond the frontiers; they have already been governing us for quite
some time. . . . We are [therefore] waiting not for a Godot, but for
another—doubtless very different—St. Benedict."[7]

Although MacIntyre's conclusion may seem foolhardy and naïve to some, it is important to acknowledge its coherence with the
historical record. Most of the world's major religious traditions
arose in periods of great moral chaos and made their mark by establishing new patterns of community life that would later remold,
if not replace, the existing social order. MacIntyre clearly believes
that some such movement will arise again from within Catholicism.
It is certainly possible that this may happen. Nevertheless, it is
important to ask why those who are not already committed
Catholics would accept this conclusion. Might we not also find
dynamics worth renewing in traditions that MacIntyre does not
place within the virtue tradition, such as Hinduism, Buddhism,
Confucianism, and Daoism, or even within Jewish, Islamic, and
Protestant variations of the virtue tradition?

The most plausible response to this challenge MacIntyre can
make is to argue that because the modern West arose as a transformation of late medieval Catholicism, we can only repair its problems by revitalizing the Catholic virtue tradition. Unfortunately,
this argument oversimplifies the process that led from late medieval Christendom to the modern West. Certainly, the Protestant
and Enlightenment rejection of the Catholic virtue tradition did
shape the contours of European modernization. Yet these were not

the only important factors. Nonreligious dynamics of urbanization, the invention of the printing press, the advancement of natural science, the decline of feudalism, and the growing accumulation of capital each exerted a decisive influence on modern European life. Even within the realm of religion, recent scholarship has shown that the modern West did not arise under pristinely Catholic influences. Armando Salvatore, for example, has demonstrated how both Catholicism and Islam shaped the emergence of the modern public sphere, as well as how both these movements emerged within the dynamic encounters of the classical axial traditions.[8] The point here is not to deny the legacy of late medieval Catholicism, but rather to contest the claim, which undergirds MacIntyre's renewal narrative, that the modern West arose as an autonomous and internal transformation thereof.

Regardless of how we see the relationship between late medieval Christendom and the modern West, we have little reason to believe that the only way we can respond to our contemporary problems is by renewing a religious dynamic that previously declined. Indeed, the simple fact that the Catholic virtue tradition was itself at one point a new movement undermines MacIntyre's effort to present the renewal of this tradition as our only hope. Is it not possible that something new could enter history today and help us address our pressing social and moral concerns?

A second significant problem with MacIntyre's narrative concerns his uncharitable condemnation of the modern West. We live, he suggests, in the "new dark ages" in which the barbarians "have already been governing us for quite some time."[9] How, then, can we account for the leading role that modern Western societies played in abolishing slavery and giving unparalleled political rights to women, ethnic minorities, and the poor? Indeed, MacIntyre's very narrative of modern moral chaos refuses to acknowledge the many instances of moral consensus that modern Western societies have achieved. Jeffrey Stout has criticized this feature of MacIntyre's thought: "Are there no examples of ethical debates in our culture that have come to an end? MacIntyre does not ask this question. Suppose we go back to mid-nineteenth-century America. What is the most impassioned ethical debate of the day? Clearly, it is the debate over the abolition of slavery. This is not, I am happy

to add, an unfinished debate. . . . In the meantime, we have had
great debates over whether women should be permitted to vote,
whether alcoholic beverages should be banned in a society that
cares about the virtue of temperance, and whether blacks should be
allowed to sit in the front of the bus. Each of these more recent debates, so far as I can tell, is now over."[10] Indeed, MacIntyre seems
unable to acknowledge, as Charles Taylor puts it, "the humbling
degree to which some of the most impressive extensions of a gos-
pel ethic depended on a breakaway from Christendom," as doing
so would undermine his claim that the decline of late medieval
Christendom was an undiluted evil, and hence his attempt to argue
that renewing this tradition is the only viable option today.[11]

Martin Heidegger

Martin Heidegger presents modernity as a spiritual wasteland in
which everything appears as a valueless resource that can be shaped
by our will. This state of affairs, he argues, is the final stage of the
metaphysical trajectory that Plato ushered into Western civilization long ago. Yet Heidegger claims to have uncovered another
and more benevolent possibility in the work of the pre-Socratic
Greeks. He therefore recommends that we return to pre-Socratic
thought to learn how to distance ourselves from the Platonic tradition and "light up that space within which Being itself might again
be able to take man, with respect to his essence, into a primal
relationship."[12]

To clarify Heidegger's basic argument, it will be helpful to
briefly consider two roles that notions of divinity can play in
human affairs. First, "divinity" can be used in a metaphysical or
theological manner to unify a group of people around a shared
vision of higher order. Consider, for example, how a system of orthodox practices and creeds unites the global Catholic community.
Second, "divinity" can describe a revelatory dynamic that unsettles
fixed patterns of thought and action and discloses new horizons.[13]
We could think here of the massive disruptions brought about by
the Protestant Reformation or the Hebrew prophets' critiques of
the social order. Heidegger's basic claim is that, since Plato, the
West has increasingly emphasized divinity's metaphysical function

over its revelatory counterpart, even to the point where large swaths of modern society see divinity as nothing but an abstract concept that people use to impose order on the world.

Those familiar with Heidegger's use of the term "Being" and his critical relationship with Christianity might find it strange to see his thought explained in explicitly religious terms. Indeed, as Julian Young explains, "Heidegger denies many times that Being is . . . the god of Christian theology and metaphysics." However, if we think of Being as a mysterious and unknown God who transcends doctrine and makes Himself known in the inspired words of poets, philosophers, and mystics, then, "to be brief and blunt, Being is God." He continues: "Being—'the Origin,' 'the Source,' . . . 'the Other of beings,' '*ku*' as it is called in Japanese Zen Buddhism, '*Tao*' as it is called in Taoism—is . . . something 'mystical,' 'awesome,' 'holy,' is an object of something close to, or identical with, religious veneration."[14] Heidegger's hesitation to describe Being in religious terms stems from his desire to distance himself from the metaphysical tradition that has long dominated Western thought and his belief that we can only authentically encounter divinity by abandoning the metaphysical approach and reattuning ourselves to divinity's revelatory function.

On Heidegger's reading, pre-metaphysical Greek polytheism remained open to the divine's revelatory function by allowing the gods to disclose the world to human beings in many ways.[15] It was not people's job to specify beforehand what reality could be, but rather to respond appropriately to the way one or another god decided to reveal it. Plato reversed this orientation by binding divinity to an eternal cosmic order. Instead of letting things appear in myriad forms, Plato sought to demonstrate that things could only be the way the one cosmic order allowed them to be. It is precisely here that Heidegger locates the beginning of the Western elevation of metaphysics over revelation. Or, as Heidegger puts it, "*metaphysics begins* with Plato's interpretation of Being as *idea*. For all subsequent times, it shapes the essence of Western philosophy."[16]

Each of the subsequent periods of Western history extended Plato's conceptual maneuver. In the medieval period, for example, the unchanging metaphysical order was held to emanate from the mind of God and to be infallibly recorded in Holy Scripture.

Thomas Aquinas, for Heidegger, exemplifies this worldview. In the modern period, the notion arose that human beings participate in the divine mind and can therefore discover the eternal order of things through the autonomous use of reason. Descartes supposedly exemplifies this age. And finally, during the postmodern period we began seeing God as a mere concept that we create in order to control the world. Nietzsche articulated this line of thought.[17] Though clearly oversimplifying a complex tale, I might summarize Heidegger's view of Western history by saying that we proceed from the God of ideas (Plato) through the God of Scripture (Aquinas) and the God of the philosophers (Descartes) to the God of our own creation (Nietzsche).[18]

Although some read Nietzsche's announcement of God's death as a rallying cry for a new kind of muscular atheism, Heidegger points out that Nietzsche considers godlessness a problem that needs to be solved. Nietzsche recognizes that humans need a metaphysical divinity to orient and bestow meaning upon their world. The death of God is therefore a great tragedy for human life. It is for this reason that "the madman" in Nietzsche's *Thus Spoke Zarathustra* announces the death of God in the midst of his fervent search to find Him: "Haven't you heard of that madman who in the bright morning lit a lantern and ran around the marketplace crying incessantly, 'I'm looking for God! I'm looking for God!' ... The madman jumped into their midst and pierced them with his eyes. 'Where is God?' he cried; 'I'll tell you! *We have killed him*—you and I! We are all his murderers.'"[19] Then, with a dizzying mix of terror and thrill, Nietzsche suggests his own solution to the problem of godlessness: "How can we console ourselves, the murderers of all murderers! Is not the magnitude of this deed too great for us? *Do we not ourselves have to become gods merely to appear worthy of it?*" The idea here is that the only way to maintain divinity's metaphysical function after recognizing that we create God is to take up God's world-ordering work for ourselves.[20]

Heidegger appreciates Nietzsche's vision but argues that it fails to extirpate the Western metaphysical tradition.[21] His main criticism is that, despite Nietzsche's rejection of the idea that a higher, ideal reality orders the world, Nietzsche still assumes that thought aims to order the world. In other words, although Nietzsche claims that his critique of the Western tradition takes us beyond Platonic metaphysics, he simply undermines the content of Platonic metaphysics while continuing to bind thought to the same metaphysical task. Heidegger thus argues that Nietzsche leads us deeper into the Western predicament.

Heidegger claims that technology captures the essence of Nietzschean postmodernism. Within a technological worldview, everything appears as a valueless resource that can be ordered to our liking. We create the meaning that such resources possess and dupe ourselves into thinking that this meaning objectively exists. Nevertheless, we gradually realize what we have done, and thus meaning begins to dissipate. This stimulates a frenzied and ultimately futile drive for novelty. Thus, although technological culture generates many useful instruments, our feverish attempts to ignore the emptiness of our pursuits create ever-greater monstrosities, such as environmental degradation, the objectification of ourselves and the world, and the decline of aesthetic and religious sensibility. This last development is arguably the most egregious, as it "threatens man with the possibility that it could be denied to him to enter into a more original revealing and hence to experience the call of a more primal truth," which is to say that it threatens us with the possibility of forgetting that we can inhabit the world in a more revelatory manner.[22] Thus, instead of following Nietzsche's recommendation that we simply accept our role as world creators, Heidegger suggests that we must try to overcome the world-ordering impulse that Plato ushered into Western civilization long ago and learn again to submit ourselves to the revelatory function of the divine.

Heidegger argues that we can proceed in this direction by renewing our engagement with the pre-Socratic, and hence pre-metaphysical, Greeks.[23] Heidegger's wish is not to resurrect early Greek thought and religion per se, but rather to rediscover the way early Greeks inhabited the world. Thus although Heidegger often valorizes an encounter with the "divinities," he does not expect us to believe in the Greek pantheon again. His hope is that we will learn to reembody the spirit of pre-Socratic Greek religion, which is to remain open to the many sacred promptings of the world without collapsing them into a single theological schema. This is why Mark Wrathall and Morganna Lambeth describe Heidegger's ultimate position as "poly-divinism," as opposed to polytheism.[24]

Upon first reading (perhaps even upon a second or third), Heidegger's basic argument can appear bizarre. Looking back to pre-Socratic Greek polytheism contradicts our most basic sense of the developmental merit of Greek philosophy and Abrahamic monotheism.[25] Nevertheless, several contemporary thinkers have argued that Heidegger was onto something important. For example, Hubert Dreyfus and Sean Kelley turn to Heidegger's poly-divinism to think about the role that religion and spirituality can play in our pluralistic public sphere. Dreyfus and Kelley accept that religion will not disappear in modern times and that the sacred is a fundamental feature of human existence. Nevertheless, they challenge the suggestion, made recently by Jürgen Habermas, that we ought to revitalize the conjunction of faith and reason that characterized the traditions of the axial age, as these traditions were all ostensibly caught up in the metaphysical project that Heidegger identified and critiqued. Dreyfus and Kelley therefore follow Heidegger in recommending that we alternatively strive to reengage the sacred today by revitalizing non-metaphysical and pluralistic pre-Socratic spirituality.[26]

When considering the viability of Heidegger's broader renewal narrative, it helps to begin by specifying the methodological assumption that animates his work. As Richard Rorty puts it, Heidegger believes that "if you understood the history of Western philosophy you understood the history of the West."[27] Indeed, Heidegger appears to go further still and claim that we can understand the West by simply interpreting a few of its most distinguished minds. As we saw above, Heidegger believes that Plato, Aquinas, Descartes, and Nietzsche each articulated the basic assumptions of their age. Therefore, understanding their thought lets us understand the true history of the West.

Is this a legitimate maneuver? Can we grasp the presuppositions of a cultural epoch by analyzing the work of one, or even several, of its exemplary thinkers? There is clearly some insight in this approach. To use Heidegger's own examples, Plato, Aquinas,

Descartes, and Nietzsche each exerted an astounding influence on the cultural trajectory of the modern West by articulating vague sentiments and ambitions that were taking shape during their respective epochs. Furthermore, we can discern a developmental relationship between their projects, whereby each subsequent figure developed perspectives that were only latent before. A well-grounded Heideggerian-style analysis of the history of Western philosophy ought therefore to generate powerful and important insights about the broader trajectory of the West. The only question is whether such an analysis could ever discover the true meaning of the West.

Recent research gives us little reason to answer in the affirmative. David Sorkin, for one, has demonstrated that the Enlightenment was not characterized by a single monolithic project, but rather by a series of diverse yet interrelated endeavors.[28] He describes these as "religious," "moderate," and "radical" Enlightenments and explains that we can understand the Enlightenment only by considering the dynamic interactions between these three movements. Charles Taylor has similarly shown that the modern West is not defined by a single evolutionary arc, but rather by the gradual emergence of a novel, multifaceted dynamic that stimulates the proliferation of new positions and perspectives.[29] Such complexity disrupts Heidegger's attempt to collapse each cultural epoch into the work of a paradigmatic individual.

This critique also applies to Heidegger's assessment of the ancient beginnings of Western civilization. Can we plausibly say that the history of the West autonomously unfolds from the philosophy of Plato? Certainly, Plato was a figure of towering importance, and every subsequent generation has found insight and inspiration in his work. Yet acknowledging this influence is a far cry from crediting him with Western civilization. Of course, Heidegger's point is not that Plato himself founded the West, but rather that he first articulated the existential choice that Western civilization subsequently pursued. Even still, the clear implication is that, existentially speaking, all of Western history is just a "series of footnotes to Plato."[30] This means that Western civilization is a self-contained system that has long been unfolding the implications of Plato's original position. It is this assumption that leads Heidegger to reject the entire

Western tradition and to endeavor to begin again with the pre-Socratics.

Although many arguments could be marshaled to challenge this conclusion, the most damning appears when we simply note that Heidegger's desire to cast off Western civilization and renew pre-Socratic Greek spirituality encouraged him to embrace Nazism.[31] Indeed, in his recently published journals, Heidegger equates the basic features of his renewal narrative with Nazi ideology. For example, Heidegger claims that the growing power of "world Jewry," as he puts it, "finds its basis in the fact that Western metaphysics—above all, in its modern incarnation—offers fertile ground for the dissemination of an empty rationality and calculability."[32] He explains how the "original and primordial" transformation that modern Germany must pursue will forever "remain inaccessible to this 'race.'"[33] Following the war, Heidegger even argued that Germany's failure to carry out the necessary renewal of early Greek spirituality was a far greater tragedy than the Holocaust itself: "Is not the failure to acknowledge this destiny (the destiny of the German people), and repressing our will for the world, a 'fault,' and an even more essential 'collective guilt' whose enormity cannot be measured against the horror of the 'gas chambers,' a guilt more terrible than all the officially censurable 'crimes,' for which no one will apologise in future? It can already be perceived that the German people and German territory are a single concentration camp such as the world has never seen and never wants to see, a not wanting much more willed and consensual than our absence of will in the face of the feralisation of national socialism."[34] Although I do not agree with Emmanuel Faye that Heidegger's anti-Semitism taints all his philosophy, I do find it hard to give much credence to the narrative that led him to embrace the worst kind of fanaticism.[35] Indeed, the lure of backward-looking fanaticism is one of the dangers that renewal narratives must constantly face.

Muhammad Iqbal

Philosophically trained at Cambridge and Munich in the early twentieth century, Muhammad Iqbal (1877–1938) was a founding father of modern Pakistan, a key, though misrepresented, resource for the Iranian Revolution, a towering figure of modern Islamic poetry, and a leading twentieth-century Islamic philosopher.[36] His influential renewal narrative is built upon the somewhat counterintuitive idea that "European culture, on its intellectual side, is only a further development of some of the most important phases of the culture of Islam."[37] More specifically, he argues that Islamic intellectual culture was taken up by the Christian West after Islam grew encumbered by legalism and mysticism. In making this claim, Iqbal interprets modern history according to the Qur'anic verse "If you go not forth, He will chastise you with a painful chastisement, and instead of you *He will substitute another people.*"[38] It is only from this perspective that we can grasp his otherwise bizarre remark that "the British empire . . . [was] the greatest Muhammadan Empire in the world."[39] However, Iqbal also goes on to suggest that Christianity's individualistic message did not provide the modern West with the intellectual and spiritual resources it needed to properly channel Islam's great civilizational force. This is why Western civilization gradually fell into nationalism, secularism, and naturalism during the modern period. The only way to reverse these destructive tendencies is to "tear off from Islam the hard crust which has immobilized an essentially dynamic outlook on life" and reconnect modern society with its true roots in Islam.[40]

Iqbal acknowledges that this claim will be hard to accept for many in the West, because Western perceptions of Islam have for centuries been colored by prejudice and suspicion.[41] This is why he goes to such pains to clarify "the ruling concepts of the culture of Islam" and to explain how they came to influence the Christian West.[42] Iqbal focuses in particular upon Islamic concepts of knowledge, evolution, and society.

Concerning knowledge, Iqbal argues that Islamic thinkers, and not the ancient Greeks or modern Europeans, were the first to develop experimental science. Greek thinkers conscientiously disregarded concrete experience and sought to contemplate the eternal structure of things in a speculative manner. Although engaging with Greek philosophy certainly sharpened the capacities of Islamic thinkers and provided them with a theoretical basis upon which to build, they gradually realized that the "concrete spirit of the Qur'an" clashed with the "speculative nature of Greek [thought,] which enjoyed theory and was neglectful of fact." Islamic thinkers laid the foundations for modern experimental science by trying to develop a more concrete and factually oriented mode of inquiry. Of particular importance was the way they formulated the principle of doubt as the basis for all knowledge, developed sophisticated inductive critiques of Aristotelian logic, argued for the primacy of sense perception in all natural-scientific knowledge, and systematically applied these new strategies of inquiry to astronomy, optics, medicine, physics, history, anthropology, and sociology.[43]

To ground the idea of Islam's "concrete spirit," Iqbal draws attention to the notion of prophetic finality, which is commonly interpreted to mean that Muhammad is the last prophet and Islam the final religion. Iqbal instead focuses on how this idea entails the "abolition of priesthood and hereditary kingship in Islam," points toward "reason, experience, nature, and history as sources of human knowledge," and raises the idea that the spiritual life is "open to critical scrutiny like other aspects of human experience."[44] If humanity can have no supernatural authority after Muhammad, then its only course is to try to understand the world through experimental and rational inquiry. Iqbal suggests that the Qur'an explicitly urges humanity in this direction.

Furthermore, Iqbal argues that, in contrast to the Greeks' focus on eternal structures and disregard for temporal processes, the Qur'an encourages Islamic thinkers to develop an evolutionary account of reality by explaining that God's will appears within the temporal dynamics of the world:

> It is He who made the sun a radiance, and the moon a light, and determined it by stations, that you might know the number of the years and the reckoning. God created that not save with the truth, distinguishing the signs to a people who know. In the alternation of night and day, and what God has created in the heavens and the earth—surely there are signs for a godfearing people.[45]

> Divers institutions have passed away before you; journey in the land, and behold how was the end of those that cried lies.[46]

We created man of an extraction of clay, then We set him, a drop, in a receptacle secure, then We created of the drop a clot, then We created of the clot a tissue, then We created of the tissue bones, then We garmented the bones in flesh; thereafter We produced him as another creature. So blessed be God, the fairest of creators![47]

With such passages as their guide, Iqbal notes that by 1000 CE, Ibn Miskawayh had developed a sophisticated theory of material and biological evolution; and al-Biruni, a vision of nature as a dynamic process of becoming.[48] And by 1400, Ibn Khaldūn had articulated his seminal account of evolutionary historical and social process, and Rumi had incorporated the concept of evolution into his poetic rendition of the soul's journey toward God.[49]

Iqbal further argues that the Qur'anic notion of prophetic finality helped stimulate the emergence of a universal democratic ideal in the medieval Islamic world. Without a clear successor to the Prophet or an established legal system, the Islamic community was forced to choose its leader and to work out the implications of Qur'anic law on its own. And because the Qur'an accepts the "division of mankind into races, nations, and tribes . . . for purposes of identification only" and requires all believers to regularly face Mecca in collective prayer, fast during the month of Ramadan, make pilgrimages to Mecca, and give charitably of their property, he claims that Islam "gradually enlarges the sphere of human association" to the entire human race. Indeed, he even suggests that the very goal of Islam has always been to "realize [humanity's] essential unity as a fact in life by demolishing all barriers which stand between man and man." In this way, he places the desire for a global spiritual democracy at the center of Islamic practice and belief.[50]

Iqbal is under no allusions as to the current state of Islam. Its true spirit, he tells us, lies "dormant," enmeshed in "rigorous conservatism" and "dogmatic slumber," "mechanically repeating old values," "overshadowed or displaced by Arabic imperialism," immobilized by a "hard crust," "deislamized through the influence of local character, and pre-Islamic superstition," and bewitched by a "false reverence for past history" and the futile pursuit of its "artificial resurrection."[51] This is not to say that Islam's potential is sapped. Rather, Iqbal's purpose in making these claims is to demonstrate how Muslims can acknowledge Islam's decline without either embracing Western secularism or trying to reinstitute earlier Islamic ways.

To help us see how the proper renewal of Islam might proceed, Iqbal explores why Islam declined in the first place. He begins his analysis by explaining that numerous early Islamic thinkers rejected important features of Qur'anic teaching because they accepted Greek thought wholesale. In response, Islamic jurists sought to curb these thinkers' influence by belittling the value of philosophy and science and by emphasizing the integrative power of shari'a law. The legalists gradually prevailed over the philosophers, but the rational and explorative impulse was not entirely quelled, appearing again with particular force in the phenomenon of Sufism. Many of the best Muslim minds accordingly began following the Sufi path. But Sufism's preoccupation with abstract metaphysical concerns left Islamic society "in the hands of intellectual mediocrities" and the "unthinking masses . . . [who] found their security only in blindly following the schools." It was precisely at this fragile moment in Islamic history that the Mongols sacked Baghdad, the Islamic world's intellectual center. In response, conservative jurists began focusing "all their efforts on . . . preserving a uniform social life for the people by a jealous exclusion of all innovations in the law of Shari'a." Fortunately, Islamic intellectual culture had by that time taken root in Moorish Spain and was beginning to exert a strong influence on European thought. As a result, during subsequent centuries, "Europe has been seriously thinking on the great problems in which the philosophers and scientists of Islam were so keenly interested" and has achieved an "infinite advance . . . in the domain of human thought and experience" thereby.[52]

In light of this historic trajectory, Iqbal concludes that there is nothing wrong with modern Muslims turning to the West for knowledge, as long as they remain focused on the work of renewal and are not seduced by the "dazzling exterior" of Western materialism. On this front, Iqbal pays particular attention to modern science. Like many others, he considers science the contemporary paragon of human learning but questions the assumption that accepting science entails naturalism. He recognizes that natural scientists do focus on sense perception and natural laws and have no need to reference reality's spiritual dimensions in their investigations.[53] However, he also argues that naturalism makes an unwarranted leap from the success of natural science to the claim that only the natural-scientifically known world exists. In this regard, although Iqbal acknowledges that religious knowledge is currently much less developed than natural-scientific knowledge, he highlights the universality of religious experience and the apparently nonmaterialistic implications of post-Newtonian physics to suggest that it may even be possible to generate religious knowledge in a scientific way.

As a first step in this direction, Iqbal considers the difference between our encounters with physical reality and spiritual reality, claiming that the former take place via sensory perception and the latter via a mode of spiritual perception that he describes as "the heart."[54] Although his notion of heart is not thoroughly developed, Iqbal seems to describe a faculty that perceives fundamental spiritual truths and is attracted to their inherent beauty. Based on this distinction between sensory and spiritual perception, Iqbal argues that our knowledge of both physical and spiritual reality can be pursued in a sufficiently systematic and experimental manner. The knowledge system that emerges from the former is science, while the knowledge system that emerges from the latter is religion. Of course, science has generated much more reliable knowledge than religion during the modern period, but only because religious actors have not yet dedicated themselves to generating religious knowledge in a systematic and experimental manner. In this regard, Iqbal's view of the relationship between scientific and religious inquiry comes very close to Dewey's, except that Iqbal acknowledges transcendence while Dewey does not.

Iqbal mentions two areas of religious inquiry that are particularly amenable to a more scientific approach. First, there is the effort to purify and elevate inner life, a goal that mystics of various sorts have pursued throughout the ages. Iqbal believes that something similar should be done today, albeit in a way that reflects modern scientific methods. Second, there is the effort of religious communities to "realize the spiritual in a human organization"—

that is, to reconstruct human society around certain spiritual ideals.[55] Iqbal suggests that we can make this line of inquiry more scientific by systematically experimenting with ways to translate spiritual ideals into new patterns of individual and collective life. The development of a more scientific pattern of religious inquiry also requires an evolutionary worldview that fully acknowledges reality's material and spiritual dimensions. He finds Alfred North Whitehead's process metaphysics deeply insightful on this front, as Whitehead acknowledges that evolution involves the simultaneous growth of material complexity and the further appearance of spiritual ideals and potentialities in the world.

Iqbal's renewal narrative is built on four interrelated claims: (1) The diffusion of Islamic intellectual culture caused the emergence of modern Europe; (2) Christianity's individual message was unable to sustain the great civilizational forces of Islam; (3) as a result, the modern West gradually fell into decadence and decline; (4) therefore, the only way to properly channel modern social forces today is to renew our engagement with an authentic and reformed Islam. Which, if any, of these claims is defensible?

Concerning the notion that the diffusion of Islamic culture stimulated Western modernity, it is interesting to note that many of the processes that Iqbal mentions have been confirmed by contemporary research. For example, we now know that Muslim scientists powerfully advanced Greek science, in both its theory and its method, and played a foundational role in stimulating early modern science. Modern scholars are also beginning to appreciate the significant role Moorish Spain played in catalyzing the European Renaissance, as well as the influence that Islamic social forms had on the emergence of the bourgeois public sphere. Indeed, the general trend seems to be for scholars to increase their estimation of Islam's role in the genesis of Western modernity as their understanding of the dynamics of Islamic cultural diffusion advances.[56]

This is not to say that Islam was directly responsible for the emergence of Western modernity. Obviously, the state of affairs in late medieval Europe had to be such that the progressive features of Islamic culture could be taken up, energetically engaged, and transformed. Perhaps Iqbal believed that God had somehow prepared the European peoples during the medieval period to take up the mantle of Islam in this way. Unfortunately, he says nothing explicit on this front, so we can do little more than speculate. As it stands, then, Iqbal does not come close to offering a sufficiently sophisticated account of the interaction between Islamic and late medieval Christendom to support his claims.

Concerning Iqbal's suggestion that Christianity's individual message was ultimately unable to sustain the civilizational forces of Islam, several recent accounts of Western modernity have emphasized Christianity's contribution to modern individualism. For example, Larry Siedentop argues that the concept of the "individual" plays an "organizing social role in the West," and that our understanding of this idea arose out of an evolving background of medieval Christian beliefs.[57] Charles Taylor has similarly grounded modern individualism in the influence of Christianity: "The New Testament is full of calls to leave or relativize solidarities of family, clan, society, and be part of the Kingdom. We see this seriously reflected in the way of operating of certain Protestant churches, where one was not simply a member in virtue of birth, but where one had to join by answering a personal call. This in turn helped to give force to a conception of society as founded on covenant, and hence as ultimately constituted by the decision of free individuals."[58] Although these authors recognize that individualism beneficially stimulated notions of human rights, religious freedom, and scientific inquiry, they also acknowledge that it contributed to the emergence of consumerism, relativism, and the decline of traditions of public virtue and civic engagement.[59] The general dilemma for these authors, then, is to figure out how to revitalize the beneficial components of Christianity while overcoming the destructive components that support modern individualism. Iqbal claims that Christianity does not possess sufficient conceptual, institutional, or scriptural resources to do so, whereas a true and adequately reformed version of Islam does.

This critique of Christianity is certainly plausible. For many today, it is hard to imagine how Christianity alone could succeed in solving the problems of the modern world. This is not to say that Christianity is wholly obsolete or that it cannot exert a great beneficial influence on modern society. Rather, the point is simply that

it is difficult to accept the claim that its social teachings, institutions, and scriptures contain all we need in order to grapple with
the challenges of late modernity.

What, then, about Iqbal's conclusion that the only way forward
is to revitalize Islam? Let us consider the basic theological challenge he faces in recommending this path. How can he maintain
the orthodox belief that Islam is the final and consummate religion
while also arguing that the Islamic community has fallen astray and
been temporarily replaced in its world-historical role by the West?
Iqbal's solution is to give Islamic reformers a prophet-like power
to periodically reconstruct and renew Islam with the sheer force of
their will. "The only effective power," he explains, "that counter-
acts the forces of decay in a people is the rearing of self-
concentrated individuals. Such individuals alone reveal the depth
of life. They disclose new standards in the light of which we begin
to see that our environment is not wholly inviolable and requires
revision."[60] It is not hard to see why this aspect of Iqbal's thought
was picked up by Ayatollah Khamenei to justify the violence of the
Iranian Revolution. Iqbal's vision of Islamic revival explicitly rejected extremism, anti-intellectualism, and anti-Western ideology.
Nevertheless, the authority he bestows upon the singular Islamic
reformer has little ability to prohibit such violent deviations.

Acknowledging this limitation, we might still ask whether the
project of Islamic renewal could succeed if Muslims actually developed the kind of evolutionary, scientific, and global democratic reforms that Iqbal envisions. Perhaps. However, I cannot help but
wonder if such reforms would require so many departures from
traditional Islam that they would end up creating something altogether different. Some readers may disagree. Yet the conclusion
flows quite readily from extending the basic logic of Iqbal's critique
of Christianity to his own vision of Islam.

Examining these three renewal narratives helps us appreciate the
framework's basic argument: that the decline of an earlier religious
tradition caused the problems of the modern world and that the
only way to solve these problems is to renew the relevant tradition
today. In this light, the basic question we must ask of all renewal
narratives is whether it is possible to place such weight on a

specific earlier instance of religion. It is plausible to suggest that the decline of a certain religious dynamic hurt the modern world and that we could improve contemporary affairs by renewing this dynamic today. Indeed, considering only the examples provided above, the world would likely be much better if society believed more strongly in virtues, if religious believers gave up the desire to develop comprehensive theological systems and focused more on opening themselves to the revelatory promptings of divinity, and if we reestablished the kind of harmony between science and religion that arose during the heyday of Islam. Many other examples could also be given.

However, the simple fact that we can identify multiple dynamics that are worthy of renewal undermines the logic of most renewal narratives. Why should we present the decline of one specific religious tradition as the sole cause of our modern problems, and its renewal as the ideal solution to our contemporary woes? Beyond the fact that we may be personally committed to a theological vision that considers this or that tradition the divine remedy for the world, what plausible justification could we provide for such a claim? In this direction, it is somewhat ironic to note that the virtue tradition, early Greek thought, and golden-age Islam were all, at some point, novel contributions to the history of religion. They did not arise in attempts to revitalize a lost golden age, but rather in attempts to provide novel solutions to the many problems of a moment in time. Why, then, would we reject the possibility of something novel entering into the world again today? Indeed, it seems more reasonable to expect that, if we ever were to adequately respond to the crises that plague the contemporary world, something akin to a new religious movement would again need to emerge.

CHAPTER THREE

The Transsecular Narrative

THE CLAIM OF THE TRANSSECULAR narrative is that the forces of modernity do not cause religion's marginalization and decline, but rather stimulate its transformation. Thus, whereas classical secularization theorists claimed that the advancement of modern forces like science, technology, capitalism, secular ethics, and democracy gradually displace religion, those who espouse the transsecular narrative framework see these same forces as part of a broader process of religious change. The transsecular narrative is particularly popular among many contemporary scholars because it enables them to be more positively disposed toward both religion and modernity than either subtraction or renewal narratives allow. It also sets forth less robust claims about religion's broader course than subsequent narratives advance.

Charles Taylor

Charles Taylor presents the main features of his transsecular narrative in *A Secular Age*, where he examines how "exclusive" or atheistic humanism became a viable and attractive option in the West during the past five hundred years.[1] Taylor recognizes the merit of using a subtraction narrative to explain the emergence of exclusive humanism, as the marginalization and decline of Latin Christendom did figure centrally in this process. Nevertheless, he finds that subtraction narratives fail to appreciate that exclusive humanism was only one part of a broader process of religious change.

One of the key concepts Taylor uses to elucidate this claim is that of the "immanent frame." The idea here is that, unlike premodern Westerners, who saw divinity in every aspect of life, modern Westerners have the ability to understand themselves and the world without referencing transcendence. Consider natural science: it explains a wide variety of natural phenomena (e.g., electromagnetism and the operation of cells) without mentioning transcendence. Scientists can therefore believe in God or not and still examine the world in natural-scientific terms. This combination of a self-contained logic and compatibility with a wide variety of metaphysical perspectives is the key characteristic of the immanent frame, and Taylor suggests that it animates all spheres of modern life—science, politics, economics, law, ethics, religion, and education. Regardless, it is important to keep in mind that the immanent frame is not atheistic; rather, it brackets metaphysical and theological conceptions in a way that premodern cultures could not.

Taylor tells a lengthy historical tale to explain how the immanent frame emerged. He begins with early tribal religion, which ostensibly had no notion of a transcendent spiritual reality and was focused on issues of worldly flourishing (e.g., health, fertility, material wealth, and social stability). He then explains how the conceptions of transcendence (e.g., God, heaven, and Brahma) and a good beyond human flourishing (e.g., nirvana, salvation, and paradise) were introduced during the axial age (800–200 BCE). In response to these powerful new ideas, groups of believers abandoned their inherited traditions and social positions to dedicate themselves to pursuing the higher good. Thus, as Taylor puts it, "monks, Bhikkus, sanyassi, devotees of some avatar or God strike out on their own" during the classical axial period and start "unprecedented modes of sociality: initiation groups, sects of devotees, the sangha, monastic orders and so on."[2] Although most people continued practicing flourishing-oriented religion as they had for many generations before, they began offering material support to the new class of axial renunciates, while the axial renunciates, in turn,

helped their supporters through petitionary prayer, mediating ritual, accumulation of vicarious merit, or wise guidance and rule.
Indeed, Taylor explains that this pattern of "hierarchical complementarity" between the flourishing-oriented masses and the
transformation-oriented axial renunciates became the lynchpin of
the axial age.[3]

A distinctly Western trajectory began when medieval Christian
leaders rejected the axial pattern of hierarchical complementarity
and sought to bring the masses onto the path of higher transformation. Without explaining exactly why this "reform-clerical complex" emerged during the eleventh century, Taylor notes that it
involved the appearance of a new kind of spiritual elite—some
were clerics and others were lay practitioners—who saw in popular
religion only "mindless derisions from real piety" and advocated
widespread religious reform.[4] This reform-clerical complex appeared with particular force during the Protestant Reformation.

During the Enlightenment, however, the deists turned the
Protestants' critical strategies around. The Protestants argued that
true Christianity was revealed in the Bible and later obscured by
Catholicism's manufactured doctrines and superstitions, and that
eliminating these additions would therefore re-reveal the true
Christian path. The deists, in turn, argued that true religion spontaneously arose from human nature but had been obscured by
Christian doctrines and superstitions, and that removing
Christianity would therefore enable people to rediscover their inherent goodness and natural religious impulses. Thus, just as the
Protestants used a notion of primordial and universal Christian
truth to critique Catholicism and to advocate a new "flattened"
vision of society, so the deists used a concept of primordial and
universal human nature to critique Christianity as a whole and to
advocate a new vision of society that was flatter still.

Having gone this far, subsequent thinkers found little to stop
them from rejecting religious beliefs outright. The providential deists had already claimed that humans had everything they needed
to create a just, peaceful, and prosperous society, and that orthodox
religion only hindered our ability to bring these benevolent characteristics forth. Why not, then, simply abandon all religion and focus
exclusively on putting our natural capacities to work? This line of

thought—which was articulated by the likes of Baron d'Holbach, Denis Diderot, and Auguste Comte—led many progressive thinkers to embrace exclusive humanism.

Again, Taylor's claim is not that religion somehow disappeared once exclusive humanism came on the scene. Rather, exclusive humanism's emergence only signaled the appearance of the immanent frame. In other words, as soon as exclusive humanism became viable and widespread, people had the ability to think about themselves and their world in wholly immanent terms. Of course, many rejected exclusive humanism and sought to combat its growing influence. Yet the very fact that they could understand and contend with its conclusions meant that they had entered the immanent frame. The immanent frame thus had less to do with the ideals of exclusive humanism per se than with the appearance of a new cultural setting in which all worldviews were up for debate.

Taylor explains how four particular worldviews, or "cross-pressures," as he calls them, came to dominate modern culture. First is exclusive humanism, which generally claims that human reason can solve all problems, that natural science gives us an accurate picture of reality, that democracy and capitalism are the best ways to organize society, and that, while individuals have the right to believe what they choose, religion is an illusion that tends to lead otherwise reasonable and good people into irrational and immoral behavior. Second is a kind of conservative civil religion that claims that modern Western societies are and should remain grounded in Christian values, practices, and beliefs. Advocates of this perspective tend to have conservative convictions and to try solving contemporary problems by advocating some kind of religious renewal.[5] Third, as exemplified by the philosophy of Nietzsche and Jean-Paul Sartre, what Taylor describes as the "immanent Counter-Enlightenment" claims that both exclusive humanism and conservative civil religion ignore the true darkness of reality and block the radical paths that alone can enable people to lead noble and authentic lives.[6] Immanent Counter-Enlightenment thinkers thus tend to value expressive aesthetics, subversive and revolutionary political activity, and heroic individualistic ideals. And fourth, what we might call the "spiritual" Counter-Enlightenment similarly maintains that exclusive humanism and

conservative civil religion obfuscate the transformative moral resources lying deep within ourselves, but it alternatively claims that
we can reconnect with these resources only through spiritual self-
discovery.[7]

Though the modern influence of immanent Counter-
Enlightenment thought is well appreciated, at least in intellectual
circles, the spiritual Counter-Enlightenment's importance is not
yet as widely acknowledged. Initially arising among advocates of
Romanticism, the spiritual Counter-Enlightenment emphasizes individual spiritual search and presents it as a journey back to harmony, health, or authenticity from some prior imbalanced state
(e.g., rationalism, instrumentalism, consumerism, or orthodoxy).[8]
Because these "seekers" often see orthodox Christianity as a main
cause of our current state of spiritual malaise, they tend to valorize
non-Western and pre-axial religions, as well as Christianity's more
marginal and mystical dimensions. These seekers also hesitate to
identify with particular religious traditions, but prefer instead to
select from different practices and beliefs to suit their personal
needs.[9] Although spiritual Counter-Enlightenment thought often
finds immodest expression in "New Age" phenomena and involvement in drugs, raves, and the like, Taylor is encouraged by how it
currently helps many people begin reconsidering spiritual and religious themes.[10]

Taylor concludes by describing the "galloping pluralism on the
spiritual plane" that has become a distinctive feature of the late
modern age. As the four major cross-pressures continue vying
with one another, a "steadily widening gamut of new positions"
emerges.[11] Some of these new positions inhabit intermediary spaces
between two or more cross-pressures, while others resist intermix-
ing by adopting more purist, or even extremist, perspectives. He describes this pluralizing process as the "nova effect" and explains that
it will not likely diminish soon. Indeed, as he explains, "our world is
ideologically fragmented and the range of positions is growing as
the nova effect is multiplied."[12]

He believes we can navigate this nova effect by reconsidering two
ideas: that transcendence exists and that all the socioreligious forms
he considers—flourishing-oriented pre-axial religion, axial patterns
of hierarchical complementarity, universal transformative religion (a

là Protestantism), the immanent frame, exclusive humanism, conservative civil religion, the immanent Counter-Enlightenment, and the spiritual Counter-Enlightenment—authentically perceive some of its features. Unfortunately, the current norm is to choose one of these frameworks and claim that it encapsulates the whole. In Taylor's view, this dogmatic tendency has made the modern West the "scene of a total, almost obsessive identification with certain favourite schemes, driven to any wild or repellent consequences, justifying murderous schisms."[13] However, Taylor suggests that by acknowledging the existence of a transcendent reality that exceeds every finite conceptual scheme, we can begin appreciating the complementarity that such diverse strands of thought display.

Taylor's account of the emergence of the culture of modern Western religion is illuminating and profound. Let me summarize his narrative again. He claims that pre-axial religion focused on worldly spiritual powers and the requirements of human flourishing. The axial age altered this focus by introducing the ideas of transcendence and a good beyond human flourishing. A new group of renunciates began pursuing the goal of higher transformation in relative isolation from the world, while the masses continued, in a pre-axial fashion, practicing flourishing-oriented religion. The only difference was that a pattern of hierarchical complementarity had emerged, whereby the masses materially supported the renunciates and the renunciates sought to facilitate the masses' spiritual development through education, prayer, wise guidance, and the like. Medieval Christian thinkers eventually rejected this dynamic and sought to bring all people onto the path of spiritual transformation. The Protestant Reformation carried this project significantly forward, giving rise to the belief that the proper application of Christian values and beliefs would generate the ideal society. Providential deists gradually overturned the Protestants' critical strategies by arguing that humans naturally possess all the resources they need to live good lives and to build a better world. Exclusive humanists pushed this line of thought to its conclusion by claiming that people can best realize their benevolent natural capacities within a wholly immanent worldview. The appearance of exclusive humanism therefore signaled the emergence of the immanent frame. Yet advocates of conservative civil religion resisted exclusive humanism's claims by arguing that the modern West is and should remain grounded in Christian values, practices, and beliefs. Immanent and spiritual Counter-Enlightenment thinkers, in turn, rejected both options and sought to reawaken the hidden transformative resources that lie deep within the human psyche; they simply debated whether or not these resources connect with transcendence.

Taylor's analysis of Western dogmatism is also apt, as is his suggestion that a humble understanding of transcendence helps us move beyond its strictures. Consider: if no theoretical framework encompasses transcendence, but two or more each claim that they do, these frameworks will appear to fundamentally contradict each other. And because each framework does illumine certain features of transcendence, their advocates will refuse to abandon their respective perspectives, and thus will become locked in perpetual conflict with one another. However, if each group acknowledges that no theoretical framework encompasses transcendence, they should begin to approach each other's frameworks as complementary perspectives. This line of thought helps us appreciate how diverse religious insights can ossify into competing truth claims, as well as how Taylor's humble approach to transcendence can undermine dogmatic and polarizing habits of thought.

It is also interesting to note how each of the four major cross-pressures Taylor identifies resonate with one or more of the narratives presented in this book. Exclusive humanism and the immanent Counter-Enlightenment arise within the subtraction narrative framework. Conservative civil religion aligns with the renewal narrative. Advocates of the spiritual Counter-Enlightenment tend to employ postnaturalist and perennial perspectives. And Taylor's own account of the origin and evolution of the immanent frame fits neatly within the transsecular narrative domain.

Despite these many strengths, the main flaw in Taylor's narrative stems from his tendency to treat the modern West as an autonomous and globally isolated phenomenon. More specifically, he ignores entirely how encounters with Native American, Chinese, Japanese, Indian, Islamic, Mongol, and historic Middle Eastern (e.g., Manichean and Zoroastrian) socioreligious configurations shaped Western modernity.[14] To provide but one example, we now know that many ideas that proved central to both the immanent and the spiritual Counter-Enlightenments arose through European and North American encounters with Indian and Chinese practice and thought.[15] How can Taylor claim to describe the origin and evolution of modern Western culture without taking these broader interactional dynamics into view? It is understandable that he focuses on a limited range of themes. Yet by making no mention of the robust global contexts in which the modern West emerged, Taylor ends up perpetuating a falsely nativist historical view.[16]

Rodney Stark

The central idea of Rodney Stark's transsecular narrative is that Europe's uniquely low levels of religious practice and belief stem from the monopoly European Christianity has long maintained on the region's religious market. The high levels of religious commitment observed in the United States stem from its free and invigorating religious markets. Stark thus claims that European secularism is more the result of a kind of market depression than of any distinctly irreligious force.

Stark's key theoretical claim is that supernatural agents are the only source of certain rewards (e.g., salvation and immortality) that humans greatly desire. Because these rewards cannot be enjoyed in this life, believers require secondary rewards (e.g., health, fortune, happiness, community, power, virtue, and social stability) to compensate for and give evidence of their religion's postmortem claims. Every religious movement thus offers a set of compensating secondary rewards to increase confidence in its postmortem promises. And a religion's ability to generate compensating rewards increases as its resources grow. Religious groups therefore vie with one another for believers, material wealth, and social influence. But when one religious group monopolizes a religious market, its leaders become lazy and self-serving, and thus less able to generate religiously sustaining secondary rewards. Monopolized religious markets therefore sustain lower levels of religious commitment than do their competitive counterparts.[17]

Healthy competition can still exist within otherwise monoreligious societies. For example, in many Islamic countries, "competition among local mosques helps generate high levels of religiousness in Islam just as it does within American Christianity."[18] But the kind of monopoly Stark has in view arose in post-Constantine Christendom, when one religious institution was sponsored by the state and run by a group of professional priests. However, this was not the case during the first three hundred years of Christian history, when Christianity was a vigorous, innovative, and resourceful competitor within the Roman Empire's open religious market. Telling the story of this transition helps us understand how the distinct religious trajectories of Europe and the United States emerged.

The Roman Empire was unique in the pagan world for not having state-sponsored temple priests. Instead, priests competed for clientele, and many even pursued their priestly work part-time to maintain other sources of income. The empire was also influenced by numerous monotheistically inclined "oriental" religions (e.g., the cults of Isis, Cybele, and Jupiter) and monotheistic Jewish movements. Concerning the diversity of Jewish movements in the Roman Empire, Stark notes that the Sadducees advocated a worldly-oriented temple religion; the Pharisees sought to please God through moral, devotional, and legal rigor; the Essenes pursued strict asceticism; the Zealots sought to overthrow foreign rule and establish a divine kingdom; isolated mystics like John the Baptist wandered the wilderness in contemplation and prayer; and integrated diaspora Jews and a "God-fearing" community of interest upheld Jewish identity without embracing Jewish law. This was the religious "market" into which Jesus came and where he galvanized a few hundred followers.[19]

Things changed when Paul disassociated Jewish law from Christian practice, for missionaries now had more leeway to win converts from among the diaspora Jews, the God-fearing community of interest, and those with oriental faiths.[20] Additionally, Christianity's many worldly benefits gave it distinct advantages over its competitors. For example, because rudimentary nursing greatly increased survival rates in periods of sickness and plague, the ratio of Christians to non-Christians steadily increased because of Christians' tendency to provide basic health care for one another. Additionally, the Roman practice of female infanticide created a population imbalance that both lowered pagan birthrates in comparison to Christian birthrates and created the need for Romans to marry Christians, which, in turn, led to the conversion to Christianity of many spouses and mixed children. The Church also maintained high levels of enthusiasm and innovation through its commitment to communal solidarity and its willingness to accept individual initiative.[21]

When the emperor Constantine converted to Christianity, the Church's new wealth and prestige attracted a "sudden influx" of aristocrats into the priesthood. This transformed the competitive early Church into a monopoly religion whose professional leadership was often more concerned with converting kings than with transforming the masses. And with Eastern Christianity being overwhelmed by the spread of Islam, the monopolized pattern of European Christianity was thenceforth co-extensive with Christendom.[22]

The Church's spiritual orientation never entirely disappeared; it was simply displaced to its monastic margins. It began moving back to center stage when the reform-oriented Henry II (1017–56) appointed his Benedictine cousin to the papacy (Pope Leo IX, r. 1049–54), who filled the Church hierarchy with pious monastics and mobilized public support for Church reform. Subsequent popes continued these efforts, with Pope Nicholas II (r. 1059–61) going so far as to call on the public to boycott "masses and other sacraments if performed by priests who kept concubines or who had purchased their offices."[23] Lay practitioners thus became increasingly involved in reforming Church affairs.

These eleventh-century reforms help explain why an "outburst of protest movements" arose when the "Church of Power," as Stark calls it, regained control from the "Church of Piety" during the twelfth century.[24] Some of the reform movements were channeled into new monastic orders (e.g., the Franciscan and Dominican Orders) while others were labeled heresies (e.g., Catharism, the Waldensian movement, Lollardy, and the Bohemian Reformation). Regardless, Stark explains, a spirit of reform took hold of the religious public, giving rise to the conviction that if the Church "could not be reformed from within," then it might be necessary to "turn elsewhere for genuine piety."[25]

Stark points out how it was primarily "well-to-do urbanites" who participated in these early efforts of Church reform. This helps clarify why the Protestant Reformation eventually proceeded as it did. Luther's reform efforts succeeded because they mobilized the support of prominent Germans, not the masses. Indeed, Stark explains that "peasants and urban lower classes . . . were almost completely uninvolved in Luther's Reformation, both as it took place and afterwards." When the elite advocates of Protestantism drove Catholicism from its monopoly position, they simply replaced it with a Protestant church that better served their interests. As a result, the Protestant Reformation did not much improve "the low level of Christian commitment among the general population."[26]

The real transformation came when Christianity established itself in North America. Initially, settlers reestablished European patterns of religious participation within colonies that had state-sponsored churches.[27] This situation changed when the U.S. government outlawed state religion after the Revolutionary War. An "intense competition among the churches for member support" thus arose in post-Revolutionary America. This was, in Stark's view, the "miracle" that created America's vibrant religious scene, "with the result that by 1850 a third of Americans belonged to a local congregation." By the twentieth century, he continues, "half of Americans belonged, and today about 70 percent belong."[28]

Although some scholars argue that American-style religious freedom pushes groups in increasingly liberal directions, Stark contends that the opposite is actually the case.[29] As he puts it, "people do not flock to faiths that ask the least of them, but to those that credibly offer the most religious rewards for the sacrifices required." In other words, people are willing to follow very demanding religious practices that offer sufficient compensating rewards. Hence, Southern Baptists, Jehovah's Witnesses, Mormons, and evangelical nondenominational churches have grown significantly in the United States over the past forty years, while the more liberal churches have "suffered a catastrophic loss of members."[30] The lesson seems to be that religious groups with specific beliefs, particular missions, and strong communal ties offer their members greater rewards than do liberal churches that are hardly distinguishable from humanistic organizations.

Christianity's global spread also testifies to the invigorating effects of open religious markets. In Africa, Latin America, and Asia,

vigorous missionary work by American Christian groups created a
religious pluralism that inspired intense local involvement, led to
the proliferation of successful local variants, and even strengthened
established faiths. On this last point, Stark argues that Latin
American Catholicism previously functioned as a monopoly religion but was strengthened and refined by its forced response to the
rapid spread of charismatic Christianity.[31]

Stark acknowledges the apparent difficulty of explaining why
modern Europe's high levels of religious freedom have not reinvig-
orated religion, but responds by claiming that European religious
freedom is greatly overestimated. In most European countries "a
particular religion is the object of considerable government 'favoritism'" and "the government bureaucracy engages in overt and covert interference with all religious 'outsiders' and 'newcomers' that
challenge the established religious order." Brian Grim and Roger
Finke's analyses capture this reality. Most European countries score
favorably (though far behind the United States) in the authors'
Government Regulation Index, which measures the "restrictions
placed on the practice, profession, or selection of religion by the
official laws, policies, or administrative action of the state."
However, the situation is quite different in Grim and Finke's
Government Favoritism Index, which measures "subsidies, privi-
leges, support, or favorable sanctions provided by the state to a select religion or a small group of religions." There, Afghanistan and
the United Arab Emirates received the same grade as Iceland,
Spain, and Greece (7.8), Belgium was found to have a bit more favoritism (7.5) than Bangladesh (7.3), and Denmark (6.7), Finland
(6.5), Austria (6.2), Switzerland (5.8), and France (5.5) all scored
about the same as Morocco (6.3). Stark, who cites and examines
these figures, concludes that "in most European nations there is
nothing resembling a religious 'free' market."[32]

From this angle, Europe's low levels of religious commitment
appear to have little to do with any distinctly irreligious force. "It's
not that Scandinavians, for example, have stopped going to church.
They never did go." Even more, polls suggest that most Europeans
still hold distinctly religious beliefs, even if they include "New Age
beliefs in such things as reincarnation, 'healing' crystals, and
ghosts." In fact, such unorthodox beliefs are quite coherent with

the pagan beliefs that many Europeans have espoused for centuries. For all these reasons, Stark concludes that it is "absurd to call these secularized societies when what they really are is unchurched."[33]

Stark's transsecular narrative admirably inverts the Eurocentrism of classical secularization theory. Instead of seeing European secularity as a reality that all cultures and peoples will eventually embrace, he presents it as the result of a pernicious cycle of market depression that other societies, and particularly the United States, have avoided by sustaining high levels of religious freedom.

That said, the clarity and convenience of Stark's narrative should not be taken as a demonstration of its truth, as there are many places where his analyses fall short. For example, as noted above, Stark claims that the medieval Church never really engaged the masses, but rather pivoted around the interests of urban elites. Charles Taylor presents a very different argument. Though he acknowledges that elites spurred the medieval Church's rejection of the axial pattern of hierarchical complementarity, he explains that their goal really was to guide all Christians onto a higher path of spiritual transformation. And the widespread dissemination of this new orientation created the conditions in which a "secular" modern Western culture could gradually emerge. Whom, then, should we believe, Taylor or Stark? Taylor's account aligns with the explicit statements made by many medieval thinkers and Church leaders, while Stark simply applies his model to a limited range of data and claims to provide the "real" explanation of historical events. Thus, though generating an attractively comprehensible account of the follies of the medieval Church, we see here that Stark's argument stems from a cavalier application of his theory of religious economy.

Another substantive problem appears in Stark's claim that northern and western Europe's religious economies have been uniquely monopolistic. Was the state of affairs really so different, we might ask, in, say, Russia, southern Europe, China, and the Islamic world? In each instance, we see largely mono-religious societies in which there has long been a centralized religious authority, a priestly class, or a crystallized body of orthodoxy. Concerning Islam, though Stark quickly suggests that imams have traditionally competed for attendance at their prayer services, he fails to mention that many mosques have been financially supported by the state and their imams appointed for political or nepotistic reasons.[34] Thus, though there is certainly insight in Stark's argument that the legacy of state sponsorship in post-Constantine Christianity created a top-heavy European church, far more in-depth analyses are needed to support his weighty comparative claims.

Stark's narrative also faces the difficulty of disassociating secularism from irreligion. His model suggests that phenomena like naturalism and exclusive humanism are nothing more than deluded justifications of a depressed religious market. Admittedly, some people are drawn to naturalism and exclusive humanism because they are unimpressed by religion's sociopolitical fruits. To these, Stark could respond by claiming that religion would generate more impressive sociopolitical fruits if only we established sufficiently free religious markets. However, if the United States really is the paragon of religious freedom, as he often suggests, it is hard to sustain this argument, as naturalism and exclusive humanism have gained hold among American intellectual elites. Would this be possible if these lines of thought did not emanate from a reasonable and persuasive set of irreligious propositions? Thus, while we clearly cannot root European secularism in the operation of irreligious forces entirely, we must recognize that the rise and spread of irreligious doctrines like naturalism and exclusive humanism have played an important role.

Regardless, the place where Stark's theory applies best remains, unsurprisingly, the United States. The United States has very consciously encouraged a competitive religious market by minimizing state favoritism and regulation. This competition has played an important role in maintaining high levels of religious commitment and diversity. Stark's account of these distinctly American dynamics is articulated in the acclaimed book *The Churching of America*, co-written with Roger Finke.[35] Stark's theory also shows some applicability to other societies, like Ghana and India, where high levels of religious freedom and competition have historically obtained.[36] However, these few points of applicability do not warrant his efforts to use what is, in the final estimation, a quite simplistic model of religious economy as a complete explanation of the history of religion.[37]

Jeffrey Stout

Jeffrey Stout's transsecular narrative redescribes the origin and evolution of the modern democratic tradition. The modern democratic tradition, he argues, arose from the idea that public discourse should not be governed by religious orthodoxy, but rather by free, rational discourse among diverse peoples. This vision was first advanced following the sixteenth-century European Wars of Religion to help Europeans reestablish social stability and peace, not to somehow banish religion from the public sphere. However, both advocates and critics of democracy often fail to recognize this point, and thus falsely claim that democracy and religion are somehow inherently at odds.

Stout begins his narrative by exploring how the project of political secularization took shape in early modern Europe. Though most Europeans believed that the Bible was "an authoritative source of normative insight," they saw that diverse Christian groups could neither agree upon what the Bible said nor who had the authority to arbitrate between competing interpretations. As a result, efforts to ground politics in biblical truth tended to cause violence and confusion. Modern Europeans thus sought to develop a new kind of public discourse in which appeals to biblical authority would be replaced by efforts to persuade and convince one another through rational deliberation. "Notice," Stout explains, "that secularization in this sense does not reflect a commitment to secularism, secular liberalism, or any other ideology. . . . It is simply a matter of what can be presupposed in a discussion with other people who happen to have different theological commitments and interpretive dispositions." Democratic secularization thus involves "neither the denial of theological assumptions nor the expulsion of theological expression from the public sphere," but rather the recognition that "the age of theocracy is over."[38]

Unfortunately, many recent interpreters of the democratic tradition have failed to appreciate this point, as Stout points out. Richard Rorty, for example, explicitly describes religion as a democratic "conversation stopper," while John Rawls claims that religious concepts have no legitimate place in public rationality.[39] Inversely, "traditionalists" like Alasdair MacIntyre and Stanley Hauerwas contend that modern democracy pursues a "prideful and disastrous secularization of the political sphere" and that believers can thus only authentically pursue lives of faith by striving to reestablish a more orthodox pattern of public life.[40]

Though Stout is troubled by the "largely false story about the kind of society we live in" that both groups tell, he is more worried by how the resultant secularist-traditionalist dichotomy dampens our collective faith in the contemporary viability of democracy, particularly in the United States. Most Americans, he explains, are religious. Yet the dominant position among intellectual elites is that religion's public influence ought to be curtailed. Many religious people therefore feel as if their faith has no place in the public domain and begin looking to nondemocratic and premodern patterns of life for ideas about how to faithfully inhabit the world.[41] These efforts, in turn, confirm secularists' belief that religion somehow contradicts democracy, and lead them to take an even harder stance against public religion. And so the cycle continues, with both sides gradually losing faith in the idea that open democratic deliberation is still possible today.

The resultant secularist-traditionalist "culture wars" also hinder our collective ability to address the rising tide of social inequality, which is, on Stout's reading, the most substantive threat to democracy today. The globalization of capital markets and the penetration of mass media into every aspect of public and private life have given elites unprecedented abilities to "translate economic power into political power."[42] As a result, though "people retain the right to vote" and "certain constitutional protections," their "effective political voice appears to be dwindling as rapidly as the average wage earner's share in the common wealth." Indeed, the situation has become so dire that Stout wonders whether we can accurately describe the United States as a "democracy" anymore: "If our most powerful elites are now essentially beyond the reach of accountability, as they increasingly seem to be, then why suppose that our polity qualifies as a democratic republic at all? It appears to function, rather, as a plutocracy, a system in which the fortunate few dominate the rest. And if that is true, then honesty requires that we stop referring to ourselves as citizens, and admit that we are really subjects. The question of democratic hope boils down to whether the basic concepts of our political heritage apply to the world in which we now live."[43]

These oligarchical developments have been enabled by "an overall decline in the organizational strength of ordinary citizens." Though Stout does not explain why precisely this decline took place, he clearly believes that false ideas about the incompatibility of democracy and religion played a central role. Part of his proposed remedy is to help everyone see how religion can contribute to democratic struggles for justice, equality, and freedom. Indeed, if it is only the "deference and torpor of ordinary people" that allow economic elites to continue amassing power and influence, the religious systems that organize most ordinary people's lives must figure centrally in any attempt to combat oppressive elitism today.[44]

To help us consider how this process might actually proceed, Stout articulates several ways religion has advanced American democracy throughout history. He begins by noting how many prominent democratic thinkers drew upon religious thought to describe the conditions that sustain a vibrant democratic culture. Walt Whitman (1819–92), for example, argued that it is not enough for democratic societies to establish systems of checks and balances that "neutralize the evil effects of self-interest among the people"; they must also cultivate spiritual virtues like piety, hope, and love that maintain citizens' commitment to the process of democracy in the long term. Whitman thus placed a religiously inspired project of virtue cultivation—which MacIntyre considers anathema to modern public life—at the heart of the democratic tradition, as did his colleague and compatriot Ralph Waldo Emerson (1803–82).[45]

Stout then considers several instances in which religious language helped the American public achieve quintessential democratic goals. He is particularly impressed by the public addresses of Abraham Lincoln and Martin Luther King Jr., which, he explains, "represent high accomplishments in our public political culture," yet are laden with religious concepts and terms.[46] Two passages suffice to demonstrate the point. The first is from Lincoln's second inaugural address:

> The Almighty has His own purposes. "Woe unto the world because of offenses; for it must needs be that offenses come, but woe to that man by whom the offense cometh" [Matthew 18:7]. If we shall suppose that American slavery is one of those offenses which, in the providence of God, must needs come, but which, having continued through His appointed time, He now wills to remove, and that He gives to both North and South this terrible war as the woe due to those by whom the offense came, shall we discern therein any departure from those divine attributes which the believers in a living God always ascribe to Him? Fondly do we hope, fervently do we pray, that this mighty scourge of war may speedily pass away. . . . With malice toward none, with charity for all, with firmness in the right as God gives us to see the right, let us strive on to finish the work we are in, to bind up the nation's wounds, to care for him who shall have borne the battle and for his widow and his orphan, to do all which may achieve and cherish a just and lasting peace among ourselves and with all nations.[47]

The second passage is from Martin Luther King Jr.'s 1963 speech atop the steps of the Lincoln Memorial:

> I have a dream that one day every valley shall be exalted, and every hill and mountain shall be made low, the rough places will be made plain, and the crooked places will be made straight; "and the glory of the Lord shall be revealed and all flesh shall see it together" [Isaiah 40:5]. . . . With this faith, we will be able to hew out of the mountain of despair a stone of hope. With this faith, we will be able to transform the jangling discords of our nation into a beautiful symphony of brotherhood. With this faith, we will be able to work together, to pray together, to struggle together, to go to jail together, to stand up for freedom together, knowing that we will be free one day. . . . And when this happens, and

when we allow freedom to ring, when we let it ring from
every village and every hamlet, from every state and every
city, we will be able to speed up that day when *all* of God's
children, black men and white men, Jews and Gentiles,
Protestants and Catholics, will be able to join hands and
sing in the words of the old Negro spiritual: Free at last!
Free at last! Thank God Almighty, we are free at last![48]

Stout emphasizes that both Lincoln and King used religious language
in a reasonable, ethically oriented, and open way. Indeed, Lincoln and
King explicitly used religious language to help Americans overcome
their ethnic and political differences and recommit themselves to the
pursuit of democratic ideals.

Stout's purpose here is not to argue that religious language
always achieves these results, but rather to argue that religious language can contribute powerfully to democratic discourse when
used in the right way. But so can secular language, and the best
moments in American public life often have deft intertwining of
the two. Stout concludes that effective democratic discourse requires little more than a robust collective commitment to reasonable, free, and benevolent speech. Instead of outlining rules for
determining when religious language can and cannot be used in
public discourse, then, he simply encourages us all to "cultivate the
virtues of democratic speech, [to] love justice," and then to "say
what [we] please."[49] Doing so is more important than ever before,
as we have few other ways of combating the rising power of elites.
"The imbalance of power between ordinary citizens and the new
ruling class has," he explains, "reached crisis proportions," and the
crisis cannot be resolved unless "citizens who hold differing conceptions of the sacred" "commit themselves to getting democrati-
cally organized."[50]

I find it hard to argue with most of Stout's conclusions.
Secularist and traditionalist interpreters of the democratic tradition do often present overly pessimistic accounts of religion's public role, both historically and today. Stout's examples of
constructive religious contributions to public discourse also clearly
show that theorists of the public sphere would be well served by
shifting their attention from the metaphysical content of public

speech to the virtues that should characterize public deliberation. It is difficult to imagine how the general populace can combat social inequality today without developing a more unifying pattern of public discourse. And democratic societies would certainly improve if more religious actors modeled their public speech on the examples of Lincoln and King. Nevertheless, the limitations of Stout's view appear once we consider how these developments might actually take place.

To begin, though Stout consistently encourages religious actors to participate in public deliberation in charitable, civil, and reasonable ways, he offers surprisingly little analysis of what this entails in practice. Admittedly, Stout presents the public addresses of Lincoln and King as paragons of religiously inspired public discourse. But he does not specify why this is so. Were Lincoln and King's addresses ideal because they de-emphasized abstract theological doctrines that divide religious communities and concentrated instead on the more straightforward tasks of religious ethics? Did their addresses focus on issues of common concern instead of on spreading tradition-specific practices and beliefs, as many conservative Christians do today? How did Lincoln's and King's religious speeches help diverse people transcend resentment and self-interest and embrace a wider vision of human solidarity? And how can others do the same? My purpose in posing these questions is not to surreptitiously advance my own account of the ideal characteristics of religiously inspired public speech, but rather to highlight the kinds of important questions Stout does not address.

Additionally, Stout's desire to highlight the imbalances and oversights that plague traditionalist critiques of the democratic tradition leads him to discount the legitimate reasons that incline many people toward traditionalist conclusions. Without aligning myself with MacIntyre's ultimate vision of social change, a brief review of his conclusions is instructive. As I mentioned earlier, on the final page of *After Virtue*, MacIntyre concludes that "what matters at this stage [of history] is the construction of local forms of community within which civility and the intellectual and moral life can be sustained through the new dark ages which are already upon us."[51] Stout agrees with the idea that we can reform democratic public life only by establishing local forms of community in which "civility and the intellectual and moral life" can be nurtured and grow. The only difference is that Stout believes that these local communities should appear within the democratic tradition, whereas MacIntyre believes they will somehow emerge from within a revitalized version of the Catholic tradition. Stout's suggestion is plausible; but so too is MacIntyre's, as it may very well be that the modern democratic tradition is beyond repair, at least in its current form, and that the only way forward is to gradually establish a new tradition and pattern of sociopolitical life. Stout's outright dismissal of those who find in the profound teachings of religion a call to build such a world is therefore unfair. This is particularly true when we adopt a longer historical view. During earlier epochs of history, religion often helped humanity move beyond declining patterns of social and political life. Why, then, should we reject the possibility of similar transformations happening again today, or even accuse those who pursue them of unnecessary idealism and despair?

I have placed these authors' work within the transsecular narrative domain because they each argue that modernizing forces do not cause religion's marginalization and decline, but rather facilitate its transformation. The transsecular narrative thus helps us move beyond the polarity of subtraction and renewal narratives by denying the very idea that there is an inverse relationship between modernity and religion. From a transsecular perspective, then, subtraction narratives rightly point out that premodern patterns of public orthodoxy are incompatible with diverse modern societies, while renewal narratives correctly highlight the enduring social relevance of religious language and ideas.

Nevertheless, most transsecular narratives remain mired in Western-centric assumptions. As we saw above, Taylor misrepresents modern Western culture by presenting it as a globally isolated phenomenon, Stark falsely interprets religious history in terms of an American vision of "free" religious markets, and Stout refuses to consider the viability of sociopolitical projects that do not arise from the democratic tradition. Western-centrism, albeit now in a more American than European guise, thus continues influencing transsecular perspectives. The analysis of two editors of the *Economist* clearly demonstrates the growing influence of this view: "Ever since the Enlightenment there has been a schism in Western thought over the relationship between religion and modernity. Europeans, on the whole, have assumed that modernity would marginalize religion; Americans, in the main, have assumed that the two things can thrive together.... For most of the past two hundred years the European view of modernity has been in the ascendant.... [But] the world seems to be moving decisively in the American rather than the European direction. The American model of religion—one that is based on choice rather than state fiat—is winning."[52]

Admittedly, it is not wrong to argue that religion in democratic and democratizing societies will likely behave more as it does in the United States than in western Europe, if only because the United States more aggressively seeks to remold the world in its image today. But evidence also suggests that quite different approaches will also appear. Thus, although some societies, like Ghana and India, may continue embracing "free market" religious conditions, others will strongly regulate public religious life (e.g., China), or even explicitly promote religious homogeneity (e.g., Saudi Arabia). The concept of "multiple modernities" becomes very useful in this regard and should therefore be used to help us develop more complex and globally nuanced accounts of the modern transformation of religion.[53]

CHAPTER FOUR

The Postnaturalist Narrative

LIKE "SECULAR" AND "SECULARISM," the terms "nature" and "naturalism" are used in many ways. Nevertheless, "nature" is typically used to describe the domains that natural science studies; hence, "naturalism" generally refers to the belief that only the kinds of causes, laws, and phenomena that the natural sciences study exist.[1] Admittedly, some use the term "naturalism" to describe the methodological principle that knowledge should be continuous with the concepts and methods that the natural sciences employ. Though such "methodological" naturalism is technically coherent with belief in transcendence, it is often used as an indirect way of banishing religious considerations from serious debate. When using the term "naturalism" in this chapter, I describe the general belief that reality is limited to the kinds of causes, laws, and phenomena examined by the natural sciences, and consider atheism a logical extension of this view.

The basic thrust of the postnaturalist narrative can be stated as follows: Natural science rightly disrupted premodern views of nature and helped us radically extend our understanding of the world. But modern interpreters of natural science were falsely led by antireligious sentiment and a problematic desire to turn modern science into a complete metaphysical system to claim that accepting modern science entails naturalism. Nevertheless, critical philosophical analyses of naturalism and recent developments in natural science have helped reclarify how certain spiritual concepts are consistent with a scientific worldview. Like subtraction narratives, then, postnaturalist narratives highlight the value of modern science, and like renewal narratives, they appreciate the value of certain premodern religious ideas. Yet postnaturalist narratives also uniquely argue that embracing modern science does not rule out religious convictions; it simply forces us to deepen and modify our understanding of their claims.

The postnaturalist narrative is in many ways a subvariant of the transsecular narrative lens. Whereas transsecular narratives claim that forces of modernization do not cause religion's wholesale marginalization and decline, but rather stimulate its transformation, postnaturalist narratives describe how this transformation has played out in the domain of modern science. It would therefore have been conceivable to include the postnaturalist narrative within a broader account of the transsecular narrative, and thus to name six, not seven, prevalent narratives of religion. I pondered taking this route several times while writing this book. However, in the end, I concluded that the postnaturalist discourse on science and religion has become so prominent in Western intellectual circles, and particularly in the United States, that it deserves to be treated on its own. The following discussion of Thomas Nagel, Hans Joas, and Alfred North Whitehead should help substantiate this claim.

Thomas Nagel

In Thomas Nagel's view, the current intellectual climate makes it difficult to develop the kind of teleological account of nature that best explains the appearance of subjective beings like ourselves in the world, for any attempt to do so is met with rabid hostility by those who claim to be the protectors of science. This tendency emanates from an excessive fear of religion and the unwarranted belief that reductive naturalism is the only viable alternative. As Nagel says, "The political urge to defend science education against the threats of religious orthodoxy, understandable though it is, has resulted in a counter orthodoxy, supported by bad arguments, and a tendency to overstate the legitimate scientific claims of evolutionary theory. Skeptics about the theory are seen as so dangerous, and so disreputably motivated, that they must be denied any shred of legitimate interest."[2]

The reception of Nagel's recently published *Mind and Cosmos* confirms this diagnosis: his efforts to critique "neo-Darwinian" naturalism and argue for a form of Platonic naturalism stimulated an eruption of vitriol from numerous philosophers and scientists.[3] For example, psychologist Steven Pinker casually described Nagel's work as the "shoddy reasoning of a once-great thinker," while philosophers Brian Leiter and Michael Weisberg called his book an "instrument of mischief" in their derisive review.[4]

Sagely analyzing the reactionary tendencies several years before personally suffering critics' wrath, Nagel explains that they are intimately associated with the rise and success of natural science. Many early practitioners of natural science were eager to differentiate the knowledge they pursued from scholastic theology, and often did so by arguing that "the purposes and actions of God, if there is a god, are not themselves, and could not possibly be, the object of a scientific theory." This demarcation was meant not only to facilitate more effective inquiry, but also to protect natural science from the incursions of religious institutions. Unfortunately, to achieve this end, many scientific thinkers went to the opposite extreme and embraced a "world-flattening reductionism" that anathematized all ideas that seemed in any way to legitimize a religious worldview.[5]

This reductionism emanates from an intellectual fallacy that Nagel describes as the "view from nowhere." The fallacious idea is that we can and should develop a wholly objective account of reality, which is to say one that explains all apparently subjective phenomena in terms of underlying objective realities. Nagel acknowledges that our understanding of subjective phenomena like mind, value, and meaning becomes more objective as we "transcend our personal viewpoint and develop an expanded consciousness that takes in the world more fully." Yet, because we ourselves are undeniably subjective beings, he rejects the idea that we can ever achieve a wholly objective perspective. He therefore argues that we should begin from the assumption that the "subjectivity of consciousness is an irreducible feature of reality—without which we couldn't do physics or anything else—and [that] it must occupy as fundamental a place in any credible world view as matter, energy, space, time, and numbers." This assumption requires us to locate mind within "the general constituents of the universe and the laws that govern them."[6]

Nagel acknowledges the angst many will feel when considering accepting this claim, gripped as they are by the conviction that reductive naturalism is the only sure defense against the oppressive incursions of a religious worldview. To help dissipate these worries, Nagel analyzes the rationality of what he calls the "religious impulse."

According to Nagel, the religious impulse constitutes a "yearning for cosmic reconciliation," which is to say a yearning to "live not merely the life of the creature one is, but in some sense to participate through it in the life of the universe as a whole."[7] This impulse is fundamental to human rationality and arises from our awareness that we are a part of a wider cosmic reality.[8] Certainly, the religious impulse can be fulfilled by the idea that "there is some kind of all-encompassing mind or spiritual principle in addition to the minds of individual human beings and other creatures—and that this mind or spirit is the foundation of the existence of the universe, of the natural order, of value, and of our existence, nature, and purpose."[9] Yet Nagel believes that nonreligious concepts might also work. Unfortunately, most attempts to develop such concepts have failed because they do not properly address the legitimate religious desire for cosmic reconciliation. Nagel endeavors to show how this is true of deflationary naturalism, humanism, and what he calls neo-Darwinism in particular.

In deflationary naturalism, the religious impulse is considered an illusory and unfulfillable expression of an underlying conceptual confusion. The claim, therefore, is that we can eradicate the religious impulse by clarifying our thinking and dedicating ourselves to problems we can actually address. Indeed, science, conceptual analysis, and practical know-how provide all the knowledge we need, and more than enough mystery, wonder, and awe for us to happily exist.[10] Though acknowledging this position's allure, Nagel argues that the evasion of the question of cosmic reconciliation is disingenuous, as this question universally arises from our recognition that "we are products of the world and its history, generated and sustained in existence in ways we hardly understand."[11] He therefore concludes that no amount of deflationary therapy can quell the religious impulse on a wide scale.

Humanism also deploys a deflationary strategy, but claims that we can find wider purpose and meaning by connecting ourselves to the flow of human history. The belief here is that "we ourselves, as a species or community, give sense to the world as a whole" and are thus embedded within a grand historical project to create ourselves and our world.[12] Although humanism does locate our existence within a wider horizon than does deflationary naturalism, Nagel claims that it fails to provide us with a greater sense of cosmic meaning and purpose, as human history remains nothing more than a blip in an overwhelming sea of metaphysical darkness.

Neo-Darwinism responds to this void by placing history within the wider arc of cosmic evolution. Human life, neo-Darwinians explain, arose through a long and tortuous evolutionary process. Recognition of this should generate wonder, awe, and appreciation of nature, as well as a commitment to the species-preserving powers of rational thought. Neo-Darwinism thus endeavors to empower us to take charge of our own evolutionary future. Yet its message is ultimately that life has no meaning beyond self-preservation. Though thinkers like Nietzsche have tried valiantly to infuse this perspective with religious fervor, Nagel concludes that it, too, fails to fulfill the religious impulse by denying the existence of any higher, cosmic goal.[13]

Despite these failures, Nagel does believe that another nonreligious theory might work, albeit contemporaneously less prominent: namely, "some kind of Platonism." According to this Platonic framework, "the natural order is such that, over time, it generates beings that are both part of it and able to understand it. . . . Each of us is part of the lengthy process of the universe gradually waking up." Nagel argues that this kind of naturalized Platonism is the most successful nonreligious way of fulfilling the religious impulse because it locates the emergence and development of subjectivity within the cosmos's inherent purpose. And, though the Platonic view does reintroduce a nonmaterial, mind-oriented teleology into nature, Nagel argues that we need not postulate a transcendent, spiritual entity operating behind it.[14]

Unsurprisingly, Nagel acknowledges that distinctly religious concepts can also fulfill our religious impulses. However, he tries to downplay their potential merits by presenting them as the inverse of neo-Darwinian naturalism. As he says, the idea of "guided evolution, with God causing appropriate mutations and fostering their survival," is neo-Darwinian naturalism's inverted twin, as both push "teleology outside of the natural order, into the intentions of the creator—working with completely directionless materials whose properties nevertheless underlie both the mental and the physical."[15] To anyone even vaguely familiar with the longer tradition of religious thought, it is not hard to see that this characterization is false. The visions of divinely guided evolution found in the work of Plato, Aristotle, Laozi (Lao Tzu), Plotinus, Augustine, Aquinas, Avicenna, Rumi, Ibn Khaldūn, Hegel, Peirce, Whitehead, and Teilhard de Chardin, to name a few, do not espouse the kind of crass mechanistic dualism between divine purpose and the natural world that Nagel attributes to religious belief. They instead identify a spiritually directed teleology operating within the dynamic evolution of the world. Why, then, does Nagel ignore the potential merits of these more nuanced accounts of divinity?

The only conclusion I can reach is that Nagel, despite the many steps he takes beyond reductive naturalism, is simply not interested in the merits and possibilities of religion. Indeed, as he himself admits, he seems to fear the possibility that religious ideas might actually be true:

> In speaking of the fear of religion, I don't mean to refer to the entirely reasonable hostility toward certain established religions and religious institutions, in virtue of their objectionable moral doctrines, social policies, and political influence. Nor am I referring to the association of many religious beliefs with superstition and the acceptance of evident empirical falsehoods. I am talking about something much deeper—namely, the fear of religion itself. I speak from experience, being strongly subject to this fear myself: I want atheism to be true and am made uneasy by the fact that

some of the most intelligent and well-informed people I know are religious believers. It isn't just that I don't believe in God and, naturally, hope that I'm right in my belief. It's that I hope there is no God! I don't want there to be a God; I don't want the universe to be like that.[16]

After moving beyond the antireligious prejudice of reductive naturalism, Nagel himself apparently falls prey to the very same prejudice, albeit at a higher level of complexity.

This point can be appreciated by considering how Nagel's own naturalized Platonism stumbles before the same weakness he identifies in deflationary naturalism, humanism, and neo-Darwinism. Consider: Nagel argues that deflationary naturalism fails to achieve its goal because the religious impulse stems from a legitimate and irrepressible rational concern; that humanism fails because the religious impulse is not satisfied by a mere recognition of our place within history, but requires a meaningful cosmic setting; and that, despite locating human history within cosmic evolution, neo-Darwinism fails because it lacks the idea that there is any authentic purpose in the world. Similarly, though Nagel's naturalized Platonism posits a mind-oriented teleological purpose in nature, it does not escape the problem of meaninglessness, because everything still comes to naught. Each individual will die, as will the human race, every planet and star, and perhaps even the universe itself. What meaning, then, does human life have in this great process? Even if the universe is born again after its own demise and begins evolving toward mind once more, the whole process would still be absurd. Such has been the insight of the many Hindu and Buddhist thinkers who, upon embracing the idea of an endless cosmic cycle, saw that true reconciliation could come only from escaping the cycle outright. My purpose here is not to embrace such a worldview, but rather to show that even Nagel's naturalized Platonism fails to fulfill the religious impulse. Indeed, it seems likely that only an authentically religious response can suffice.

I would argue that an implicit recognition of this point animated much of the harsh criticism that secular intellectuals heaped upon Nagel's *Mind and Cosmos*. Nagel argues that the main naturalistic options fail to either deflate or fulfill humanity's religious impulse. He then tries to provide a better, nonreligious alternative. Yet if his naturalized Platonism does not ultimately work, we have no other option but to turn to some kind of theism—hence Leiter and Weisberg's description of Nagel's work as an "instrument of mischief." Though I agree that accepting Nagel's critique of naturalism will more likely enhance the status of religious ideas than convince readers of the merits of naturalized Platonism, I do not find the "instrument of mischief" argument convincing. It is very similar to the now-debunked claim that allowing religious voices in the public sphere will generate conflict and violence. As Toft, Philpott, and Shah demonstrate, the opposite actually seems to be the case; the more that religious actors are incorporated into public discourse, the more beneficial and benevolent their public influence tends to be, whereas placing more restrictions on them tends to foment conflict and reactionary conservatism.[17] It seems reasonable to suggest that something similar may be true concerning religious interpretations of the natural world. Instead of blocking the conversation for fear of the incursions of religious conservatives and biblical literalists, we should invite reasonable religious perspectives into the conversation in order to undermine the influence of overzealous and antiscientific ones. Nagel's arguments help us appreciate the lines of thought that such reasonable contributions might productively pursue.

From a different angle, Nagel's claim that we should reintroduce teleology into our worldview because it fulfills our religious impulse and makes sense of how subjective beings appeared in the world might seem to be wishful thinking. Certainly, it would be nice if a cosmic teleology existed, as it would legitimize certain religious aspirations and overcome the problem of explaining how mind emerged from nature. But how can we argue from this desire to the claim that a cosmic teleology actually exists? There is some truth in this accusation of wishful thinking, for we cannot simply concoct positions that make philosophical problems go away and our metaphysical aspirations come true. However, Nagel's "common-sense realism" is more sophisticated than it might initially appear.

Nagel's strategy is to begin from certain commonsense propositions and consider how we must think about the world in order for them to be true. In this regard, first, he claims that humans are subjective beings and that we exist in the world. Hence, the world must be such that subjective beings like ourselves could have appeared within it, and no amount of fascination with this or that scientific theory should lead us to conclude otherwise. Positing some kind of mind-oriented teleology in nature thus provides us with an elegant and straightforward way of explaining our own existence while preserving the many other insights that natural science provides.

Second, Nagel argues that people must use their rational faculties to make sense of the world. And history shows that these faculties are, on the whole, remarkably good at guiding us to solid conclusions. Thus, when we find the near-universal religious desire for cosmic reconciliation in human beings, we should assume that this desire exists because there is some kind of cosmic meaning and purpose to be found. We can therefore reject philosophical positions that fail to fulfill our religious impulses. Though Nagel concludes this argument by advancing his vision of naturalized Platonism, it resonates with C. S. Lewis's commonsense argument for the existence of an eternal life:

> Creatures are not born with desires unless satisfaction for those desires exists. A baby feels hunger: well, there is such a thing as food. A duckling wants to swim: well, there is such a thing as water. Men feel sexual desire: well, there is such a thing as sex. If I find in myself a desire which no experience in this world can satisfy, the most probable explanation is that I was made for another world. If none of my earthly pleasures satisfy it, that does not prove that the universe is a fraud. Probably earthly pleasures were never meant to satisfy it, but only to arouse it, to suggest the real thing. If that is so, I must take care, on the one hand, never to despise, or to be unthankful for, these earthly blessings, and on the other, never to mistake them for the something else of which they are only a kind of copy, or echo, or mirage. I must keep alive in myself the desire for my true country, which I shall not find till after death; I must never let it get snowed under or turned aside; I must make it the

main object of life to press on to that country and to help others to do the same.[18]

Again, my purpose here is not to align myself with Nagel's argumentative strategies and views, nor Lewis's, for that matter, but rather to show how, despite the many controversies that surround his recent work, his arguments are reasonable and sound.

Hans Jonas

Hans Jonas (1903–1993) studied under Martin Heidegger and sought to bring his teacher's existentialism closer to both natural science and religion. In this regard, Jonas's postnaturalist narrative explores how people moved from an ancient framework in which life was the organizing principle of the world to a modern framework in which all things are rooted in the operations of lifeless matter.[19] He argues that Cartesian dualism facilitated this transition by placing mind and matter in two wholly separate domains. "Dualism," he explains, "is the link that historically mediated between the two extremes"; it was "the vehicle of the movement which carried the mind of man from the vitalistic monism of early times to the materialistic monism of our own."[20] Jonas argues that naturalism and existentialism gradually arose within Cartesian dualism's wake, with the former trying to reduce mind to matter and the latter trying to salvage mind's autonomy after this reduction had taken place. Jonas then seeks to chart a new path of thought by developing an evolutionary account of nature in which mind and matter are intimately intertwined.

In seeking to understand Cartesian dualism's emergence, Jonas makes much of the movement's similarities to ancient Gnosticism. The Gnostics believed that "the Divine is alien to the world and has neither part nor concern in the physical universe" and that "the world is the creation not of God but of some inferior principle whose law it executes."[21] Like the Greeks before them, the Gnostics believed that the material world was infused with spiritual purpose. However, they did not consider this spiritual purpose benevolent; it was rather dark and demonic and sought to prevent human souls from returning to their true heavenly abode. The

Gnostics thus claimed that humans should strive to extricate themselves from this world and to find their way into the spiritual world beyond.

Gnosticism arose in the context of Greek city-states, where each polis helped cultivate a sense of ontological holism among its citizens. Citizens depended upon the city-state for their well-being and found purpose and meaning in glorifying and improving the city-state. The organizing idea of this holism was that the parts of things are inferior to and given meaning by the overarching whole. However, as the system of Greek city-states declined and was subsumed by the vast and impersonal Roman Empire, it became harder to preserve this intimate sense of holism. Roman intellectuals nevertheless tried to do so by developing a cosmopolitan worldview and a unified legal code. Although some appreciated this new and broader form of holism, others considered it alienating and oppressive. The Gnostics were among the most radical of this latter group, and they developed their dualistic worldview and otherworldly asceticism in response to this sense of oppression.

Jonas sees a similar pattern in the rise of Cartesian dualism. Under the Church's direction, medieval Christendom achieved the kind of intimate yet universal holism that the Roman Empire failed to establish after the decline of the Greek city-states. When medieval Christendom began to decline, however, a fast-rising modern European society tried to preserve its holism through the creation of secular and bureaucratized nation-states. Cartesian dualism developed a vision of the relationship between mind and nature that supported this view; mind was a spiritual reality that existed outside the inert natural world, but ruled over nature through the powers of reason.

Cartesian dualism was later challenged by evolutionary biology, which appeared to effectively explain mind's distinctive qualities in terms of the effects of complex material processes.[22] Existentialism later arose in order to, like Gnosticism before it, reject the material world as an "absolute vacuum, the really bottomless pit," and to advocate a radically inward turn with salvific fervor. However, the existentialists did not hope for eternal salvation in a spiritual beyond. They claimed that there is ultimately "nothing but death" and that we are "alone with [our] contingency and the objective meaningless of [our] projecting meanings." Humanity's sole hope is thus to find a more authentic way of inhabiting its finitude by accepting the true bleakness of its situation and embracing the contingency of subjective life. This is why Jonas describes modern existentialism as "infinitely more radical and more desperate than [Gnosticism] ever could be."[23]

Jonas believes we can avoid the destructive naturalism-existentialism dichotomy by conceptualizing nature as a dynamically evolving system in which mind and matter intimately interrelate. Like Nagel, Jonas begins his line of thought by explaining that because humans are part of nature, our subjective characteristics must somehow animate nature as a whole. Jonas goes on to suggest that nature's latent subjective characteristics gradually appear as its material organization and complexity grow. Chemical entities are more complex than physical ones, and thus manifest greater degrees of spontaneity, and hence subjective life. Biological entities are, in turn, more complex than chemical ones, and thus display greater degrees of subjective existence. And human entities are more complex still; hence they exhibit even higher degrees of subjective life, to the point of becoming conscious of the subjective depths of the cosmos as a whole.

Unlike Nagel, however, Jonas admits that we can plausibly describe this subjectivity-realizing teleology as "God," though he rejects the idea that such a God could be said to transcend the world. Indeed, for him, all ideas about divine transcendence end up perpetuating the dualistic dialectic that plagues modern thought. Jonas thus argues that we should see "God" as a mere descriptive characterization of the spiritual potentialities of nature, and humans as these potentialities' most recent and profound expression: "The image of God, haltingly begun by the universe, for so long worked upon—and left undecided—in the wide and then narrowing spirals of prehuman life, passes with this last twist, and with a dramatic quickening of the movement, into man's precarious trust, to be completed, saved, or spoiled by what he will do with himself and the world."[24]

Jonas's postnaturalist narrative very deftly identifies and critiques the existentialist assumption that modern science reveals a lifeless material world, since existentialists use this idea to justify their refusal to engage modern scientific ideas. Jonas is thus right when he says that "no philosophy has ever been less concerned

about nature than Existentialism, for which it has no dignity left."²⁵
Consider, in this regard, the opening remarks of Jean-Luc Marion's
Being Given, widely considered an excellent recent work in existentialist thought: "In all science—therefore in metaphysics—it is a
question of proving. To prove consists in grounding appearances in
order to know with certainty, leading them back to the ground in
order to lead them to certainty. But in [existential] phenomenology—that is to say, at least in what it intends, in the attempt to
think in a non-metaphysical mode—it is a question of showing."²⁶
Though presented as a moderate demarcation of scientific and
existential-phenomenological approaches, Marion's argument aims
to justify his complete disregard of natural-scientific ideas. Indeed,
equating science with metaphysics has the same belittling implication for existential phenomenologists as equating religion with
metaphysics does for logical positivists; it turns it into something
that responsible thinkers simply do not do. The crucial point Jonas
makes is that acknowledging a spiritual teleology in nature helps us
overcome this fragmented pattern of thought and see scientific and
existential inquiry as complementary sources of insight into the integrated and dynamically evolving system of the world.²⁷

Jonas also deepens our understanding of how views of nature
shape the socioreligious projects we pursue. Gnostics conceptualized nature as a hellish realm of demonic purpose; they therefore
sought to escape the natural world through strict asceticism.
Cartesians saw mind as radically separate from, but rationally ruling over, nature; they therefore strove to create rational-
bureaucratic states that organized all human affairs. Existentialists
believed that the scientifically known world was lifeless and inert,
but also rejected the dualistic idea of a transcendent spiritual
realm; hence, they shunned nature and sought to uncover a more
authentic path of finite subjective life. And those who, like Jonas,
see nature as an evolutionary system in which spiritual potentialities gradually emerge as material organization and complexity
grow should, Jonas believes, dedicate their energies to helping
greater states of material and spiritual prosperity co-emerge in the
world today. Although Jonas's formulations simplify the full complexity of these nexuses of practice and thought, his point about
the link between our views of nature and society is well taken.

Still, it is important to acknowledge that Jonas's efforts to present God as the immanent teleology of cosmic evolution are problematic. Of course, it is perfectly legitimate for Jonas to advance this view as his own. Problems arise, however, when he claims that all notions of divine transcendence fall into the same dialectical trap that emerged in Cartesian dualism's wake. Perhaps I am being naïve, but it seems quite easy to imagine an account of divine transcendence that avoids this problematic by conceptualizing divinity as a reality that simultaneously grounds and transcends the teleological process Nagel and Jonas describe. Indeed, some of the figures I mentioned above to rebut Nagel's uncharitable description of religious views of evolution, such as Charles Peirce and Pierre Teilhard de Chardin, articulate precisely this view. Thus, instead of banishing the concept of transcendence outright, as Jonas thinks we must in order to avoid repeating the past, the more relevant question seems to be how to avoid twisting the concept into the kind of excessive dualism that Jonas rightly seeks to avoid.

A similarly problematic reductionism characterizes Jonas's attempt to use "Gnosticism" as a privileged framework for interpreting the modern world.[28] Admittedly, Jonas is not alone in claiming that modern Western societies repeat ancient Gnosticism in thinly secularized terms.[29] Had Jonas and these other thinkers simply claimed that we can gain insight into the religious and intellectual transformations of the modern West by drawing comparisons to ancient Gnosticism, we would have no grounds for critique. However, by arguing that the modern West somehow repeats the Gnostic movement of thought, Jonas falls prey to same kind of false nativism that we found animating Taylor's thought. For if the modern West really does repeat ancient Gnosticism, then we are committed to the claim that Western civilization evolves only by unfolding the logic of its own inner principles, not by interacting with and responding to other cultures and traditions in any significant way.

Alfred North Whitehead

Alfred North Whitehead (1861–1947) was a polymath in the truest sense, making significant contributions to mathematics, formal logic, theoretical physics, educational theory, the history and philosophy of science, epistemology, the philosophy of language, the philosophy of religion, metaphysics, and intellectual history.[30] As philosopher F. S. C. Northop writes, "Few men since Leibniz and Aristotle have touched so many fields with such originality, precision, and profundity."[31] Beyond his inherent expansiveness of mind, Whitehead was driven into so many intellectual domains by his conviction that the modern West's fragmented account of reality had led it into an endless series of internal conflicts and crises. To repair this state of affairs, he endeavored to weave insights from every domain of inquiry into a coherent and process-oriented account of reality. He spent a great deal of time late in life investigating the phenomenon of religion, focusing in particular on its historic development and its relationship to broader strands of philosophical and scientific thought.

Whitehead organizes his postnaturalist narrative around an analysis of how the "scientific mentality" came to characterize the modern West. He defines the scientific mentality as a "union of passionate interest in the detailed facts with equal devotion to abstract generalization" and argues that the modern West was the first civilization to ever display this mentality on a wide scale.[32] Though European thinkers grasped the importance of the scientific mentality during the Scientific Revolution and the Enlightenment, they falsely equated it with embracing a worldview built upon the concepts of Newtonian physics. This confusion caused numerous problems, among the most disastrous of which was the emergence of the idea that science and religion, "the two strongest general forces . . . which influence men," are fundamentally at odds.[33] Nevertheless, Whitehead believes that we can learn to see modern science and religion as complementary by reexamining both the scientific mentality and the limitations of Newtonian physics.

Whitehead begins his narrative by examining the historical conditions that enabled the scientific mentality to emerge among early modern Europeans. First, a general trust in the exact order of nature had to appear. Throughout history, most people believed that some things are orderly (e.g., life cycles and seasons), while others are unpredictable (e.g., droughts and disease). "Men expected the sun to rise," Whitehead explains, "but the wind bloweth where it listeth." The Greek dramatists were arguably the first to claim that all things are governed by a single, necessary force. However, they did not make this point conceptually, but rather by artistically exploring the "remorseless inevitableness" that characterizes human affairs. The resultant vision of fate inspired Greek Stoicism, which shaped the Roman legal tradition, which, in turn, influenced the mentality of all European peoples via its inclusion into Catholicism. It is this causal link that led Whitehead to describe the Greek dramatists as the "pilgrim fathers of the scientific imagination."[34]

Second, an attitude that combined speculative theory and careful attention to empirical detail had to arise. Medieval Catholic thinkers believed that they could discern the complete structure of the world by rationally amplifying revealed biblical truth. Medieval Catholic theology was thus scriptural, speculative, and rationalistic. In Catholic monasteries operating under the rule of St. Benedict, however, monks were simultaneously educated in this pattern of theological inquiry and taught to pursue practical activities like farming and crafts. This gave rise to a unique blend of speculative rationalism and vigorous attention to practical detail. And this mentality gradually made its way beyond the monastic walls through the dissemination of monastic artworks that carefully depicted the natural world. Figures like Leonardo da Vinci took up and systematically developed this orientation, and the subsequent spread of naturalist art helped growing numbers of Europeans learn to bring theoretical sophistication to bear upon their empirical perceptions of nature. Whitehead thus describes da Vinci as "more completely a man of science than was [Francis] Bacon," because the "practice of naturalistic art is more akin to the practice of physics, chemistry and biology than is the practice of law."[35]

Third, the ancient endeavor of using mathematics to describe the basic features of the world had to be revitalized. Pythagoras and Plato first sought to use mathematics to explain the world because they believed that mathematical structures gave reality its form. Subsequent ancient and medieval thinkers abandoned this project because they felt that Aristotle's methods of description and classification were more accurate and efficient. Yet when seventeenth-century thinkers like Descartes, Galileo, Kepler, and Newton rejected Aristotelian physics, they turned again to the examples of Pythagoras and Plato and began working to renew their mathematical approach. "It was an age of great physicists and great philosophers," Whitehead remarks, "and the physicists and philosophers were alike mathematicians." Though he acknowledges the difficulty of explaining precisely why this mathematical resurgence took place, he notes many similarities between ancient Greece and early modern Europe. In both settings, for example, we see the general disintegration of traditionally held beliefs and the emergence of challenging new religious movements (e.g., the Dionysian cult and the Protestant Reformation) and schools of philosophical thought (e.g., Socratic philosophy and the Renaissance's rediscovery of ancient wisdom).[36] Regardless, pure mathematics had advanced to such a degree by the seventeenth century that early modern thinkers were able to mathematically analyze the world with unprecedented profundity and detail.

Having highlighted these three significant background conditions for the emergence of the scientific mentality among modern European peoples, Whitehead explains how the mentality became unduly associated with reductive naturalism. For over two thousand years, scientists followed Aristotle in assuming that material entities tended toward a resting state, as this assumption perfectly describes our everyday experience. When a ball rolls, there is a force that makes it roll, and it gradually stops rolling unless another force acts upon it. Galileo first went beyond this commonsensical view by claiming that the movement of material entities tends to remain constant: if things are at rest, they tend to remain at rest, and if they are moving, they tend to keep moving at the same speed. We should therefore not conceptualize physical force as a power that combats a thing's tendency to remain at rest, but rather as a power that causes the velocity of an object to change. Isaac Newton built upon this conclusion by conceptualizing physical force f as the amount of energy required to move a body of mass m at rate of acceleration a. Force = mass × acceleration. This equation enabled physicists to use abstract mathematics to explain the minute operations of the physical world, and modern Europeans were understandably so impressed by the results that they employed the framework of Newtonian physics as a foundation upon which to build a complete vision of the world.[37]

Unfortunately, the mechanistic worldview that subsequently emerged led European thinkers to embrace highly problematic views. Newtonian physics depends upon the idea that matter possesses a definite location in space and time; in a Newtonian worldview reality is nothing more than a collection of discrete material entities. The thoughts and experiences that constitute human life must therefore be either projected outside the world into a dualistic beyond or collapsed into the operations of matter. Either way, nature becomes an irremediably "dull affair, soundless, scentless, colourless; merely the hurrying of material, endlessly, meaninglessly."[38]

This natural imaginary transformed modern Europeans' understanding of the relationship between science and religion. Premodern Christians grounded their theology in an Aristotelian, which is to say teleological, view of nature. Faced with the claim that accepting a Newtonian worldview was equivalent to "being scientific," many Europeans felt like they had to either choose between science and religion or embrace a stark form of religious dualism. Either way, science and religion began to appear fundamentally at odds.

Whitehead argues that this state of affairs emanates from a common fallacy of thought, which he calls the "error of mistaking the abstract for the concrete," or the "fallacy of misplaced concreteness."[39] To appreciate what this fallacy entails, consider Whitehead's claim that we learn about the world by isolating certain phenomena, examining the patterns these phenomena exhibit, and constructing a simplified model of these patterns to learn more about their operation. No matter how accurate and profound such models may be, they always ignore the full complexity of the world. The fallacy of misplaced concreteness arises when we lose sight of this fact and claim that our models actually encapsulate reality.[40] Medieval Christians and modern naturalists both fell prey to this line of thought; hence the conceptual systems they developed appear to fundamentally contradict each other. And the Cartesian attempt to remedy this contradiction by proposing a third, dualistic alternative does not alter the underlying epistemic confusion. Whitehead thus claims that we cannot reconcile science and religion as long as we continue to equate them with the overzealous conceptual systems that modern philosophers and medieval theologians created.

However, once we disassociate science and religion from these fallacious conceptual schemes, it becomes easy to appreciate their fundamental complementarity. As Whitehead explains, science helps us understand "the general conditions which are observed to regulate physical phenomena," while religion is "wholly wrapped up in the contemplation of moral and aesthetic values." "On the one side," he continues, "there is the law of gravitation, and on the other the contemplation of the beauty of holiness. What one side sees, the other misses; and vice versa."[41] Whitehead's point here is not, as Stephen Jay Gould would later argue, that science and religion constitute two "non-overlapping magisteria," but rather that they examine the same infinite reality from different vantage points.[42]

Whitehead argues that the findings of post-Newtonian physics support this view. He is particularly impressed by how quantum physics shows that electrons do not move continuously through points of space-time, but appear at distinct points without having ever existed in between, as this finding undermines the idea that nature is a collection of material entities and supports the view, advanced by many of the world's great religious systems, that nature is an expression of a deeper domain of mind-like energetic activity.[43]

Whitehead recognizes that modern Westerners will not overcome the ingrained belief that science and religion are fundamentally at odds through theoretical arguments alone; religion must also learn to infuse itself with the scientific mentality. Or, as Whitehead puts it, religion "will not regain its old power until it can face change in the same spirit as does science." Though religion's "principles may be eternal," the "expression of those principles requires continual development," and the scientific mindset provides us with the most expedient means of developing their expression in the world today.[44]

Whitehead elaborated his postnaturalist narrative during the first decades of the twentieth century, so many of the historical and scientific details he presents must be revised. Nevertheless, most of the general points he makes remain just as relevant today as they were nearly a century ago. For example, historian Stephen

Gaukroger has confirmed the viability of Whitehead's effort to separate the scientific mentality from the mechanistic naturalism that arose around it during the Enlightenment. Gaukroger argues that Enlightenment thinkers sought to utilize modern physics to establish a new and more effective "basis for morality, politics, religion, and philosophy." This project was animated by the belief that modern physics succeeded precisely because it inverted the concepts and methods of premodern religion: whereas the scientific method was autonomous, empirical, and quantitative, religious inquiry was authoritative, dogmatic, and bound by tradition; and whereas modern physics posited nothing more than material entities and blind natural laws, religion claimed that nature was governed by a wide variety of spiritual forces. Gaukroger's own historical analyses reveal that, to the contrary, "the success of science in the West in the early-modern era was due to its close association with religion, rather than any attempt to dissociate itself from religion."[45] Thus, though Gaukroger does not follow Whitehead in trying to envision a new relationship between science and religion, his historical findings clearly demonstrate the need to move beyond a narrative of conflict that is based more on ideological prejudice than on a fair consideration of history's actual course.

Whitehead's analysis of how the fallacy of misplaced concreteness generated the modern conflict between science and religion also resonates with insights that Taylor and Dewey advance. As explained in previous chapters, Dewey argues that Western thought has long been animated by the conviction that reality is a "realm of fixed Being which, when grasped by thought, formed a complete system of immutable and necessary truth," while Taylor explains how pursuit of this belief has made the West the "scene of a total, almost obsessive identification with certain favourite schemes, driven to any wild or repellent consequences, justifying murderous schisms."[46] Both authors go on to argue that this intellectual fallacy lies behind the emergence of the idea that science and religion inherently contradict, and suggest that we can overcome this enduring conviction by adopting an alternative intellectual orientation, either a broad-based experimentalism (Dewey) or a humble appreciation of the complementarity of different modes of thought

(Taylor). Together, these views bring us very close to Whitehead's own conclusions about how science and religion can be reconciled in the world today.

Ongoing research also supports Whitehead's claim that post-Newtonian physics helps us imagine a world in which scientific and religious views ultimately cohere. Without wanting to dive into the intricacies of these debates, it suffices to note that John Polkinghorne has influentially argued that chaos theory and quantum physics provide us with a scientifically coherent way of thinking about how God interacts with the world, while Henry Stapp, Keith Ward, and David Bohm have forcefully claimed that the antimaterialistic conclusions of quantum physics point us toward the kind of panpsychist, or even panentheistic, understanding of nature that many religious systems have long espoused.[47] The arguments these authors present are neither conclusive nor immune from legitimate challenge and debate. Yet they do demonstrate the real possibility of developing rigorous interpretations of the scientifically known world that fully cohere with reasonable religious beliefs.

However appreciative we can be of Whitehead's points, he does tend to conflate the declining influence of Christianity among Western intellectual elites with the decline of religion as such. Admittedly, the declining intellectual influence of Christianity among Western-educated elites is not without wider consequence, as such elites are largely responsible for providing "official" definitions of reality in many societies. Insofar as Western-educated elites conflate Christianity with "religion" and embrace the problematic idea that science and religion fundamentally contradict each other, these ideas will influence discourse and practice throughout the world. Nevertheless, it is important to be much more precise when speaking about modern processes of religious decline than Whitehead is.

In any event, Whitehead is to be commended for the ample humility with which he presented his thoughts, acknowledging as he did that his theories might not prove the test of time: "There remains the final reflection, how shallow, puny, and imperfect are efforts to sound the depths in the nature of things. In philosophical discussion, the merest hint of dogmatic certainty as to finality of statement is an exhibition of folly. . . . The proper test is not that of finality, but of progress."[48] From this angle, Whitehead's postnaturalist narrative constitutes an enduring success.

In considering the general merit of the postnaturalist narrative, I find it helpful to note John Hick's concept of the religious ambiguity of the cosmos, which holds that reality "is capable from our present human vantage point of being thought of and experienced in both religious and naturalistic ways" without running afoul of fact or reason.[49] This means that we can neither conclusively prove nor conclusively disprove a religious interpretation of reality. My purpose in mentioning this concept, which I will discuss at greater length in chapter 6, is to suggest that we should not expect postnaturalist narratives to develop conclusive arguments for the concepts they advance. Rather, we should see them as attempts to critique naturalism and to consider how certain spiritual concepts can be reasonably reincorporated into a scientific worldview.

Of course, Hick's ambiguity need not be the final word, as we could conceivably acquire a kind of practical proof of divinity if the concept generated enough social and intellectual fruits. The point here is that evidence for the existence of transcendence is not exclusively achieved through rational argumentation and scientific analysis; it can additionally be acquired by observing the transformative effects of religious practices and beliefs.[50] Consider in this light the open-mindedness with which Buddhist disciplines and ideas are received by many who would otherwise be quite hostile to so-called Western religions; the former are seen as generating impressive individual and collective fruits while the latter are not.[51] Admittedly, the situation in the West is skewed by the disproportionate intellectual energy that is directed toward describing religion's destructive potential. This state of affairs has been somewhat alleviated by the growing body of literature that analyzes the contributions that religious actors are making within processes of humanitarian aid, peace-building, democratization, achieving psychological well-being, value formation, and the like. But much work still remains to be done.

We might therefore approach the postnaturalist narrative framework as a limited effort to articulate and marshal evidence for a series of coherent and scientifically acceptable ideas about the dynamic relationship between reality's material and spiritual dimensions. This is a great service indeed, as the sheer sophistication of naturalistic perspectives often works as a kind of tacit proof of their intellectual superiority. The disparity between the sophistication of naturalistic and religious perspectives is largely the fault of religious thinkers who have spent more time critiquing and reacting to nonreligious modes of thought in order to buttress outworn theological systems than moving boldly and confidently into new areas of inquiry. But possessing a new and fecund set of postnaturalist concepts is not enough to change this state of affairs, as religious thinkers must also find ways to build a veritable research program that will examine and extend the relevant ideas. This is a step that many religious thinkers have failed to envision, acting instead as if humanity will find its way back to a world in which everyone organizes their lives around God once more persuasive arguments for His existence are deployed. To the contrary, I would argue that such a shift could only occur once the sheer productivity of religious concepts and the transformative power of religious practices and beliefs become so abundantly clear that only an irrational few would deny their truth.

What might such a research program look like? On one level, it would require sophisticated theoretical and empirical work like the work we saw Nagel, Jonas, and Whitehead advance. At another level, however, it would require advancing knowledge about how religion can contribute to constructive, as opposed to destructive, processes of individual development and social change. Such knowledge need not be developed only within the academy; it could also be generated by diverse religious communities. This research program could traverse boundaries between religious communities and traditions in a manner that, out of a misguided association of relativism and particularism with tolerance and equality, current academic mores often discourage.[52]

Though I have gone somewhat beyond the domain of the postnaturalist narrative in these concluding remarks, my purpose has simply been to show how debates about the relationship between science and religion should be located within a wider social perspective. Although postnaturalist narratives rightly identify the limitations of naturalism and the need to consider reincorporating certain spiritual concepts into a scientific worldview, they struggle to account for the ways that the science-versus-religion debates are shaped by assessments of the productive merits of religious concepts, practices, and methods of inquiry.

CHAPTER FIVE

The Construct Narrative

CONSTRUCT NARRATIVES DESCRIBE HOW a distinctive
concept of "religion in general" arose during the modern period and consider whether this concept is an illusion, a discovery, a political project, or some mix of all
three. Construct narratives thus differ from other narrative frameworks by focusing more on intellectual history than on the history
of religion as such. Nevertheless, these narratives do make general
claims about religious history by arguing that the construction of a
general concept of religion has fundamentally altered human affairs. I focus here on the construct narratives of Talal Asad, Guy
Stroumsa, and Jason Josephson.

Talal Asad

Talal Asad locates his account of the construction of a general concept of religion within his broader analysis of the "modern project." As he puts it, "modernity is a *project*—or rather, a series of
interlinked projects—that certain people in power seek to achieve,"
and the modern concept of "religion" was developed to help specify the way in which "modern living is required to take place."[1]
This modern project, he argues, arose through the transformation
of medieval Christian monasticism. Hence, we can gain much

insight into the meaning of the modern concept of religion by examining how this transformation took place.

Medieval Christian monasticism employed the doctrine of original sin to systematize and extend the Aristotelian notion that humans are born with a latent spiritual potential that must be cultivated by discipline and education: "According to medieval Christian doctrine and practice, sin is a constant danger to the soul, and so calls for perpetual combat. The entire life of the Christian should be devoted to dealing with the corrupting effects of Original Sin, to restoring with God's grace the soul made impure and disordered by an original transgression. . . . It is for this that the monastic program was instituted, for the performance of practices specified in that program are in effect attempts at reforming the soul." Medieval monasticism sought to transform the sinful desire for lower goods into a sanctified desire for spiritual virtue through a rigorous system of practice that "determines for disciples what is to be done, how, in what order, and by whom."[2] Individuals were responsible for monitoring both themselves and their monastic brethren to ensure the highest levels of obedience to this system. Infractions were met with discipline and even physical punishment to help spur the individual's spiritual reformation. Despite the now-popular idea that monastic discipline was a kind of fetishized self-repression, Asad argues that it coherently arose from the concept of human nature that was employed at the time.

Asad explains how a slight shift in this vision of human nature stimulated Inquisitional torture during the late Middle Ages. Around that time, new Christian orders were working to extend Christian discipline from the monasteries into the "expanding, mobile population of the towns in which irreligion and heresy both seemed to thrive." The assumption was that most people were neither conscious of their sinfulness nor willing to pursue the necessary reformations. The thought therefore arose that most people's sinfulness had to be forcibly and painfully revealed in order to awaken contrition and desire for change.[3] Thus, while continuing to conceptualize human nature in terms of sin and spiritual reform, the Inquisition attributed a new measure of interiority to human beings and characterized it as a space of potential dissimulation.

Inquisitional practice coherently reflected this new vision of human nature.

When the modern project later arose, it preserved the idea of a potentially dissimulating inner space but dropped the underlying Christian view of human nature. More specifically, instead of claiming that human progress required the reform of sinful inner life, modern thinkers argued that we only needed to adopt the proper set of external behaviors. The potential conflict between external action and inner belief thus became inconsequential; one could feel, believe, or identify with anything at all as long as one followed the required behavioral rules. Within this framework, religious concerns were confined to "private belief and worship" and defined as "part of what is *inessential* to [modern] politics, economy, science, and morality."[4] Any attempt to bring religion into the public domain was seen as dangerous and illegitimate.

This privatized concept of religion shaped the modern study of religion. Asad demonstrates this point by examining Clifford Geertz's paradigmatic definition of religion: Religion is "(1) a system of symbols which act to (2) establish powerful, pervasive, and long-lasting moods and motivations in men by (3) formulating conceptions of a general order of existence and (4) clothing these conceptions with such an aura of factuality that (5) the moods and motivations seem uniquely realistic." All the terms Geertz employs—"moods and motivations," "clothing," "aura"—imply that religious symbols do not reference objective realities, but only create subjective states in believers.[5]

Unfortunately, such a privatized notion of religion obscures the operations of many religious traditions, both historically and today. For example, in contrast to the subjectivist idea that ritual is a "type of routine behavior that symbolizes or expresses something," monastic and Inquisitional rituals sought to help people train their habits of thought and action.[6] Yet because modern scholars tend to overlook these practical aims, they end up describing monastic and Inquisitional practices as gratuitous expressions of psychological mania. Inversely, because the extensive violence associated with state-sponsored war and economic manipulation are today considered legitimate tools for shaping external behavior, they are often presented as unavoidable, or even necessary.[7] It is such skewed and ideological perspectives that, according to Asad, lead many otherwise thoughtful people to advance the absurd claim that "religion" is a main cause of conflict and violence in the world, while secular politics is the agent of prosperity, order, and peace.

Asad also notes how privatized notions of religion obfuscate the operations of contemporary Islamic societies. The modern project assumes that modern societies should facilitate the "rational administration and care of entire populations" and avoid the "moral disciplining of individuals." However, most Islamic societies believe that "a well-regulated polity depends on its members being virtuous individuals who are partly responsible for one another's moral condition."[8] Those who view Islam through a privatized religious lens will therefore find its social practices illegitimate and even question whether Muslims can effectively participate in the modern world.

The main limitation of Asad's construct narrative concerns his claim that the modern project employs a privatized concept of religion. There is almost certainly no monolithic modern project, and, hence, no monolithic "modern" conception of religion.[9] Modernity involves a diverse set of social configurations that often approach religion quite distinctively. Thus, for example, modernity is very different in France and the United States, and while the French arguably conceptualize religion in a very privatized way, in the United States many people embrace a much more publicly oriented understanding of religion. Indeed, Andrew Preston has shown the tremendous role that religious convictions played in shaping the foreign policies of Abraham Lincoln, Woodrow Wilson, Franklin Roosevelt, and Harry Truman.[10] If these public figures are not part of the modern project, then who is?

A second problem with Asad's construct narrative stems from his claim that modern societies assume that people's interior lives are irrelevant to the external tasks of modern living. To the contrary, as Charles Taylor has persuasively demonstrated, growing contingents of modern peoples orient their personal, ethical, and political decisions around the idea that all external activities should "authentically" express the imperatives of their inner lives.[11]

One way to preserve the insights of Asad's construct narrative is to acknowledge that it examines how one theory of religion came to prominence during the modern period. Influential theorists like Clifford Geertz developed a privatized conception of religion. These theorists shaped how many Western-educated elites thought about religion. These elites, in turn, influenced how religion was engaged in Western public settings. And, by way of the West's aggressive global influence, this influence gradually spread throughout the world. Even though many modern people do not embrace a privatized concept of religion, this concept, as Asad rightly points out, has therefore significantly influenced global affairs.

Guy Stroumsa

Guy Stroumsa argues that early modern scholars made one of the great scientific discoveries of the modern age when they developed a generic concept of religion. Though these scholars were often motivated by the hope of converting others and examined different cultures through a narrow biblical lens, their insights set the stage for the rigorous scientific investigation of religion that would later emerge. In this regard, Stroumsa criticizes the current scholarly preference for highly specialized knowledge of a single religious tradition, claiming that it leaves us without the tools we need to think intelligently about how religion operates, both historically and today. To remedy this situation, he recommends that contemporary scholars reengage with early modern scholars' belief in the unity of humankind and their richly cross-cultural and interdisciplinary methodologies.[12]

Stroumsa organizes his analyses around three important early-modern events: the Great Discoveries, the Renaissance, and the European Wars of Religion. Concerning the Great Discoveries, Stroumsa explains that "the intellectual and religious shock caused by the observation of formerly all-but-unknown religious rituals and beliefs in the Americas and Asia provided the trigger without which the new discipline [of the science of religion] could not have been born." Concerning the Renaissance, he highlights the role that the "new interest in antiquity and growth of modern philology" played in enabling a more scientific study of the panoply of Near Eastern religions. And the savagery of the European Wars of Religion led many Europeans to question Christianity's superiority to other traditions. From this threefold shift, he explains, sprang the "hitherto unknown" notion that "beyond the multiple forms of religion . . . all religions [reflect] the unity of humankind."[13]

Stroumsa begins his narrative by describing Catholic priests' early encounters with Native American religion. The existence of Native American religion was particularly problematic for these priests, as there had almost certainly been no previous contact between Native Americans and other European or Near Eastern civilizations. How, then, did Native American ideas about divinity develop, if not by some sort of biblical transmission? These priests were also faced with the challenge of understanding Native American rituals and beliefs without any historical or linguistic context. They addressed these two dilemmas by developing an early form of ethnographic inquiry, comparing what they knew about Native American rituals and beliefs to Greek and Roman paganism, and extending their account of the universality of religion. Jesuit José de Acosta exemplified this strategy: he learned Quechua people's language and studied their rituals and beliefs by living in their villages; he compared his findings to Greek and Roman paganism; and he conceptualized Native American religion as an example of the natural religion that arises within all human beings.[14]

The Jesuits' early encounters in China proceeded differently, though with similar results. When the Jesuits went to China in 1582, they quickly dismissed Buddhism and Daoism as examples of popular idolatry but were deeply impressed by Confucianism's suppression of superstition and promotion of elevated morality. Again, the question was, How had the Chinese developed an advanced civilization and religion without interacting with revealed biblical truth? The Jesuits resolved this dilemma by claiming that Confucianism was not a religion per se, but rather a "civil religion" that strove not to "express truth about the divine but rather to offer a moral code for the people that is grounded in religious principles." Indeed, Confucian elites were often presented as atheists, though some Jesuits claimed that they espoused natural religion through their worship of "the supreme deity, the King of Heaven." The Jesuits made such distinctions to protect Confucianism from being condemned by the Church as idolatrous. They were not wrong in recognizing this risk, as they soon found themselves

mired in "la Querelle des rites" with Church leaders who claimed
that "by accommodating the Chinese," the priests "were actually
flirting with idolatry and accommodating nothing less than pagan
mores and rituals."[15] Despite these controversies, the resultant
debate deepened European awareness of the universality of religion, further articulated notions of civil and natural religion, and
enhanced the nascent practice of comparative and ethnographic
methods.

As these events were taking place, scholars in Europe were learning how to apply new philological methods to the comparative study
of the Bible and the Homeric epics. Initially, they thought that biblical Palestine was the oldest civilization and thus saw the Homeric
epics as a series of "allusions, quotations, or else parodies of the biblical texts." Some even attributed the authorship of the *Iliad* and the
Odyssey to "refugees from Palestine who concealed their original
traditions within the Greek text." Nevertheless, further analysis
began to reveal that both the Bible and the Homeric epics were part
of a broader and older Near Eastern context than had been previously imagined. "Liberation from the chains of the Bible," Stroumsa
explains, "permitted scholarly imagination to spread its wings. The
East was vast, one dreamt of it. It was now multiform, colored,
mythical."[16]

This broadened appreciation of the Near Eastern context allowed Judaism, Christianity, and Islam to be placed within the
same Abrahamic-monotheistic family. Previously, post-Christian
Judaism had rarely been the object of serious study, and Islam was
glibly presented as the paramount Christian heresy. However, in
comparison to the dizzying range of Near Eastern religious phenomena that were being discovered, the resonances between these
three faiths became harder to ignore.

It was within this context that serious study of Zoroastrianism
also emerged. Zoroastrianism had long been a topic of fascination
and controversy in European intellectual circles; there was much
debate about whether Zoroaster had actually existed or was simply
a Persian appropriation of Moses. However, after discovering the
Zend Avesta and learning more about Zoroastrian practice and
thought, the debate shifted to Zoroastrianism's status within the
history of religion. More specifically, it was unclear to early

modern scholars whether Zoroaster had taught a pure form of Abrahamic monotheism that was later corrupted by idolatry or had advocated heretical dualistic teachings.

Partly because of this renewed interest in Zoroastrian dualism, but also because of growing concern with Christian apocryphal material, Manichaeanism also became an object of intense investigation. Previously, Manichaeanism had largely been known in Europe through Christian polemics, particularly those of Augustine. But with the discovery and translation of new textual sources, scholars began evaluating Mani and his movement in a new light. Some saw in Manichaeanism as a precursor to the Protestant Reformation, while others saw it as the carrier of true Eastern wisdom. Though debate on the status of Manichaeanism still rages today, it was during this period that European scholars began approaching the movement on its own terms and not simply as a Christian heresy.

A similar trajectory took place with the study of Islam. Throughout the Middle Ages, Muhammad had been presented as "an impostor, a manipulator of dubious mores who concocted his own religion while pretending to have received revelation."[17] The first serious European translations of the Qur'an and studies of Islam were carried out within this polemic framework. However, as travelers to Islamic lands sent back tales of impressive religious tolerance, sophisticated culture, and wide learning to a European society plagued by religious wars, perceptions began to change. These changing perceptions ultimately led European scholars to accept the notion of Abrahamic monotheism, which, in turn, strengthened the idea of the unity of humankind and supported the growing belief that a perennial Eastern wisdom awaited European rediscovery. However, the changing perceptions also helped bring Christianity further into doubt within European intellectual circles. If Jesus and Moses were, after all, not so different from Muhammad, who had long been considered a religious impostor, then perhaps they, too, were false prophets.

European scholars remained perplexed by the "origin of the striking dispersion of the diverse peoples on earth" and the resultant religious plurality. A popular strategy at the time was to locate the origin of religious diversity in the story of the dispersal of

Noah's sons after the flood: "These are the descendants of Noah's sons, Shem, Ham, and Japheth: children were born to them after the flood.... These are the families of Noah's sons, according to their genealogies, in their nations; and from these nations spread abroad on the earth after the flood" (Genesis 10:1). Scholars employed this story as the "basis for their reflection on the origins of ethnic taxonomies as well as of languages, cultures, and religions throughout the various continents." They read the myth of the Flood as a "prelude to world history," which is to say that they took the Flood-induced "dispersal of peoples across the earth as the earliest departure point for any historical inquiry."[18]

Stroumsa goes on to explain how the Flood myth served as a matrix for three narratives of religious history that arose during the early modern period. The first narrative held that "truth always comes first, and error always comes later," which is to say that religion was truest in its Noahide beginnings and was subsequently corrupted by idolatrous influences. This line of thought lends itself to a Christian narrative about Christ's renewing and salvific function. A second narrative identified "the various gods of past civilizations with one another" and presented them all as reflections of the same underlying perennial truth.[19] A third narrative saw in religion's history a process of divine condescendence, whereby God gradually sublimates and improves humanity's flawed efforts to follow His will. This narrative maintained that "there was an evolution in history and that God revealed Himself and His will gradually: Moses offered a religion truer than that of the Sabians. Jesus permitted a higher, more spiritual way of serving God than the ritual laws of Moses. And finally, the Reformation proposed a better Christianity than Catholicism, a religion with too many rituals, remnants, as it were, of earlier stages of religious life."[20] Scholars working within this last narrative framework sought to understand each religion's place within a broader developmental arc. We can therefore clearly see in the early modern discourse on religion the beginnings of what I have called the renewal, perennial, and developmental narratives.[21]

The purpose of Stroumsa's construct narrative is to show how the development of a general concept of religion facilitated an unprecedented expansion of our understanding of human affairs. He even goes so far as to suggest that "religion" is one of the great scientific discoveries of early modernity. This does not mean that early modern scholars conceptualized religion perfectly. Indeed, Stroumsa's entire narrative describes how early modern scholars developed narrow and problematic accounts of religion and then refined their understanding over time. But this is to be expected, since gradual refinement is precisely how well-grounded scientific inquiry ought to proceed.

Stroumsa also argues that early modern scholars' efforts to understand diverse religious phenomena in a cross-cultural and interactional manner were more fruitful than the fragmentary approaches that many scholars employ today. Born from a growing critical awareness of the Christocentrism and Eurocentrism that have long plagued the academic study of religion, as well as a just desire to consider different cultures and peoples on their own terms, the current tendency is for scholars to focus on one religious tradition, and usually on only one small section thereof. Though comparative projects are tolerated, the claim is often made that they overlook the rich complexity and nuance that characterize particular religious traditions. In contrast, early modern scholars recognized that religious history is animated by constant interaction, borrowing, reaction, and cross-fertilization between different traditions. From this vantage point, there is no pristine Christian, Jewish, Islamic, Buddhist, Hindu, Manichaean, or Confucian tradition, but rather a complex global-interactional dynamic in which these traditions directly shape one another's evolution. Stroumsa argues that we still have much to learn from this framework of research and thought.

Stroumsa adds that early modern scholars' belief in the unity of humankind sustained their cross-cultural, interactional approach. By the "unity of humankind," he refers to the ideas that human nature is universal and that all human beings interact with the same reality—physical, social, and spiritual. He then suggests that contemporary scholars cannot reclaim a richly cross-cultural and interactional approach without reengaging this concept today. The point here seems to be that we should not approach different religious traditions as if they inhabit existential, metaphysical, and historical silos. Rather, we should see them all as diversely engaging common features of human nature, addressing common features of reality, and navigating a single historical stream. Admittedly, investigating religion in this way requires researchers to develop a greater breadth of knowledge and understanding. Yet anything less, Stroumsa rightly suggests, will only perpetuate the tendency to isolate different religions, as well as their respective believers, from one another.

The main challenge to Stroumsa's optimistic construct narrative comes from the argument that "religion" did not exist during premodernity. Rather, sacred practices and beliefs were simply facets of every premodern cultural matrix. Only during modernity, and particularly in the modern West, did people begin differentiating "religion" from other aspects of society, such as science, politics, ethics, and art. When scholars identify instances of "religion" in non-Western and premodern settings, then, they are actually applying a sociological concept derived from the modern West to settings where it does not belong.[22]

Stroumsa does not rebut this claim with sufficient rigor. Yet his argument can endure the critique. Every concept was constructed at some point in history. Unless we embrace the most aggressive forms of relativism and subjectivism, we all already accept the idea that a concept can be constructed and true. Articulating a concept's genealogy therefore does not suffice to undermine its validity. Additionally, a concept need not be perfect from the outset in order to constitute a discovery. No one would argue that, for example, Copernicus's theory of planetary orbits is entirely valid today. Yet it is widely recognized that his heliocentric framework enabled subsequent astronomical discoveries. The same point can be made about early modern conceptions of religion. We can now see that early modern thinkers conceptualized religion in problematic ways. However, without their initial insights, our knowledge of the religious dimensions of human history and culture would be much less advanced. Thus, even though our understanding of religion has evolved, and must continue to evolve, Stroumsa rightly argues that the development of this concept has helped us radically extend our understanding of social reality.

Jason Josephson

Jason Josephson examines how the concept of religion developed in Japan in order to critique the kind of Eurocentric construct narrative that Asad and others advance. Or, as Josephson puts it, by showing how "Japanese intellectuals, leaders, policymakers, and diplomats were involved in a process of negotiation that produced religion in Japan," he seeks to contest "the narrative that understands modernity to be simply the product of Euro-American culture exported to an imitative or passive 'Asia.'"[23] Though Josephson admits that "the discourse on religion emerged in the context of Western Christendom," he claims that it "is no longer exclusively Western in its current formulations." It has been "reformulated in the *inter*stices, the *inter*national—in the spaces between nations and cultures."[24]

Josephson begins his construct narrative by describing the first encounters between Japanese and Christian Europeans in the 1500s. Just as medieval Christians presented all other religious movements as Christian heresies, the Japanese first conceptualized Christianity as a Buddhist heresy. This was driven in part by one Japanese translator's decision to equate "heaven with the Buddhist pure land (*jōdo*), hell with the Buddhist underworld (*jigoku*), angels with the deities of the Brahma-Heaven (*tennin*), and, most problematically, God with the Cosmic Buddha (*Dainichi*)," lacking as he did any better terms.[25] It was also influenced by Japanese efforts to make sense of the similarities between Buddhism and Christianity by positing some kind of causal historical influence, seeing, for example, Israel's proximity to India as a sign of Jesus's having been inspired by Buddhist teaching.

Unfortunately, the idea of a historical and theological connection between Buddhism and Christianity did not generate a spirit of affection, as Christianity came to be seen as a demonic imitation that could lead people astray. Japanese Buddhist texts had long warned of impostors who would claim to represent Buddhism while actually being demons who cause great social harm. Thus, when in 1557, after some positive Christian-Buddhist encounters, Jesuit priests began burning Buddhist texts and destroying Buddhist statues, the Japanese felt that they had found the long-prophesied demonic imposters. This interpretation was strengthened when the Japanese later witnessed Portuguese merchants "purchasing Japanese slaves, forcibly converting them to Christianity, and then selling them abroad"; heard news of Spanish attacks upon the

Philippines; and were forced to respond to the rebellion of Japanese peasants armed with European guns and "waving banners with an image of angels worshiping the Eucharist and the slogan *'Lovvado seia o Sãctissimo Sacramento'* (Praised be the Blessed Sacrament)." Christianity thus came to be seen as a "method for in-doctrination and conquest and a set of teachings that resemble that of Buddhism reflected through a dark mirror," and the idea arose that Christianity needed to be "literally wiped off the map" in Japan.[26] This conclusion set the stage for Japan's response to Western powers' efforts to introduce "religious freedom" to Japan during the nineteenth century.

On July 19, 1858, the USS *Powhatan* sounded its cannons in Tokyo Bay and forced Japanese officials to sign a treaty with the United States. This was not an isolated event, but rather the culmination of five years of intensive efforts by Western powers to use international law to force the Japanese to open their ports to Western trade. Throughout this process, Japanese officials and intellectuals struggled to translate many concepts and terms from Western international law that had no ready equivalent in Japanese. Of particular importance was the concept of religion as articulated in the principle of religious freedom.

During the period of treaty drafting, the Japanese sought to define religion in a way that would let them simultaneously uphold religious freedom, a major sticking point for the United States, and "quarantine Christianity and forestall missionary activity."[27] Though some may read this move as a crass betrayal of the spirit of religious freedom, the reality was not so straightforward, as Western powers were hoping that the Japanese treaty would open the country to "the blessed rule of Christianity." Consider in this light the following extract from the personal journal of the first U.S. consul general to Japan, Townsend Harris (1804–78), some months after the U.S. treaty was signed: "I shall be both proud and happy if I can be the humble means of once more opening Japan to the blessed rule of Christianity. My Bible and Prayer Book are priceless mementos of this event, and when (after many or few years) Japan shall be once more opened to Christianity, the events of this day at Yedo will ever be of interest."[28] The Japanese were thus correct in seeing the West's advocacy of religious freedom as a covert effort to spur politically oriented missionary activity.

In this context, it is fascinating to consider how the Japanese framed the relevant issues in the treaty. As the document states, "Americans in Japan shall be allowed the free exercise of their religion (*shūhō*), and for this purpose shall have the right to erect suitable places of worship. No injury shall be done to such buildings, nor any insult be offered to the religious worship (*shūhō*) of the Americans. American Citizens shall not injure any Japanese temple or *mia*, or offer any insult or injury to Japanese religious ceremonies (*shinbutsu no raihai*), or to the objects of their worship (*shintai butsuzō*). The Americans and Japanese shall not do anything that may be calculated to excite religious animosity (*shūshi*). The Government of Japan has already abolished the practice of trampling religious emblems (*fumie*)."[29] Though the English appears straightforward, the Japanese terminology is ingeniously complex. *Shūhō* (sect-law) refers to the "practices, regulations, and laws governing each specific Buddhist sect." By guaranteeing Americans the right to practice their *shūhō*, the Japanese granted them the "freedom to engage in the practices and obey the codes of their sect" and "construct special places in which to carry out such practices." The phrases *shinbutsu no raihai* (ritual for the gods and Buddhas) and *shintai butsuzō* (embodied gods and images of the Buddhas) alternatively presented Japanese practices and beliefs as the actual way of the gods and not a religious sect. When the Japanese prohibited Americans from exciting *shūshi* (sect-doctrine) animosity, they therefore forbade Americans from disrupting the way of the gods as practiced in Japan by engaging in missionary activity.[30] Thus, while appearing to grant full religious freedom, the Japanese actually developed a quite novel concept of "religion" in order to hamper Christian missionary activity and inscribe certain Japanese practices and beliefs in the public sphere.

The notion of Shinto was developed to name this newly conceptualized Japanese tradition. Shinto was not meant to be a religion like Christianity or Buddhism, but rather the "science of the gods" that had been established at the beginning of Japanese history. This definition allowed the Japanese to "interweave Shinto into the fabric of government, and to mandate the performance of

Shinto rituals without contravening new guarantees of religious freedom." Historically, the term "shinto" was used in the medieval period to describe the gods' behavior. As Josephson puts it, "Shinto was not a religion but rather a description of the conduct of the gods." During the Kamakura period (1185–1333), the term was used to describe the rituals performed for local gods, but there was no distinctly Shinto set of rituals; Buddhist and Confucian priests both performed their own sorts of "shinto."[31]

To explain how the notion of a Shinto tradition emerged, Josephson highlights the conjunction of a renewed interest in "rediscovering the spirit of early Japan" and the growing recognition of the superiority of modern Western science that arose during the nineteenth century. Efforts to rediscover the spirit of ancient Japan stemmed from a growing sense of weakness and backwardness in relation to Western powers. The thought was that Japan had grown weak because it had fallen away from its true cultural essence and that by rediscovering and renewing this essence Japan would become strong again. The crucial factor in the growing Japanese appreciation of Western science was the demonstration of the superior predictive power of Western astronomy: "like other societies under the influence of Chinese models of statecraft, it was thought that synchronizing the official calendar with the changes of the seasons and occurrences of celestial events such as eclipses would bring the heavens and the human world into harmonious relation."[32] The challenge was thus to draw what was true from Western science without taking what were considered its unnecessary and corrupting Christian accretions.

A new group of scholars known as "National Scientists" arose to achieve these tasks. They developed "new methodologies for philology and historical research" that were meant to help them recover "Japan's pre-Buddhist mythic past" through the careful study of ancient texts. They argued that "in previous eras [Japan] had formed a coherent whole in which the people were united in a common vision and sense of belonging to the family of the divine ancestor." Unfortunately, Japan fell into weakness when this unity was lost. To restore Japan to its former glory, Japanese unity needed "to be reattained" by rediscovering Japan's "true common essence." Shinto was the name given to this imagined ancient unity and also to the ritual practices that were to facilitate its reemergence. National Science scholars employed the Shinto framework to reinterpret the findings of Western science. Indeed, some National Science scholars went so far as to attribute "the birth of Western sciences to the manifestations of the will of Japanese deities." Josephson explains that "National Science was an all-inclusive project that needed to engage universal forms of learning. The sciences were another 'text' to be hierarchically included in the formation of Shinto discourse. The writings of Western scholarship—from medicine to Christian sources—became at least metaphorically part of the Shinto canon."[33]

Some have argued that National Science scholars attempted to establish a Japanese state religion, but Josephson alternatively claims that they sought to create a "Shinto secular" in which "religions" like Buddhism, Christianity, and Confucianism would be limited to the private sphere while Shinto would be woven throughout the public sphere. In this way, "Shinto was the condition for the eventual invention of religion in Japan, because it was the form of the political from which religion could be distinguished." Or again, "the existence of 'religion' was premised on its differentiation from both education and politics, both of which were understood in Shinto terms."[34]

Josephson then shows how a distinctively Japanese account of religion influenced the West. Contrary to Edward Said's claim that Orientalism was largely focused on the Middle East, Josephson explains that "the principle focus of the inaugural conference on international Orientalism was not the Middle East, not North Africa, not colonized India, not newly dominated China," but rather Japan. Additionally, though Said claims that "orientalism was a conversation among Europeans *about* non-Europeans," Josephson points out that there was an official and highly influential Japanese delegation at the first international Orientalist conference. Indeed, the Japanese were invited both as one among the modern nations and as "the true Orientalists, the true masters of Asia." Here, the Japanese convinced the Europeans that Shinto was not a religion, that Buddhism was not authentically Japanese, and that Confucianism was a freethinker's philosophy. They also stimulated a major shift in the Western discourse on religion by arguing, whether correctly or not, that Buddhism and Confucianism have no concept of God. Previous Western definitions of religion had always connected religion with worshiping God.[35]

Beyond the many historical merits of his account, Josephson's construct narrative makes three major conceptual contributions. First, he counters the overly Western-centric conclusions of most construct narratives by showing how at least one non-Western society did not simply accept the Western discourse on religion, but rather developed its own conception of religion through a complex process of negotiation and exchange. Peter van der Veer found similar dynamics in his examination of the origin of the discourses on religion in China and India.[36] One implication of this is that "modernity" is not simply a Western product that has been globally exported; it is, rather, a complex global dynamic that takes various shapes as Western and non-Western peoples interact with and respond to one another. Another implication is that, for better or worse, it is not only modern Westerners who have found the notion of religion to be a useful conceptual tool.

Second, Josephson's construct narrative forces us to qualify the widely accepted notion that the Protestant Reformation uniquely caused the secularization of modern public life, whatever precisely we imagine this process of secularization to entail. Japan clearly differentiated Christianity, Buddhism, and Confucianism from public life and modern scientific inquiry before similar differentiations happened in the West. Thus, as Josephson explains, "Taylor's so-called secular age seems to have happened first outside of Europe, at the periphery rather than the center, or in exactly those parts of the globe Taylor explicitly fails to consider." This means that "if the secular is supposed to be Protestant in character, then Japanese thinkers would seem to have out-Protestanted the nations of Europe."[37] Josephson's point is not to deny the tremendous influence the Protestant Reformation had on the transformation of modern European societies, but to challenge the claim, still widely made, that the Protestant Reformation was the necessary and sufficient cause of secularization.[38]

This conclusion has far-reaching, and thus far little-considered, implications, as we can see from just one example: Josephson demonstrates how the Shinto secular did not disenchant (or

de-spiritualize) nature and public life. To the contrary, Shinto secularists specifically sought to locate the powerful findings of modern
science and elements of a modern Western political order within
an enchanted Japanese worldview. The Japanese example thus
helps us see how a modern public sphere can explicitly pursue
sacred practices and disseminate religiously charged virtues and
ideas without falling into the kinds of public orthodoxy and
antiscientific authoritarianism that many Westerners would expect
to see.[39]

When considering the relative strengths and weaknesses of the
construct narrative, a first point to mention is that it rightly highlights how a novel, generic concept of religion crystallized as the
West modernized. This does not mean that there were not important historical precursors. Steven Wasserstrom, for example, has
persuasively demonstrated how the modern European discourse
on religion was deeply influenced by the extensive comparative
religious inquiries pursued by the twelfth-century Islamic scholar
Al-Shahrastani.[40] Yet the point remains that a new and explicitly
generic concept of religion arose in the modern West.[41] This new
concept had its limitations, and still does today. But it has undeniably helped expand our understanding of human affairs. This is a
point that many critical construct narratives fail to consider.

I would suggest that the best way to combine these appreciative and critical perspectives is to strive to use the concept of
religion in an increasingly accurate and profound way. Toward
this end, I will conclude by briefly considering one way that the
concept of religion could currently be improved.

Religion is an irreducibly normative phenomenon; it seeks to
tell us how things are and how we ought to live. Nevertheless, contemporary academics endeavor to use the term "religion" in a descriptive way. Consider, in this light, Geertz's definition cited
above: It is a "(1) a system of symbols which act to (2) establish
powerful, pervasive, and long-lasting moods and motivations in
men by (3) formulating conceptions of a general order of existence
and (4) clothing these conceptions with such an aura of factuality
that (5) the moods and motivations seem uniquely realistic."[42]
To put it crudely, there is nothing in this definition that helps us

distinguish Mother Teresa's religion from Osama bin Laden's. We cannot say that Mother Teresa was more religious than bin Laden, because he too organized his life around such a system of symbolic practices and beliefs. Our only recourse, then, is to utilize some external ethical criteria to defend the intuitively obvious claim that Mother Teresa's religious practices and beliefs were better.

To get a sense of the difficulties involved in this dynamic, imagine using the term "science" to describe all efforts to learn about and control the natural world. This would mean that modern science is no more "scientific" than shamanistic healing or medieval alchemy. We do not normally wrestle with such absurdities when discussing science, as most people think about science in a normative way, which is to say as a phenomenon that must be evaluated by its nearness to or distance from certain ideals. This means that there is such a thing as good science and bad science, and that research is scientific only to the extent that it embodies scientific ideals. Most scholars therefore have no problem saying that shamanistic healing and medieval alchemy are less scientific than particle physics or evolutionary biology, though they do appreciate how these endeavors presaged more mature forms of scientific endeavor.

Modern scholars did not initially employ the concept of religion descriptively. Indeed, diverse religious practices and beliefs were long judged according to their nearness to prevalent Christian practices and beliefs, particularly of a Protestant sort.[43] Yet this approach became increasingly difficult to maintain as Christianity lost its grip on Western academic inquiry. And after removing Christianity from its pedestaled position, it was impossible for scholars to replace it with another tradition. They therefore began conceptualizing religion in a descriptive manner and using secular ethical standards (e.g., liberalism or Marxism) whenever normative evaluation was needed. I find this state of affairs unsatisfactory, as religion is not simply an instrument of secular ambitions, however laudable they may be. Rather, religion is permeated by certain distinctive normative ideals that should be recognized and incorporated into our broader understanding of the term. How, then, can we think about these ideals without falling into the pedestaled tradition trap that ensnared so much modern research?

One possibility is that philosophers of religion could begin examining admirable instances of religious practice, inquiry, and deliberation in order to better understand how they exhibit certain religious ideals. This inquiry would be somewhat analogous to the demarcational investigations that philosophers of science pursued during the past decades. The goal of such inquiry would be to gradually articulate a vision of religious normativity that could be used to ground a more robust general conception of religion. The perspectives such a framework offered would help us study diverse expressions of religion, both historical and contemporary, and think more profoundly about how religion can contribute to the betterment of the world. As we will see in the next chapter, John Hick has taken some noteworthy strides in this direction. Nevertheless, a great deal of constructive work remains to be done if we are to ever develop a normative concept of religion that can be confidently deployed in our increasingly global and interconnected age.

CHAPTER SIX

The Perennial Narrative

THE PERENNIAL NARRATIVE CLAIMS that all religions exhibit common characteristics. For some, the word "perennial" immediately calls to mind the school of thought known as *philosophia perennis* or perennial philosophy, which argues that all great religious thinkers have uncovered a single system of thought. Beginning with the Christian engagement with Neoplatonic thought, perennial philosophy expanded during the modern period to include a broader range of sources through the efforts of philosophers, theosophical occultists, neo-Vedantists, advocates of the Traditionalist School, and scholars of comparative religion. Yet the domain of the perennial narrative exceeds that of perennial philosophy per se. Figures like John Hick and Rudolf Otto, for example, use the perennial narrative framework to argue that all the world's religions conceptualize the same spiritual reality differently. Likewise, Søren Kierkegaard, Friedrich Nietzsche, and countless dharmic thinkers argue that human subjectivity displays a cyclical pattern of religious existence, while Ibn Khaldūn and Arnold Toynbee see a perennial pattern in the rise and fall of religious civilizations.[1]

In striving to understand the distinctive features of the perennial narrative, it is important to appreciate its resonances with several other narrative frameworks considered in this work. Thus, for example, a perennial narrative that describes humanity as locked in a cycle of spiritual decline and renewal would likely lend itself to an interpretation of the current period of history as one in which we have fallen away from the eternal truth and now require some kind of spiritual rebirth, bringing us close to Alasdair MacIntyre's and Martin Heidegger's renewal narratives. Alternatively, a perennial narrative claiming that, after a period of blindness, modern science is beginning to rediscover the eternal spiritual truths that were known by earlier generations correlates with Alfred North Whitehead's postnaturalist narrative. And a perennial narrative that views human history as the gradual expression of certain spiritual ideals resonates with the development narrative that we will see Karl Jaspers discuss in the subsequent chapter. Thus, while the perennial narrative framework does retain a distinct overall tone—it concentrates on the phenomena of perpetuity and recurrence within religious history, and not on those of renewal or development, or the postnaturalistic transformation of modern science—we should not view it as a perspective endorsed only by esotericists and New Age enthusiasts.

Aldous Huxley

Aldous Huxley (1864–1963) is known primarily as a novelist. Indeed, Huxley was a belle-lettrist in the truest sense, penning in addition numerous collections of short stories and poems, as well as a substantial body of nonfiction, screenplays, plays, travel logs, and children's books. In 1939 he developed a strong interest in neo-Vedantist perennialism and started an extensive exploration of mysticism that would eventually lead to the publication of *The Perennial Philosophy*.[2] Widely and energetically engaged by British and American readers, this work was heralded as a healing response to the moral failings of Western civilization, with one *New York Times* reviewer going so far as to describe it as "the most needed book in the world."[3]

Huxley begins his perennial narrative by arguing that the most perceptive religious thinkers have uncovered a common set of truths about human nature and reality. This "perennial philosophy," as he calls it, involves two basic ideas: first, that all things, including human subjectivity, emanate from a single spiritual ground; and second, that the purpose of human life is to unite—in thought, action, and existential orientation—with this spiritual ground. Though the articulation and enactment of this perennial philosophy differ from culture to culture and epoch to epoch, its basic truths have been known since humanity's early tribal beginnings. There is therefore no real progress in religious history, but only varying degrees of nearness to or distance from the eternal truth.

Huxley proceeds to argue that we cannot understand the content of the perennial philosophy via abstract reflection. Instead, we must strive to remove all "God-eclipsing obstacles" from our lives and learn how to meet "all, even the most trivial circumstances of daily living . . . with love and understanding," as detachment, purity, and selfless compassion enable us to engage spiritual reality in an objective manner. To support this conclusion, Huxley quotes William Blake's verse "If the doors of perception were cleansed every thing would appear to man as it is, Infinite."[4] This epistemological vision resonates with Nagel's view of objectivity, briefly discussed in chapter 4: "Objectivity is the driving force of ethics as it is of science: it enables us to develop new motives when we occupy a standpoint detached from that of our purely personal desires and interests, just as in the realm of thought it enables us to develop new belief."[5] Huxley adds to this the idea that objectivity is also the driving force of religion and that this spiritual objectivity emerges only when we develop detachment, purity, and selfless compassion.

Huxley employs the notion of spiritual objectivity to make sense of the phenomenon of divine prophets or messengers (e.g., Krishna, Moses, Zoroaster, the Buddha, Jesus, and Muhammad). Each of these figures, he argues, became a clear reflection of the life and will of God by abandoning his ego and his lower impulses: "the 'I' was purged away so as to make room for the divine 'not-I.'" Huxley explains that Jesus came to be thought of as Christ because "he had passed beyond selfness and had become the bodily and mental conduit through which a more than personal, supernatural life flowed down into the world." Because of their selflessness, divine messengers seek to help people grow spiritually and realize their latent potentialities. Yet, over time, their teachings are hijacked by "speculative barristers and metaphysical jurists" and thus robbed of their transformative force.[6] Divine messengers must therefore return from age to age to realign religion with the perennial truth. Huxley cites the Bhagavad Gita to corroborate this view:

When goodness grows weak,
When evil increases,
I make myself a body.

In every age I come back
To deliver the holy,
To destroy the sin of the sinner,
To establish righteousness.[7]

Huxley claims that humanity is currently proceeding through one such period of spiritual decline and cites three pervasive forms of modern idolatry to corroborate his view. First, technological idolatry, which involves the belief that technological innovation can fix humanity's problems, has led to the creation of nuclear weapons, to the mass production of firearms, and to unprecedented environmental degradation. Second, political idolatry, which worships redemptive social and economic organizations, has animated not only the rabid nationalism that spurred two world wars, but also the bloodthirsty competition between communism and capitalism that emerged in their wake. And third, moral idolatry, which worships the ethical ideal of freedom, has created rampant consumerism, stultifying legalism, and pervasive anomie and aimlessness.[8] Huxley thus blames the modern proliferation of "wars, revolutions, exploitation and disorder," of "waste and exhaustion of irreplaceable resources," and of "ignorance of the reason and purpose of human existence" on religion's abandonment of the perennial truth.

Though the widespread renewal of perennial philosophy would vanquish these idolatries and repair the problems of the modern world, Huxley despairs of this ever taking place, barring the arrival of another prophet whose power rivals, or even exceeds, that of Jesus, the Buddha, or Muhammad. He therefore concludes that "any individual's chances of achieving man's final end" are relatively thin and that "societies on a national and super-national scale" will almost certainly continue to be "ruled by oligarchical minorities, whose members come to power because they have a lust for power."⁹ Though Huxley does acknowledge that small groups could establish a more ideal pattern of life by building new communities in relative isolation (as narrated in his novel *Island*), he concludes that even these communities would be perpetually threatened by ignorant outsiders.¹⁰

Huxley's perennial philosophy has suffered a fate similar to that of two other widely popular religious thinkers of his day, Pierre Teilhard de Chardin and Arnold Toynbee. All were simultaneously accused of naïveté and wishful thinking by scholars and rejected by religious thinkers for straying too far from the orthodox pale. Certainly, Huxley deserves many of these critiques. He does seek to transform the profound spiritual resonances between the world's religious traditions into a higher, esoteric tradition. His thinking does lend itself to the kind of cafeteria spirituality that elevates the individual's path above community and tradition. And his experiments with mescaline did lead him to develop an overzealous interest in occult phenomena.¹¹ Nevertheless, these criticisms should not blind us to his many positive contributions.

Consider, for example, Huxley's claim that cultivating detachment, purity, and selfless compassion helps us interact with spiritual reality in a more objective manner. As we saw above, this line of thought aligns with Thomas Nagel's influential claim that objectivity arises when we detach ourselves from individual ways of viewing and valuing the world; Huxley simply applies this conclusion to transcendence. Thus, just as good science and good ethics depend upon the practice of scientific and ethical objectivity, Huxley quite plausibly argues that good religion depends upon our willingness to engage spiritual reality objectively.

Admittedly, this notion of spiritual objectivity clashes with prevalent ideas about the non-objective nature of religious experience. Friedrich Schleiermacher (1768–1834) first articulated this viewpoint when he claimed that religion emanates from a "sense and taste for the Infinite" that has nothing to do with the rational deliberations of "knowledge and science."¹² Yet upon closer investigation, Schleiermacher's and Huxley's views can be seen to align. Schleiermacher argues that we should stop conceptualizing God because God transcends our powers of comprehension and instead either refrain from speaking about God outright or only use poetic language to enhance our experiential encounters with Him. Though Schleiermacher would not use this language, his point is clearly that representational theology is less objective than humble and poetically inclined mysticism, as the latter more accurately responds to the reality of divine transcendence. My purpose here is not to espouse Schleiermacher's views, but to show how even they cohere with Huxley's notion of spiritual objectivity.

There is also much insight in Huxley's claim that spiritual powers are released when people respond to suffering in the right way. Suffering, he explains, constitutes a kind of spiritual "intelligence test" that forces us to choose either greater spirituality and selflessness or greater attachment to the material world. When we choose correctly, we are rewarded "by spiritual growth and progressive realization of latent potentialities," as well as new powers to exert a "beneficent influence on individuals and even on whole societies." However, when we fail our tests, we fall into personal "self-stultification" and collective decline. Huxley thus explains that the "effects of suffering may be morally and spiritual bad, neutral or good, according to the way in which the suffering is endured or reacted to. In other words, it may stimulate in the sufferer a conscious or unconscious craving for the intensification of his separateness; or . . . it may mitigate it and so become a means for advance towards self-abandonment and the love and knowledge of God. Which of the . . . alternatives shall be realized depends, in the last analysis, upon the sufferer's choice."[13]

There are numerous examples of movements and groups that have used similar assumptions to ground powerful processes of social change. Gandhian satyagraha, for example, arose from the resonant idea that there is an active spiritual force in the world that releases its transformative potentialities when people respond to hatred, ignorance, and oppression with love, justice, and compassion. As Gandhi explains, "Truth (*satya*) implies love, and firmness (*agraha*) engenders and therefore serves as a synonym for force. I thus began to call the Indian movement Satyagraha, that is to say, the Force which is born of Truth and Love or non-violence."[14] The success of the Indian liberation movement demonstrated the soundness of this conviction, as did the efforts of American civil rights and South African anti-apartheid activists. We can also see a deep awareness of the transformative power that stems from responding to suffering with justice and compassion in the words of the Universal House of Justice, the senior administrative body of the global Bahá'í community, when they encouraged persecuted Iranian Bahá'í youth to maintain a posture of "constructive resilience": "With an illumined conscience, with a world-embracing vision, with no partisan political agenda, and with due regard for law and order, strive for the regeneration of your country. By your deeds and services attract the hearts of those around you, even win the esteem of your avowed enemies, so that you may vindicate the innocence of, and gain the ever-increasing respect and acceptance for, your community in the land of its birth. . . . Service to others is the way. . . . Strive to work hand-in-hand, shoulder-to-shoulder, with your fellow citizens in your efforts to promote the common good."[15] Although Huxley's account of the relationship between suffering and transformation does not align with each of these examples precisely, his arguments help us better appreciate the premises upon which their efforts are based.

Additionally, though the most problematic feature of Huxley's perennial narrative is clearly his claim that all religious practices, traditions, and systems of thought can be reduced to a single brand of philosophical mysticism, it is hard to not be struck by the fact that religious thinkers and practitioners who inhabit vastly different cultural and historical settings often develop deeply resonant ideas. The oft-cited recurrence of the Golden Rule bears elegant testimony to this dynamic, as does the largely shared conceptual terrain that the world's great religious philosophers have long explored.[16] Thus, though there are many problems with the particular perennial narrative that Huxley articulates, it is not without reason that his *Perennial Philosophy* continues to be widely read and engaged with some seven decades after it was originally released.

John Hick

John Hick's perennial narrative is based on three interrelated claims. First, we can reasonably interpret the universe in either a religious or a naturalistic manner. Second, spiritual reality exceeds finite human comprehension. And third, true knowledge of spiritual reality reorients individual and collective life from a posture of self-centeredness to one of Other-centeredness. With the first point, Hick aims to bypass interminable debate about the nature and existence of God and to focus instead on questions associated with a religious interpretation of reality. Simply put, if both religious and naturalistic frameworks are rationally coherent and empirically adequate, then our time is better spent developing one of these frameworks than trying to prove its superiority over the other. With the second point, he seeks to establish the basis of a religious conceptual framework that makes sense of religious plurality. The idea here is that if spiritual reality exceeds finite human comprehension, then different religious traditions can authentically respond to transcendence without conceptualizing it in the same way. With the third point, he seeks to shift debate from theological apologetics to more practical considerations of how religion actually contributes to the betterment of the world. I follow this sequence of thought in elaborating his positions below.

Hick develops his argument for the "religious ambiguity of the universe" by demonstrating the inconclusiveness of arguments both for and against the existence of God.[17] His purpose in doing so is not to disparage efforts to provide good reasons for our metaphysical convictions, but rather to undermine the idea that it is possible to develop a conclusive argument one way or another. He claims that no argument for God's existence will make it rationally necessary for nonbelievers to believe, while no argument for naturalism will make it rationally necessary for believers to abandon their faith. Instead, reality displays a constitutive religious ambiguity such that we can adopt either a religious or a naturalistic viewpoint without flying in the face of fact or rationality.

To understand Hick's point, let us consider his critique of the cosmological argument for the existence of God. As the argument normally goes, in trying to explain how the universe arose, we are either led into an infinite causal regress or led to posit a first cause. Because reason cannot accept an infinite regress, we must posit a first cause. However, for any supposed first cause to truly be a *first* cause, it must be the eternal and self-subsisting creator of all that exists, including mind. Another word for such an eternal and self-subsisting creator of all things, including mind, is God. Therefore, explaining the existence of the cosmos leads us to posit the existence of God. Hick responds to this argument by asking why we cannot simply posit nature as the eternal and self-subsistent creator of all things. With either God or nature we still face an ultimate mystery. Why would an eternal, self-subsistent, and creative God exist? He just would, and there is no more explanation than that. Alternatively, why would an eternal, self-subsistent, and creative nature exist? It just would, and there is no more explanation than that. The only question, then, is whether we find it more convincing to believe in an ultimately mysterious God or in an ultimately mysterious nature, and history shows that very intelligent people embrace both views. Hick therefore does not deny that the cosmological argument provides a good reason to believe in God; rather, he denies that it rationally necessitates such belief.[18]

Hick similarly critiques antitheistic arguments that hinge on the perceived incompatibility between the concept of an omnipotent and benevolent God and the reality of evil. If a supposedly omnipotent and benevolent God allows great evil to exist, the claim is that we must question His omnipotence, His benevolence, or His existence. Since no one is particularly interested in arguing for the existence of a non-benevolent God, we can reject that idea outright. Likewise, though some are willing to deny God's omnipotence, most feel that such a compromise leaves us with an abstract God who hardly compels worship and belief, so this idea can also be ruled out. Therefore, the most likely explanation for the existence of evil is that God does not exist. Hick responds, as most other philosophers of religion do, by explaining how ideas of free will and a wider temporal and metaphysical horizon for God's goodness can plausibly reconcile the idea of a good and omnipotent God with the reality of evil. Again, his point here is not to deny that evil is a problem that might reasonably lead some people to embrace naturalism. Rather, he seeks to undermine the claim that the existence of evil requires all rational people to abandon religious belief.

Because such metaphysical ambiguity characterizes all our encounters with the world, Hick suggests that philosophers should stop trying to determine whether or not there is a God and dedicate their time instead to understanding why some people adopt religious beliefs while others do not. Generally speaking, whenever we explore reality—physical, ethical, or spiritual—we accept that doing so could change our patterns of thought and action. We cannot continue as before when we discover that, for example, Aristotelian purpose does not animate biological life, that slavery is incompatible with the principle of freedom, or that spiritual forces operate in the world. Those who love truth relish such changes, while those who remain attached to their current habits would rather deny reality than change their lives. This is particularly the case, Hick argues, with spiritual reality, as its truths demand a more fundamental transformation than do either physical or ethical reality. Physical truths demand that we change the way we interact with nature. Ethical truths demand that we change our values and relationships. Yet religious truths demand that we undertake the "profoundly threatening" process of renouncing self-centered aspirations and orienting ourselves toward service of the divine: "To give up one's personal projects, desires, hopes and ambitions, as also one's fears and aversions, in absolute surrender to God, or in a fading away of the ego point of view, or in acceptance of one's existence as but a fleeting moment within the interdependent flux of life, inevitably seems to most of us like plunging into darkness— even though there is the promise beyond it of peace with God . . . or of union with Brahman . . . or of the indescribable joy of the ego-free state of Nirvana."[19] Hick argues that most people who deny the existence of transcendence today do so because they do not witness the reality of such transformations, or even the benefit of pursuing them, although they might express their doubt in terms of debates about spiritual reality's place within a natural-scientific framework. He therefore does not spend much time trying to convince nonbelievers of religion's truth. Instead, he seeks to develop and explore the internal rationality of religious belief, paying particular attention to the problem of religious diversity.

Hick's basic claim on this front is that if spiritual reality is infinite, we cannot encompass it within a single theoretical framework or historical tradition. To the contrary, any particular conceptualization, however profound, can offer no more than a partial and finite perspective. Hick argues that all the major religious traditions have, in one way or another, realized this point. Within Hinduism, there is an acknowledged difference between the Brahman without attributes (*niguna*), who exceeds all human comprehension, and the Brahman with attributes (*saguna*), who appears to human minds as the creator and governor of the world. In Buddhism one finds the distinction between the ultimate Dharmakaya and the diversified Buddhas and Boddhisattvas who are its incarnations. The *Daodejing* begins by stating that "the Tao that can be expressed is not the eternal Tao."[20] Jewish philosopher Maimonides clearly distinguishes between the essence and the various manifestations of God. Islam highlights God's ultimate transcendence while also acknowledging that He periodically makes Himself known to people through messengers and scriptures. And Christian mystics like Meister Eckhart distinguish between the unknowable Godhead and the personal face of God who is known to human beings. Hick believes that these claims all suggest that multiple finite accounts of spiritual reality can be true simultaneously.[21]

The main difficulty Hick must address in making this claim concerns how Buddhism, Daoism, Confucianism, and the higher forms of Hinduism apparently orient themselves around belief in an impersonal spiritual essence, while Judaism, Christianity, and Islam concentrate on a personal God. How can such different concepts refer to the same reality? Hick tackles this problem by drawing an analogy with quantum wave-particle duality. Though we cannot observe the pure structure of light, we find that it behaves like a "shower of particles" under certain conditions and like a "succession of waves" under others. Thus, physical reality can be "validly conceived and observed in both of these ways." Why would the same not hold true for transcendence? In this way, Hick concludes that "when human beings relate themselves to [transcendence] in the mode of I-Thou encounter they experience it as [a] personal . . . He or She." But when they relate "themselves to [transcendence] in the mode of non-personal awareness they experience it as non-personal, and in the context of this relationship it *is* non-personal."[22]

By accepting this pluralistic interpretation of religion, Hick suggests that philosophers should begin shifting their attention from debates about the viability of religious belief to analyses of how religious practices and beliefs actually operate. In this regard, Hick argues that all the major axial traditions (i.e., Judaism, Hinduism, Buddhism, Confucianism, Daoism, Zoroastrianism, Greek philosophy, Christianity, and Islam) focus on ultimate salvation or liberation. Whereas pre-axial religions were conservative in nature, seeking to protect human society against periodic breakdown by prescribing perpetually reenactments of an unchanging set of rituals and myths, axial religions imparted "to our present existence the positive character of movement towards a limitlessly good end." "Christianity," Hick explains, "speaks of redemption and eternal life; Judaism of the coming kingdom of God; Islam of judgment and paradise; Hinduism of *moksa;* Buddhism of enlightenment and *nirvana.*" Hick thus presents the various religious traditions that arose during and after the classical axial period as "alternative soteriological 'spaces' within which, or 'ways' along which, men and women can find salvation / liberation / ultimate fulfillment."[23]

Despite their differences, Hick finds a common structure among these soteriological visions, namely the goal of transforming self-centeredness into Reality- or Other-centeredness. "In all these forms," Hick explains, religious soteriology "involves a transposition of the individual's existence from a state of self-centredness to a new centredness in the Real experienced and responded to as the divine Thou."[24] Each axial tradition states that we should liberate ourselves from attachments and desires and orient our lives instead around the divine Other. In doing so, however, we need not turn away from the world and other people, for they are both created and sustained by the divine. We should instead respond to them with great compassion and appreciation. Certainly, articulations of this transformative project differ from tradition to tradition. Yet Hick still maintains that the overall structure remains consistent, and he accordingly presents the project of transforming self-centeredness into Other-centeredness as the normative core of religion.

Based on this conclusion, Hick encourages us to evaluate the merit of diverse religious practices and beliefs by considering the extent to which they actually stimulate such spiritual transformation.

Many in the West would argue that Christianity has the clear edge
on this front, as it is presumably responsible for generating modern
science, democracy, humanitarianism, and human rights. But this
line of thinking obscures not only the fact that various other religious, cultural, and philosophical sources contributed to the emergence of these remarkable modern forces, but also that the modern
West is responsible for the two most atrocious wars in human history, the threat of global thermonuclear destruction, religiously
sanctioned racial oppression, the spread of consumerism, unprecedented and life-threatening environmental degradation, and an explosion of divorce, drug use, and depression, to name a few. In this
regard, Hick suggests that Islam has historically exhibited far superior levels of racial equality, while Hinduism has nurtured stronger
and more supportive family units, and Buddhism has cultivated
more sustainable relationships with the environment.[25] Of course,
these traditions also struggle with certain moral failings, such as
gender inequality and violent extremism in the Islamic world and
the caste system in South Asia. Hick's point is simply that the longer
historical record does not allow for an easy assertion of one tradition's soteriological superiority over the others. Instead, it shows a
mixture of triumphs and failures, in which certain strands within
certain traditions advance the cause of transformation for a time,
while others ossify, decay, and become entangled in blatant immo-
rality. Indeed, from Hick's perspective, one tradition's preoccupation
with asserting its own superiority over the others already betrays its
failure to remain committed to the project of transforming self-
centeredness into Other-centeredness.

One way to make sense of this aspect of Hick's thought is
through the analogy of Imre Lakatos's theory of scientific research
programs.[26] In Lakatos's view, science is populated by a number of
competing research programs, each of which employs distinct conceptual frameworks, methodologies, empirical standards, and technological instruments. Over time, some research programs prove
themselves "progressive" by generating novel predictive insights
about the world, while others show themselves to be "degenerative" by protecting their core theoretical vision with a series of
ad hoc alterations. Still, every research program aims to increase
our knowledge of and control over the same physical reality,

locates itself within a common sphere of scientific endeavor, and can contribute to the advancement of the scientific enterprise. Analogously, Hick sees all religious traditions striving to generate knowledge about how to transform self-centeredness into Other-centeredness and developing different practices, strategies, and beliefs as they do so. At any moment, the "research programs" some traditions pursue may be developing and advancing, while others may be undergoing a process of degeneration and decline.

Some have criticized Hick by claiming that his pluralistic view of religion undermines our ability to fully embrace one system of religious practice and belief. If all religious traditions constitute authentic ways of engaging transcendence, then it seems impossible to say, for example, that Jesus alone was the son of God or that Buddha uncovered to true path to enlightenment. In one sense, these critics are correct, as Hick's view of religion is not compatible with exclusivist or finalist doctrines. Nevertheless, his views are fully compatible with the claim that one religious system is the most relevant and beneficial in the world today. As explained above, Hick argues that the merit of all religious practices and beliefs stems from their demonstrated ability to transform individual and collective life from self-centeredness to Other-centeredness. For this reason, one community or tradition could presumably demonstrate its superior merit by generating fruits that are notably superior to those produced by others. This is arguably how natural science gained its current global ascendency, not by proving a priori that its concepts are true, but rather by yielding undeniably powerful results.

I must admit that I am partial to Hick's conceptualization of transcendence. At least within the "major" religious traditions found throughout the world today, the spectrum of conceptions of transcendence do range from the personal to the impersonal. As he suggests, in the face of this conceptual diversity, we can see all as equally false, only one as true, or several as providing some insight into a reality that must, by definition, transcend finite human comprehension. Thus, unless one clings to the idea that just one community has received true knowledge of divinity, it seems hard to avoid adopting some version of the last claim. The alternative would be to reject transcendence outright. How, after all, can there not be more than one way of looking at an infinite reality?

I am also attracted to Hick's claim that the goal of transforming self-centeredness into Other-centeredness lies at the center of the normative project that all of the major world religions pursue. Of course, we should be suspicious of any attempt to arbitrarily impose outside criteria on all religious practices and beliefs. Yet even according to Hick's own logic, his formulation could never claim to exhaust the normative content of religion, as transcendence exceeds our powers of comprehension by definition. Hick's soteriological ideal should therefore be seen as but one generalization that can help us begin thinking about the normative dimensions of religion in a more penetrating and productive way.

Rudolf Otto

Rudolf Otto's perennial narrative argues that different religious traditions arise by variously schematizing a common core of religious experience, which he describes as the experience of *mysterium tremendum*. Otto suggests that this experience of *mysterium tremendum* arises from our encounter as finite beings with an infinite, loving, yet all-powerful spiritual reality. These encounters are schematized in different ways because of the different cultural and historical contexts in which they emerge. Otto observes that these schematizations evolve in a progressive manner, whereby the "daemonic dread" that characterized early tribal religion is gradually transmuted into the loving encounter with divine grace that we see in modern Christianity.

Otto begins his account of *mysterium tremendum* by explaining how the divine essence is, in relation to finite human beings, "wholly other," "transcendent," and "supernatural."[27] As an infinite reality, the divine always exceeds human comprehension. Nevertheless, contrary to what Kant claims, this transcendence does not prevent us from experiencing the divine. Rather, to use the phrase recently coined by Jean-Luc Marion, we encounter the divine via a "counter-experience," which is to say via the experience of our finite human capacities being surpassed and overwhelmed.[28] Otto uses the term *mysterium tremendum* to describe this religious counter-experience.

The word *mysterium* denotes "that which is hidden and . . . beyond conception or understanding, extraordinary and unfamiliar," while *tremendum* describes how this mystery "may burst in sudden eruption up from the depths of the soul with spasms and convulsions, or lead to the strangest excitements, to intoxicated frenzy, to transport, . . . to ecstasy, . . . and can sink to an almost grisly horror and shuddering."[29] *Mysterium tremendum* thus refers to the mix of love and fear that arises from our experiential encounter with a spiritual reality that radically exceeds our powers of comprehension. Otto argues that every form of religion, from early tribal ritual to the most exalted heights of philosophical mysticism, emanates from this same experiential core.

To clarify how this common experience generates the dizzying variety of religious forms that have appeared throughout history, Otto introduces the idea of "analogical arousal." His claim is that "any form of [religious] consciousness may be stored by means of feelings analogous to it of a 'natural' kind."[30] This means that worldly phenomena that evoke, for example, a feeling of mystery, awe, or terror (e.g., a fortuitous turn of events, the beauty of an ancient forest, or a natural disaster) tend to become linked with the mysterious, awe-inspiring, and terrifying elements of *mysterium tremendum*. Certain analogical links resonate across all cultural settings; others operate within the cultures in which they originally arose. Regardless, once there is an analogical link between a worldly phenomenon and an aspect of *mysterium tremendum*, recalling this worldly phenomenon helps evoke the relevant religious experience. The skill and intricacy of our efforts to utilize such analogical connections gradually increase over time, just as musicians gradually become more skilled at evoking certain emotions through regular practice. Religious diversity is thus, for Otto, somewhat like diversity in world music; all music interacts with the same set of human emotions, albeit by employing historically and culturally specific patterns of musical expression.

Otto considers the process of analogical arousal the key to the developmental arc of religious history. In the earliest forms of tribal religion, the experience of *mysterium tremendum* was charged with feelings of fear. This led tribal religions to focus on devising means to withhold the wrath and win the favor of certain spiritual beings. Furthermore, tribal religion tended to involve high degrees of nature worship, since spiritual beings had not yet been distinguished from the material world.[31]

Over time, the more benevolent and transcendent facets of *mysterium tremendum* came to the fore. This process of sublimation found its highest expression in the Jewish, Greek, and Christian traditions. Judaism's main contribution was to help us see that although divinity is both wrathful and benevolent, the aspect of benevolence ultimately prevails. Although the God of the Hebrew Bible was not beyond destroying errant populations or purifying His believers with violent tests, His goal was to redeem history and to bless the world. In a somewhat different fashion, the Greek philosophers, Plato in particular, added depth and precision to our understanding of divinity's transcendence: "The most remarkable characteristic of Plato's thought is just that he himself finds science and philosophy too narrow to comprise the whole of man's mental life.... He abandons the attempt to bring the object of religion into one system of knowledge with the objects of 'science,' i.e. reason, and it becomes something not less but greater thereby.... No one has enunciated more definitively than this master-thinker that God transcends all reason, in the sense that He is beyond the powers of our conceiving, not merely beyond our powers of comprehension." Later, Christianity synthesized the Jewish and Greek strands of thought by advancing the concept of an infinite and transcendent God who leads us, via Christ's atoning sacrifice, out of sin and into a state of eternal grace. Otto thus suggests that Christ's sacrifice was the mechanism by which primordial religious fear was transmuted into religious love. This is, for him, proof of Christianity's truth: "no religion has brought the mystery of the need for atonement or expiation to so complete, so profound, or so powerful expression as Christianity."[32] Nevertheless, Otto still finds in Christianity the same encounter with *mysterium tremendum* that animated all the religious movements that came before.

Given the setting in which Otto wrote—he was a German Lutheran theologian whose *Idea of the Holy* was first published in 1917—his Christo- and Eurocentric biases are unsurprising. His was an epoch in which European thinkers were simultaneously discovering the spiritual wealth of the world's diverse religious traditions, struggling with the rise of an aggressive and ideologically motivated form of naturalism whose proponents were eager to abandon the rich harvests of Christian tradition, and firmly ensconced within a Eurocentric vision of world history. It is therefore important to differentiate the gold of Otto's enduring insights from the dross of his limited historical perspective.

There is little support for his claim that tribal religion was fundamentally characterized by a sense of "daemonic dread." To the contrary, as Robert Bellah demonstrates, while there was an experience of precariousness in tribal religion, there was also deep assurance that the proper execution of ritual would facilitate the restoration of harmony and well-being. From this angle, there is no more dread in tribal religion than in any later stage of religion.[33]

Otto's attempt to use Christianity, and particularly Lutheran Christianity, as the goal toward which all religions have been historically proceeding is also deeply flawed. Admittedly, as a Lutheran theologian, Otto naturally believed that Lutheran Christianity was true and thus somehow exemplary in relation to other religious traditions. However, Otto provides such little argumentation for his claim that we can only attribute his conclusions to the influence of ideological prejudice. Regardless, Otto's work is not so much remembered for its developmental narrative as for its claim that *mysterium tremendum* provides religion with its perennial experiential core. That is why I include Otto in this chapter and not the next.[34] Let us therefore turn to the more enduring elements of his thought.

There is nothing fundamentally wrong with Otto's efforts to articulate the common core of religious experience. Indeed, the facts that human beings are one species, inhabit a single reality, and constantly engage in cross-cultural borrowing, translation, and interaction make the idea that religious experience displays certain universal structures immensely plausible.

What, then, about Otto's claim that *mysterium tremendum* is religion's experiential core? Clearly, the concept of *mysterium tremendum* usefully describes certain aspects of religious experience. For example, it helps us see how many forms of religious experience overwhelm our finite capacities. Philosopher Jean-Luc Marion has persuasively developed the first line of thought in his philosophy of "givenness" and "saturated phenomena."[35] Additionally, the concept of *mysterium tremendum* explains how most religious experience involves an interplay of love and fear: both benevolent spirits and demons populate tribal and archaic religious myths; invocations of the love and fear of God constantly arise in biblical and Qur'anic texts; and the Buddhist and Hindu writings present the divine as both the life-giver and the destroyer of worlds.

At the same time, however, *mysterium tremendum* does not adequately account for some of the more mundane characteristics of religious experience. For example, experiences of communal solidarity arising through collective prayer do not figure into Otto's conceptual scheme, nor do experiences of being sustained during a difficult period of life, nor even the feeling of being connected with a sacred tradition through celebrations and ritual observance. Certainly, there is an element of "counter-experience," to use Marion's phrase, in all these phenomena. But the experience of "being overwhelmed" is not fundamental, nor is the interplay of love and fear. There is rather a sense of gentle nourishment and assistance, in which we are not so much "countered" by divine transcendence as helped to become better versions of our individual and collective selves. Otto's notion of *mysterium tremendum* offers few resources to think about this everyday aspect of religious life.

Many critics are quick to point out problems with the perennial narrative framework. This comes from a distaste for the contemporary popular tendency to present esoteric and superstitious phenomena as the high road to spiritual truth. It is also influenced by a growing recognition of how efforts to articulate universal theories of religion have been historically intertwined with oppressive colonial endeavors. Though legitimate, these critiques should not lead us to overlook the many merits of the perennial narrative's conviction that the world's diverse religions display certain common core features. Consider, in this regard, how people from remarkably different cultural contexts and historical settings have long found insight and truth in the Confucian *Analects*, the *Daodejing*, the Bhagavad Gita, the *Dhammapada*, the Hebrew Bible, the Gospels, and the Qur'an, texts which themselves have remarkably different cultural and historical origins. Consider also the significant consensus among different religious traditions about many fundamental ethical and spiritual precepts, including the Golden Rule. Admittedly, it is certainly possible to overemphasize such patterns of unity and thus to do violence to the real and meaningful diversity that exists. Yet it is also possible to overemphasize difference to the point where we ignore the real and meaningful patterns of unity that also exist.

The question, then, is how to engage perennial narrative perspectives on religion without overzealously collapsing all religious difference into an easy unity. My own view resonates with John Hick's. I consider transcendence to be a reality that simultaneously transcends and interacts with human beings. This means that there is more than one legitimate way to conceptualize transcendence, and also that different systems of religious practice and belief have arisen throughout history as diverse peoples sought to respond to their encounter with divinity in an authentic and faithful way. Even still, the different religious systems display a great deal of overlapping consensus on issues of fundamental ethical and spiritual concern. We can therefore reasonably use these instances of overlapping consensus to develop a more robust normative understanding of religion. Such a perspective would help us begin exploring the intuitively obvious fact that not all religious practices and beliefs are equally meritorious. And it would also help us redirect our intellectual energies from abstract theological debates to more grounded explorations of how individuals, communities, and institutions can draw upon the powers of religion to stimulate constructive processes of transformation.

Not everyone will accept this way of conceptualizing religion. Indeed, some might even claim that any attempt to describe the perennial features of religion in a normative way will simply re-create the colonialistic and Romantic patterns of thought that have long entranced Western minds. However, in our age of rapid globalization, in which diverse religious communities and traditions are being forced to interact with one another in increasingly frequent and substantive ways, we must develop new and more sophisticated ways of engaging in a collective normative discourse on religion. The line of thought articulated above offers one plausible way of beginning this inescapable task.

CHAPTER SEVEN

The Developmental Narrative

DEVELOPMENTAL NARRATIVES ARGUE THAT the broader arc of religious history exhibits a staged process of development and growth. Some authors present this developmental process as progressive, claiming, for example, that we gradually learn more about God or further unfold the implications of certain spiritual ideals. Others describe it more neutrally as involving the expansion of human capacity or the growth of religious complexity, which can be used for either evil or good. Developmental narratives first arose in the West when early modern thinkers sought to make sense of the religious diversity they were encountering throughout the world by claiming that all other religions were somehow steps along the path toward European Christianity.[1] However, such triumphalistic developmental narratives have recently given way to attempts to describe the historical development of religion in a more globally nuanced and open-ended way. In what follows, I consider one classically Christo- and Eurocentric developmental narrative—that of G. W. F. Hegel—and then examine Karl Jaspers's and Robert Bellah's attempts to offer a more balanced global view.

G. W. F. Hegel

The central premise of G. W. F. Hegel's (1770–1831) developmental narrative is that religion evolves alongside humanity's maturing understanding of God.[2] Humanity, he claims, has proceeded from the idea that God is diffusely present in nature, to the idea that God stands over and against the world, to the "consummate" Christian idea that God is present in the self-actualization of human life. Hegel's developmental narrative forms an integral part of his broader philosophical system. It is therefore difficult to understand the former without also understanding the latter. Although it is not possible to elaborate Hegel's system in its entirety in the short pages that follow, we can gain sufficient insight into its basic features by briefly considering Hegel's relationship to Kantian thought.

We can helpfully approach Kant's "critical" philosophy as an attempt to reconcile the conflict between empiricists and rationalists that raged during his day.[3] Simply put, the empiricists attacked metaphysics by claiming that all knowledge must be rooted in sense experience, and hence that knowledge of non-sensory phenomena like "being" or "God" is impossible. The rationalists countered by claiming that metaphysical knowledge is possible because human minds are created in the image and likeness of ultimate reality; hence, when we discern the necessary structures of thought, we also uncover the metaphysical structures of the world. Kant synthesized these two positions by arguing that mind creates the experienced world by applying its innate conceptual framework to received sense impressions. By attributing the creation of the experienced world to the human mind, Kant accepted the empiricist claim that humans cannot know supersensible reality, but preserved the rationalist conviction that there is a fundamental likeness between the conceptual structure of human thought and the metaphysical structure of the world.

One of the key concepts Kant develops to support this claim is that of the "transcendental" imagination.[4] The transcendental imagination is the mental activity that transforms apprehended sense impressions into a robust image of the world. The word "imagination" suggests the constructive dimension of this activity, while "transcendental" conveys how this activity precedes and enables our normal encounter with the world. Kant argues that a series of innate a priori concepts (e.g., notions of space, time, quantity, quality, relation, and modality) structure the constructive activity of our transcendental imagination. Hence, these innate a priori concepts also structure the experienced world.[5] Although the rationalists were right to highlight the likeness between our minds and the world, a true understanding of this likeness should lead us to see that the likeness originates in the creative activity of the human mind.

Although this brief summary of Kant's critical philosophy inevitably simplifies what is, by any estimation, a vast and complex intellectual endeavor, it provides us with a useful angle from which to approach Hegel's work. From this vantage point, Hegel's entire philosophical project can be seen as an effort to elaborate and critique Kant's notion of the transcendental imagination. Hegel does this in two specific ways. First, he rejects the idea that the transcendental imagination has an unchanging conceptual structure and argues instead that it evolves throughout history. This means both the structure of the mind and the structure of the experienced world change from age to age. Hegel uses the term "Spirit" to describe this history-embedded rendition of the transcendental imagination. Second, Hegel rejects Kant's claim that ultimate reality is unknowable, which he does by abandoning the idea that ultimate reality transcends human experience. Instead, he argues that humans are already the self-conscious expression of the one reality that exists. In other words, Hegel rejects the idea of a transcendent God, equates ultimate reality with the evolving system of the world, and consequently claims that we are the self-consciousness of this one, evolving world.

Secondary debates have long raged around this aspect of Hegel's thought. In rejecting the idea of transcendence, is Hegel merely claiming that only the natural world we encounter every day exists? Or is he making the more heterodox claim that humans are the self-expression of some kind of immanent world-soul or deity? Contemporary "analytic" interpreters like Robert Pippin and Terry Pinkard generally adopt the first approach, while "Continental" and theological readers like Cyril O'Regan, William

Desmond, and Peter Hodgson tend to adopt the latter. Inevitably, the interpretation one chooses shapes how one reads Hegel's philosophy of religion.[6] Without diving into the intricacies of these debates, my own assessment is that Hegel does espouse a kind of heterodox mystical theology whereby humans are the self-conscious expression of an immanent deity.[7] Regardless, this reading will not unduly influence my account of the basic features of Hegel's developmental narrative of religion.

As mentioned above, the basic premise of Hegel's developmental narrative is that religion evolves alongside humanity's maturing understanding of God. Within this schema, each of the world's religions operates as a stage of consciousness that leads gradually, and in a cumulative manner, to the "emergence of the true religion" and to the "authentic consciousness of spirit" in European Protestantism.[8]

Hegel claims that religion first appears among early humans just after they step beyond the animal condition. Although early humans live, like animals, in constant fear "of the forces of nature," they believe that spiritual forces enjoy complete "dominion, power, and lordship over nature." Religion arises as a way of tapping these spiritual forces in order to ward off "such unstable conditions as earthquakes, thunderstorms, protracted drought, flood, rapacious beasts or enemies." "Charms and fetishes" are often used to facilitate this process. Hegel accordingly describes early religion as "magical" and "superstitious" and claims that it was still practiced during his day by Eskimos and many African tribes.[9]

Magical religion acquires a more sophisticated and disciplined form in the ancient Chinese emperor cult and in Daoism. In Hegel's account, the ancient Chinese emperor cult is organized around the notion of Tian, or heaven, conceptualized as a universal spiritual will that rules nature and "dispenses or withholds its blessings according to moral deserts and conduct." However, Tian itself does not establish "the laws of religion and ethical life," but receives them from the emperor, whose will alone ultimately secures harmony and stability. The Daoists develop a similar notion of individual authority over the spiritual forces that govern nature, but seek to use these powers to achieve individual immortality.[10]

For Hegel, Buddhism surpasses magical religion by shifting the balance of power from the individual to the spiritual. Whereas advocates of magical religion endeavor to control spiritual forces in order to manipulate the world, Buddhists strive to annihilate individuality in order to merge themselves with the spiritual absolute. Toward this end, Buddhists dedicate themselves to disciplines that aim to help them to "will nothing, to want [nothing], and to do nothing." Hegel continues: "The principle cultus for [Buddhists] is the uniting of oneself with this nothing, divesting oneself of all consciousness, of all passions. The cultus consists of transposing oneself into this abstraction, into this complete solitude, this total emptiness, this renunciation, into the nothing. When one has attained this, one is then indistinguishable from God, eternally identical with God." The fully enlightened Buddhist neither gains magical powers nor physical immortality, but experiences the perfect bliss of uniting with God. "When one is no longer subjected to the burdens of stress, old age, sickness, and death, nirvana has been attained; one is then identical with God, is regarded as God himself, has become Buddha."[11] Though Hegel uses the term "God" to describe Buddhist belief, he still considers Buddhism a "natural religion" because it conceptualizes the spiritual absolute as the immanent ground of the natural world.

In Hinduism the spiritual absolute (Brahma) is "the substance from which everything proceeds or is begotten" and "the power that has brought forth or created everything," but in Hegel's view, Hinduism goes beyond Buddhism with the argument that Brahma gives rise to a series of "independent deities" or "universal powers" that each animate some region of the world.[12] Hindus thus believe that people can approach Brahma by worshiping any of its various manifestations (e.g., Vishnu, Shiva, Krishna, or Hanuman).

Zoroastrianism posits a radical gap between God and nature by claiming that God creates the world yet exists separately from it. The drama of Zoroastrianism comes from the idea that God's creatures fall prey to the evil idea that they are self-subsistent. "Hence we have two principles," Hegel explains, "the realm of the good and that of evil. . . . The good is indeed the true and the powerful, but it is in conflict with evil, so that evil stands over against it and persists as an absolute principle." This narrative of conflict between good and evil, between the recognition of God's creative authorship and the foolhardy attempt to assert creaturely independence, states Hegel, is the central feature of Zoroastrianism, and all Zoroastrian practice aims to tilt the balance back toward divinity.[13]

Ancient Egyptian religion develops the idea of a gap between God and nature by positing the idea of an immortal soul. The Egyptians introduced this idea through the myth of Osiris. As the story goes, the primeval Egyptian king Osiris was killed and dismembered by his brother, who sought to usurp his throne. Osiris's wife gathered her husband's severed body parts and organized them for ritual burial. This act so impressed the gods that they reincarnated Osiris and made him ruler of the underworld. On Hegel's reading, this myth reconceptualizes the dead as those who "endure by themselves on a higher plane" and suggests that our behavior in this world shapes our life in the next.[14]

Hegel suggests that the ancient Greeks also embrace the ideas of an immortal soul and transcendent spiritual reality but additionally claim that humans can manifest transcendent realities in the natural world. The Greeks develop this insight through the myth of the war of the gods, in which the humanlike gods (e.g., Zeus and Apollo) overthrow the nature-like titans (e.g., Chronos and Oceanus). The Greek gods, however, are not content to simply rule nature after winning; they want to manifest themselves within it. Accordingly, Greek poets, priests, sculptors, dramatists, architects, and the like all endeavor to incarnate the gods through their creative works. Greek religion thus "consists in making [the gods] representational, in enabling consciousness to represent to itself something divine. . . . Hence the gods of the Greeks are products of human imagination or sculptured deities formed by human hands."[15]

Judaism surpasses Greek religion by gathering all the "particular spiritual powers" into a single "spiritual unity" and claiming that this one God creates the world ex nihilo, gives reality a unified rational order, and directs all things toward the achievement of His purpose and will. The ideas of "revelation" and "miracles" both emerge in this context in order to emphasize the priority of divine will over the created world. Indeed, the Jewish religion as a whole seeks to embody this priority by claiming that obedience to God's revealed teachings and laws is the only way for the Jews to achieve prosperity and stability.[16]

Roman religion overcomes the Jewish idea that God "is only a national God, [who] has restricted himself to this nation," by gathering all the deities that the Roman Empire's subjects worship into "one pantheon, assembled under one destiny." Whereas Jews seek to create a prosperous and divinely illumined Jewish nation, the Romans seek to create a prosperous and divinely illumined world empire.[17] Toward this end, the Romans reconceptualize the gods as distinct powers that help humans realize certain practical ends, and believe that creating a universal pantheon would let them utilize all the divine powers.

Christianity consummates religion's developmental arc by advancing the notion of a self-manifesting Trinitarian God. God the Father exists over and against the world; created humans exist in a fallen state within the world. God manifested Himself in the person of the Son, Jesus Christ, in order to reconcile humanity with Himself once and for all. And when people accept Jesus as the Son of God, God manifests Himself within their individual and collective lives in the form of the Holy Spirit. The work of the Holy Spirit begins with the formation of a distinct Christian community, but its ultimate aim is to manifest "the spirituality of the community . . . in the [entire] worldly realm." The process began when the church established itself as an imperial power. However, in pursuing an imperial path, the church took "worldliness up into itself" and became corrupt.[18] In response, two powerful reform efforts emerged. The first strove to purify Christianity. In his 1827 *Lectures*, Hegel attributes this function to Protestantism—pietism in particular.[19] The second reform effort, which Hegel identifies with the Enlightenment, rejected Christianity's external form and sought to use the Christian sense of reconciliation to promote a new pattern of autonomous rational inquiry. Hegel's point here is that Enlightenment thinkers only trusted free rational inquiry because they already believed that God perfectly manifests Himself in the lives of Christian believers. In the final stage, Protestant and Enlightenment reform efforts reconciled, and Christianity became an agent of enlightened social formation. In this context, learned people recognize that Christianity found its highest expression in the autonomous intellectual activity that Enlightenment thinkers pursued. Yet they also appreciate how traditional Christianity must endure in order to cultivate a "reconciled" consciousness in each new generation, as well as to orient the masses who will likely never rise to the stage of rational inquiry. Thomas Lewis aptly describes Hegel's conclusions on this front:

> The church's vital pedagogical role requires that the religious community or its functional equivalent—an institution that instills a consciousness of the absolute in representational form—endure. Only through practices of this sort do individuals come to view themselves in the manner appropriate for participation in modern life—as free individuals. The appropriate religious upbringing cultivates a self-understanding that enables individuals to be at home in institutions that realize this conception of ourselves—i.e. for Hegel, modern political institutions. Moreover, because religion makes this content accessible to everyone—in a way that philosophy does not—the consummate religion is the religion that can function as social glue in the modern world.[20]

The major interpretive question is whether Hegel argues that Christianity should endure for purely pragmatic reasons or because he believes that it cultivates an awareness of ourselves as the world-soul's own self-consciousness. The former reading aligns with analytic interpretations of Hegel, the latter with the more theologically oriented Continental ones. Glenn Magee's *Hegel and the Hermetic Tradition* has convinced me that the latter interpretation is more apt.[21] Regardless, the main point is that Hegel concludes his developmental narrative by presenting Christianity as an essential force of modern social formation that is perfected by a pattern of autonomous rational inquiry that locates all the powers of divinity within human life.

When evaluating Hegel's developmental narrative today, it is important to acknowledge that his account of world religion is based upon the highly problematic information that was available in Germany during the early decades of the nineteenth century. It is therefore not possible to consider here each of the many factual and conceptual errors that plague his text, since doing so would require narrating the entire history of religion anew. Indeed, recent interpreters have found Hegel's treatment of non-Christian religions, which takes up half of the one-volume edition of his *Lectures*, so problematic that they choose to ignore it entirely in their book-length examinations of his philosophy of religion.[22]

Of course, it is still possible to defend the basic arc of his developmental narrative. This is not something I want to do. However, I do appreciate how someone who believes that Protestant Christianity is true, that there is some validity in other religions, and that modern Western civilization is the logical expression of European Christianity's roots might be led to embrace a vaguely Hegelian view. Rodney Stark has elaborated precisely this line of thought, as well as sought to avoid dealing with the European colonial legacy by placing American Protestantism and the project of global liberalism at the pinnacle of human history.[23]

At the same time, it is interesting to note how such a Hegelian developmental narrative can give way to a subtractivist view. If one believes that Protestant Christianity is the consummate religion and that it finds its highest expression in modern Western civilization, then, if Protestantism (or Christianity more broadly) begins to lose its ability to influence the modern West even though the positive features of modern Western civilization endure, it becomes easy to conclude that, as Gauchet comments, Christianity is the *"religion for departing from religion."*[24] Many classical secularization theorists developed their subtraction narratives by applying this logic to western Europe.[25] And, though Stark seems to protect himself from this inversionary tactic by placing the United States at the pinnacle of religious history, the same problem arises if the United States also undergoes a wide-ranging process of secularization, as some recent surveys suggest is taking place.[26]

Despite these problematic aspects of Hegel's thought, his ultimate account of the relationship between religion, culture, and politics is profound. According to Hegel, religion plays a unique role in cultivating the ethical virtues, the forms of consciousness, and the cultural norms out of which forms of political organization and intellectual activity arise. Yet when it strives to enter directly into the partisan bickerings that characterize contemporary political order, or to intervene in public discourse in an overly dogmatic and theological way, its ability to productively influence modern culture diminishes. This view does not require religion to refrain from influencing public life. Hegel's point, which contemporary sociological analysis appears to support, is that religion best contributes to the advancement of modern societies by remolding the cultural and intellectual systems upon which these societies depend, as opposed to either pursuing partisan political activity or reasserting orthodox convictions in public discourse.[27]

At a methodological level, it is important to distinguish Hegel's dialectical narrative of religious history from his attempt to articulate a dialectical typology of religious worldviews. Hegel's dialectical developmental narrative depends upon the idea that each religion has a static and monolithic form. This assumption lets him speak about the essential characteristics of, for example, the "Zoroastrian" and "Jewish" religions and to specify their respective places on the religious totem pole. Yet we now know that religious traditions are much more complex than this: they involve diverse communities and schools of thought; they constantly interact with one another; and they evolve in response to emergent social realities. One has only to consider Josephson's analysis of the Protestant-like impact of modern Japanese Shintoism to appreciate the significance of these conclusions, since Hegel's historical schema would fix Shinto within the high-magical stage of East Asian imperial cults.

The same critique does not apply to the project of analyzing the dialectical relationships between different forms of religious consciousness, which does not require us to equate each form of religious consciousness with a specific religious tradition. It may be that some religious traditions inculcate certain kinds of religious consciousness more frequently than others—for example, Zoroastrianism and cosmic dualism. However, this is not the same as saying that Zoroastrianism has a dualistic core, because relevant forms of dualism may appear in other religious settings, and other forms of religious consciousness may appear within the complex and multifaceted tradition that we have come to call Zoroastrianism. The point here is not to embrace Hegel's particular account of the structures of religious consciousness, but to generally defend the project of ahistorically analyzing the dialectical connections between different forms of religious consciousness, the likes of which William Desmond has effectively pursued in his account of the various "ways to God" that philosophers have advanced throughout the ages.[28]

Karl Jaspers

The Second World War was difficult for Karl Jaspers, who was married to a Jewish woman and refused to provide intellectual support for the Nazi regime. He was forced out of his university position, banned from publishing, and constantly threatened with removal to a concentration camp. Although many colleagues tried to protect him, others, such as his longtime friend Martin Heidegger, rejected him completely.[29] The wartime experience significantly shaped Jaspers's subsequent thinking. However, it was not merely his personal difficulties that influenced his views. For Jaspers became convinced by the horrors of the war that the Western-centric framework of history long employed by European intellectuals was blatantly false. The European people had just been gripped by a wave of violent and fanatical totalitarianism and led by its state-worshipping ways to foment the most violent and destructive war that humanity had ever known. How could such a people claim to be the apotheosis of human history?

Jaspers was not the only intellectual wrestling with this question in the postwar period. Indeed, postwar European thought was dominated by the desire to understand what had gone wrong with modern Europe, particularly with Nazi Germany, and to make sure nothing similar ever happened again. Generally speaking, two schools of thought emerged. The first, represented by Austrian philosopher of science Karl Popper, claimed that American-style liberal democracy was the way forward. The second, represented by German social theorists Max Horkheimer and Theodor Adorno, felt that only a revised form of Marxist social critique could properly chasten and reorient the modern West.[30] Both approaches perpetuated Western-centric views of history; they simply disagreed about how precisely Europe had failed to live up to modern Western ideals, defined now by either liberal-democratic or Marxist-socialist norms. Jaspers was unpersuaded by both options largely because of their Western-centrism.

Jaspers felt that all Western-centric views of history arose from the idea that Christianity was the pinnacle of religious history. If Christianity consummated all the religious developments that came before, then it was quite natural to imagine that Western civilization, which is the civilization that Christianity influenced most directly, consummated all previous civilizational developments. To move beyond such Western-centric conclusions, Jaspers argues that religion's turning point was not the advent of Christianity, but rather the series of sociospiritual revolutions that occurred between 800 and 200 BCE. "The most extraordinary events are concentrated in this period," he explains. "Confucius and Lao-tse [Laozi] were living in China, all the schools of Chinese philosophy came into being . . . ; India produced the Upanishads and Buddha and, like China, ran the whole gamut of philosophical possibilities down to scepticism, to materialism, sophism and nihilism; in Iran Zarathustra taught a challenging view of the world as a struggle between good and evil; in Palestine the prophets made their appearance, from Elijah, by way of Isaiah and Jeremiah, to Deutero-Isaiah; Greece witnessed the appearance of Homer, of the philosophers—Parmenides, Heraclitus and Plato—of the tragedians, Thucydides and Archimedes." Collectively, these figures articulated "the fundamental categories within which we still think today" and established the world religions "by which human beings still live."[31] Jaspers thus described this period as the "axial age," or the turning point of human history.[32]

To grasp the significance of Jaspers's notion of the axial age, let us briefly consider his account of the preceding "mythical" or "ancient" period. Ancient civilizations, Jaspers explains, arose between 4000 and 2000 BCE in the Mediterranean, Indian, and Chinese regions.[33] Each of these civilizations, including ancient Egypt and Mesopotamia, employed a mythic pattern of thought that located all things within an encompassing narrative of spiritual cosmogenesis. Such mythological frameworks enabled dispersed ancient peoples to see themselves as part of the same civilizational unit as others who lived far away but also inhabited the same mythological system. Thus, alongside other notable achievements, such as the creation of densely populated cities, monumental works of art and architecture, and processes of sustained technological advancement, it was during the ancient period that civilizational empires began to emerge.[34]

Over time, however, the authority of ancient rulers waned, and their empires devolved into a "multitude of small States and cities."[35] Many ancient peoples felt that civilization was declining and that something radical needed to happen to return things to their proper course. Each of the great axial figures arose in such a context of crisis and presented their revolutionary teachings as the solution.

One of the central features of each set of axial teachings was the idea that spiritual reality transcends the current social order and thus requires us to transform our individual and collective ways of life. The central axial figures accordingly tended to reject established social norms, even to abandon the existing civilization outright. Their followers, in turn, established new forms of religious community (e.g., monasteries, sanghas, and academies) in which they could pursue their founder's radical teachings in relative isolation from the world. Within these new religious spaces, "hitherto unconsciously accepted ideas, customs and conditions" were questioned, and the first distinct traditions of philosophical, scientific, and theological inquiry emerged.[36]

Each of the new religious movements that arose in this way eventually generated a new civilization. These new civilizations, in turn, were forced to water down their founding axial teachings, since it was impossible, for example, to build a civilization around the Buddhist ideal of monastic renunciation. Nevertheless, ongoing efforts in each to venerate the life of the founding axial figure and to codify and study his teachings maintained the link to their axial foundation.[37] The teachings of the central axial figures continued to influence and transform the axial civilizations, albeit in a slower and more gradual manner than at first.

Not everyone, however, was content with gradualism. Powerful reform movements arose from time to time to revitalize the original axial teachings and to reorient the axial civilizations. Jaspers describes these endeavors as "axial renaissance" movements and includes Christianity, Islam, Vedic Hinduism, and neo-Confucianism in their ranks.[38] Yet even these movements underwent a process of banalization as they later established their own civilizational trajectories.

Up through the medieval period, all the axial and axial renaissance civilizations displayed roughly similar levels of sophistication. Then, around 1500, European Christendom began to rapidly advance. Jaspers rejects the idea that the European breakthrough was stimulated by Christianity's special merits and credits instead the influence of modern science.[39]

Though Jaspers says very little about how modern science arose, he forcefully differentiates science from the materialistic worldviews that have crystallized in the modern West. Science, on Jaspers's reading, is distinguished by its systematic, methodical, empirically oriented, and collective manner of investigating the world. Though this approach animates all fields of scientific inquiry, each field generates different concepts and methods as they investigate different regions of the world.[40] Jaspers thus argues that "the sum-total of the sciences does not give us reality in its entirety," but rather a "mobile," "manifold," and "forever incomplete" collection of theories and methods.[41] The attempt to turn "science" into a comprehensive materialistic worldview undermines the very provisional and pluralistic approach upon which science's distinctiveness depends. Seen from this perspective, "scientific" materialism resembles old models of dogmatic theology more than it does modern scientific inquiry.

Unfortunately, conflating science and materialism has caused many people to assume that modernization entails accepting a materialistic worldview. Although this conflation has had many negative results, Jaspers is particularly troubled by how it perpetuates a Western-centric view of history in which increased rates of material consumption are considered the hallmark of civilizational progress.[42] He is highly critical of ongoing efforts to unite the world by globalizing consumerism and capitalist markets. Nevertheless, in contrast to many contemporary critics who claim that we should respond to capitalistic globalization by revitalizing premodern social configurations, he articulates a vision of globalization that is based on his theory of the axial age.[43]

Toward this end, Jaspers correlates the current dynamics of Western-led globalization with pre-axial patterns of material development. Although ancient civilizations made many important developments, their main contribution was to use new technologies to unite ever-greater swaths of humanity into discrete civilizational units, for the collapse of these ancient civilizations created the conditions in which the axial revolutions could emerge. Similarly, Jaspers suggests that the current phase of materialistic globalization should be seen as an initial process of world unification that will, through its eventual disruption and collapse, allow a second axial age to emerge.

Although Jaspers does not claim to know what exactly the second axial age will entail, he describes several plausible trajectories. As current dynamics of globalization advance, many will see that materialistic Western norms provide a woefully inadequate framework for world affairs and will therefore endeavor to revitalize traditional patterns of religious life.[44] Those engaged in such projects of religious renewal will struggle to achieve their stated goals, for none of the axial or axial renaissance movements possesses sufficient resources to address the many challenges and opportunities of our global age. Levels of global chaos will increase as materialists and religious traditionalists vie with one another to determine our future course. It is in this context, he suggests, that something like a second axial age will appear. Jaspers envisions two ways this might happen. First, the second axial age might, like modern science, emerge as the fruit of a new pattern of inquiry that would transcend historic faith-reason dichotomies and draw insight from all the world's religions. Or, second, the second axial age might be catalyzed by "fresh revelation from God," which is to say by the emergence of a new, globally oriented religious movement. Though Jaspers himself considers the first route more likely, he acknowledges that the reality of the second axial age will remain "beyond our powers of imagination" until it has actually appeared.[45]

Interestingly, contemporary dynamics and debates are unfolding in ways that resonate with Jaspers's expectations. For example, many prominent social analysts highlight the rising tension between a global culture heavily influenced by secularism and materialism and the efforts of traditionalists to revitalize premodern religion. In addition, many people have articulated the need to develop a new vision of the role that religion can play in public inquiry. John Hick offers one plausible account of how Jaspers's vision of an inquiry-driven second axial age might unfold by suggesting that we can use the common axial goal of "transforming self-centeredness into Other-centeredness" as a pragmatic standard of religious truth within global public discourse.[46]

Other dynamics resonate with Jaspers's alternate route to the second axial age. For example, a small number of religious movements are currently striving to establish themselves as novel, globally oriented religious traditions with their own central figures, scriptures, administrative order, and distinctive vision of history. Cases in point are those like the Church of Jesus Christ of Latter-Day Saints, the Ahmadiyya, and the Sathya Sai Organization, which still operate within the parameters of their preceding religious tradition (respectively, Christianity, Islam, and Hinduism). Then there is the Bahá'í Faith, which, during the past 170 years, has effectively established itself as an independent global religious tradition.

Although some have argued that the very notion of an axial age is an exercise in wishful thinking, Jaspers's general thesis has stood up remarkably well to subsequent examination.[47] The efforts of S. N. Eisenstadt and his colleagues to elaborate the axial age thesis through rigorous, comparative sociological analysis have been decisive on this front. In particular, Eisenstadt and his colleagues have demonstrated that each of the axial and axial renaissance movements, despite their differences, involved "a broadening of horizons, or an opening up of potentially universal perspectives, in contrast to the particularism of more archaic modes of thought; an ontological distinction between higher and lower levels of reality; and a normative subordination of the lower level to the higher, with more or less overtly stated implications for human efforts to translate guiding principles into ongoing practices."[48] Though our comparative knowledge of the various axial movements will rapidly evolve, it seems safe to conclude that the axial age thesis will continue to figure centrally in academic discussions of religion for quite some time. Charles Taylor has gone so far as to claim that "any view about the long-term history of religion turns on an interpretation of the Axial Age."[49]

The most substantive criticism of the axial age thesis concerns the challenge of explaining why the particular period Jaspers identifies as axial is *the* axis of human history. Civilization was forever changed by the tribal breakthrough, the ancient-mythic empires, the so-called axial renaissance movements, and the forces of modernization that have swept the world during the past few centuries. Why, then, should we describe all these movements as either precursors to or revitalizations of the axial age, and not as distinctive periods of revolutionary sociospiritual ferment on their own? After considering this criticism at length, John Boy and John Torpey persuasively conclude that in order to preserve the insights of the axial age thesis, we should abandon the notion of a single axial age and see the broad sweep of history in terms of a succession of axial moments.[50] Eric Voegelin presents a similar argument: "In order to elevate the period from 800 to 200 B.C., in which the parallel outbursts occur, to the rank of the great epoch in history, Jaspers had to deny to the earlier and later spiritual outbursts the epochal character which in their own consciousness they certainly had. . . . [But if] spiritual outbursts were to be recognized as the constituents of meaning in history, the epiphanies of Moses and Christ, or of Mani and Mohammed, could hardly be excluded from the list; and if they were included, the axis time expanded into an open field of spiritual eruptions extending over millennia."[51]

It was again Eisenstadt who effectively elaborated Jaspers's already profound attempt to differentiate Western modernity from modernity as such. As Eisenstadt shows, each civilization that emerged from one of the axial movements underwent similar transformations during the past few centuries, including "structural differentiation, . . . urbanisation, extension of modern education and means of communication," and the growth of "tendencies to individualistic orientations."[52] Nevertheless, each modernizing society has also "developed distinct modern dynamics [and] distinctive ways of interpreting modernity" that can be directly linked to a preceding axial (or axial renaissance) movement.[53] Understanding the axial age is therefore essential in order to appreciate the "multiple modernities" that characterize the world today.

Jaspers's account of the relationship between Christianity, Islam, and the modern world, however, remains highly problematic. Admittedly, Jaspers acknowledges Christianity's significant impact upon the history of the modern West and places Islam alongside Christianity as one of the key axial renaissance movements.[54] Yet he has remarkably little to say about how these two movements, which clearly account for the most numerically extensive religious communities in the world today, actually influenced the modernizing world. Jaspers's purpose in downplaying Christianity's and Islam's significance was clearly to emphasize the impact of the original axial movements. However, in so doing, Jaspers systematically overlooks the many novel dynamics that Christianity and Islam brought into being, as well as their impact on the modern world.

Robert Bellah

According to Robert Bellah's developmental narrative, religion both stimulates and is transformed by the historical emergence of new cognitive capacities. He makes this argument by correlating psychologist Merlin Donald's concepts of mimetic, mythic, and theoretic capacity with what he describes as the tribal, archaic, and axial stages of religious history.[55] Before considering Bellah's account of the specific relationship between religion and human cognitive evolution, I will explain these three cognitive capacities.

Mimetic capacity arose some 1.8 million years ago in early hominids and is characterized by proto-linguistic gesture and collective ritual. Without these powers, it would have been impossible for early humans to generate, store, and disseminate even the most basic forms of knowledge, as they lacked not only writing technology, but also the powers of complex language and narrative. It was therefore through the power of gesture and ritual that humanity left its ape cousins behind.

Mythic capacity arose alongside *Homo sapiens sapiens* between 200,000 and 300,000 years ago and gave rise to complex spoken language and narrative myths. These developments facilitated the gradual emergence of more advanced systems of knowledge and larger and more complex societies: first, there were larger tribes; then chiefdoms appeared; and finally, archaic civilizations like ancient Egypt and Mesopotamia emerged.[56]

Theoretic capacity first emerged when humans began employing external symbolic systems like writing to generate, disseminate, and store knowledge. This process began when writing was invented at the end of the archaic period but expanded significantly when literate intellectual classes arose during the axial age. Although neither Donald nor Bellah makes this point, theoretic capacity has clearly proceeded through several internal stages of development in the subsequent millennia. I will later return to this point.

Donald does not see a direct relationship between religion and the development of cognitive capacities. Yet Bellah does, and it is important to understand why. At the most basic level, Bellah's point seems to be that religion facilitates the gradual accumulation of cultural complexity by directing human energy toward maintaining and extending the cultural structures that underlie each cognitive capacity. At a certain stage, this mounting cultural complexity stimulates a phase change of sorts whereby a new cognitive capacity, or a new stage of an already-existing cognitive capacity, emerges. When this happens, the previous religious epoch is disrupted and a new pattern of religious life that expresses and supports the current stage of cognitive evolution in a more adequate manner begins to appear. Let us consider Bellah's account of how this process has actually taken place.

Although we can only indirectly explore the earliest stages of ritual religion through later tribal societies in which myth had already arisen, we see in these examples that ritual facilitates the generation and dissemination of basic forms of knowledge. As Bellah puts it, "Once mimetic culture had evolved, . . . [we] could learn, be taught, and did not have to discover almost everything for ourselves." These cognitive benefits were maintained in the long term because tribal religion taught that its rituals should be indefinitely preserved. Tribal-ritual religion thus directly stimulated mimetic capacity's maturation and growth.[57]

Mythic religion initially arose as a support to ritual religion; hence, the first forms of mythic religion were rooted directly in ritual life. Bellah gives the example of the Brazilian Kalapalo tribe to substantiate this point, showing how their mythic narratives are called forth by and closely identified with their ritual traditions. However, as the size and complexity of tribes grew, a more "representative" pattern of mythic religion arose to maintain social unity. There were simply too many people to participate directly in the practice of collective ritual. Yet by locating themselves within a common mythological framework, individuals could participate vicariously in the rituals that their divinely chosen leaders performed on their behalf. This new mediating relationship first animated the chiefdoms that characterized many Pacific island societies even into the twentieth century. It later matured into the archaic empires of divine kingship (e.g., those of ancient Egypt, Mesopotamia, the Shang and the Zhou dynasties, the Aztecs, the Mayans, the Incans, and the Yoruba). The development of archaic-mythic religion yielded far-reaching social innovations, including the world's first cities, the invention of plows, the use of domesticated animals for labor, the establishment of expansive trading networks, the construction of monumental temples and palaces, and the development of sophisticated moral/legal codes.[58]

Although writing was invented at the end of the archaic period, it did not yield its "theoretic" fruit until the revolutions of the axial age. The fragmentation of the increasingly large and complex archaic empires could not be halted by simply reasserting the authority of one or another divine king. The axial revolutions were therefore stimulated by marginal prophetic figures (e.g., Confucius, Buddha, Moses, Zoroaster, and Socrates) who each claimed to have received special knowledge of how to appropriately reorient individual and collective life. The sacred teachings of these figures were written down and used as the basis for a new kind of written religious tradition. Thus, it is during the axial age that sacred writings and holy books begin to appear, such as the Hebrew Bible, the Confucian *Analects*, the Pali canon, the Vedas, the *Daodejing*, and later the Gospels and the Qur'an. Specialized communities of inquiry began to systematically interpret these texts and then to use their ideas to critique and reorient their social milieu. A new ability to think about things in conceptual terms was one of the crucial fruits of the period, which is why the first true traditions of philosophical, scientific, and theological inquiry arose during the axial age.

Bellah does not examine the post-axial development of theoretic capacity in any detail. However, he does claim that the growing prominence of conceptual inquiry has led humanity to discount the contributions of ritual and myth and to grossly overestimate the reach of the theoretical systems of conceptual inquiry. Hegel's claim to have revealed the inner essence of religious ritual and myth by creating a complete system of philosophical truth exemplifies this tendency. Proceeding in the opposite direction, Bellah encourages us to see that "nothing is ever lost," which is to say that all the cognitive capacities that have emerged throughout history, as well as their associated religious forms, have something essential to contribute to society today; they are not replaced, but rather augmented, by subsequent developments.[59] One of the great modern challenges is thus to learn how to employ ritual, mythic, and theoretic forms of religion in a more balanced and integrated way.

The first question we must ask when evaluating Bellah's developmental narrative is whether his typology of tribal-ritual, archaic-mythic, and axial-theoretical religion is correct. In this regard, it is important to acknowledge that Bellah developed his threefold schema through painstaking engagement with the relevant social and natural scientific literature. This does not make his framework beyond reproach, yet his basic thesis—that religion has historically proceeded through *at least* tribal-ritual, archaic-mythic, and axial-theoretic stages of development—is of such a moderate nature that it is hard to see how it could be completely overturned by subsequent investigations. Though we will certainly gain additional insight into the precise nature and number of religious-historical stages, as well as how humanity has proceeded from one to the next, Bellah's developmental narrative provides us with a sound initial framework for thinking about religious history up through the axial age.

Furthermore, though Bellah's framework does not say much about post-axial developments, we can plausibly utilize his framework to do so. Toward this end, I have found it helpful to apply to Bellah's discussion of axial-theoretic religion Merlin Donald's suggestion that each stage of cognitive capacity proceeds through several internal stages of development.

Let us assume that the first stage of theoretic capacity coincided with the classical axial period (800–200 BCE). This was the period characterized by the emergence of marginal prophetic figures who encouraged their followers to critique inherited tradition and to systematically investigate the fundamental features of the world. Because of the difficulty of disseminating knowledge during this period, those who embraced these axial movements often gathered in special locations to study, record, and enact their founder's teachings. Thus, as Charles Taylor puts it, we see "monks, Bhikkus, sanyassi, devotees of some avatar or God strike out on their own" during the axial age and start "unprecedented modes of sociality: initiation groups, sects of devotees, the sangha, monastic orders and so on."[60] Given the prevalence of critical reflection during this epoch, one can plausibly describe it as the "critical" phase of theoretic capacity. Using this terminology, critical-theoretic religion appears to have been the globally dominant form up through what Jaspers describes as the axial renaissance period.

The subsequent stage of theoretic religion can plausibly be said to have arisen in modern Europe under the impetus of the sustained encounter with Eurasian culture, the Protestant Reformation, the invention of the printing press, the Scientific Revolution, the Enlightenment, and the rapid expansion of industrialization and international trade. The key feature of this stage was the ability to rapidly disseminate identical texts among a growing number of literate people. Without these developments, researchers and scientists could not have created the kind of coherent and incrementally progressive bodies of knowledge that they did. Though much more is involved in this remarkable epoch than I can mention here, we know that the Scientific Revolution, the Enlightenment, liberalism, the science of religions, the printing press, capitalism, and the modernizing processes of China, India, and Japan, to name a few, were all significantly shaped by religion, yet they also profoundly disrupted religion's premodern operations.[61] Indeed, it was during this time that the debates about secularization, science and religion, religious diversity, and tolerance we still wrestle with today emerged. Since the word "research" arose during the early modern period and describes many of the epoch's cultural and intellectual achievements, we can describe this second stage of theoretic capacity as "research capacity," and the associated religious form as "research-theoretic."[62]

The third stage of theoretic capacity's development has thus far been characterized by the appearance of global networks of near-instantaneous information sharing. We see the first flourishing of this capacity in the telegraph and the most recent in the Internet. David Cannadine describes the nineteenth-century epoch in which this "global-network capacity"—as we might describe it—emerged as "above all a time when unprecedented amounts of knowledge were accumulated and displayed in archives, libraries, museums, exhibitions and encyclopedias, when the world was measured and mapped with a new precision, when its inhabitants were counted and classified and depicted in novel ways, and when information could be globally transmitted more rapidly than ever."[63] In his epochal history of the nineteenth century, Jürgen Osterhammel explains how religion played a fundamental role in stimulating many of these signature developments:

> There are strong reasons why religions and religiosity should occupy center stage in a global history of the nineteenth century. . . . Religion was a force in people's lives throughout the nineteenth-century world, giving them bearings and serving to crystallize the formation of communities and collective identities. It was an organizing principle of social hierarchies, a driving force of political struggles, a field of demanding intellectual debates. In the nineteenth century, religion was still the most important provider of meaning for everyday life, and hence the center of all culture associated with the mind. It took in the whole spectrum from universal churches to local cults with few participants. It encompassed in a single cultural form, and often constituted the main link between, both literate elites and those illiterate masses who could communicate only through the spoken word and religious images.[64]

Though we currently struggle to understand precisely what religious transformations global-network capacity will bring, it clearly creates an increasingly globalized religious setting in which diverse communities and traditions are forced to interact with one another more regularly and thoroughly than ever before.

In acknowledging the speculative and provisional nature of these additions to Bellah's threefold framework, if something like a global-network religious configuration is emerging in the world today, it would be important to ask whether this development is simply another moment within theoretic religion's internal evolution or whether it signals the onset of a novel stage of religious history. As we saw earlier, Jaspers claims that humanity is currently entering a distinctly new epoch of religious existence, the ultimate result of which can be likened to a second axial age. Bellah is less optimistic about this possibility. "Some have suggested that we are in the midst of a second Axial Age," he explains, "but if we are, there should be a new cultural form emerging. Maybe I am blind, but I don't see it. What I think we have is a crisis of incoherence and a need to integrate in new ways the dimensions we have had since the Axial Age."[65] Though Bellah's hesitations are reasonable, it is interesting to note how he assumes that any second axial age would emerge directly out of contemporary patterns of religious change.[66] This is not a claim that Jaspers makes. To the contrary, Jaspers explains that "if there is to be a new Axial Period it can only lie in the future, just as the first Axial Period followed, after a long interval, the period of foundation-laying discoveries which finally differentiated human life from the animal kingdom: the Promethean Age. This new Axial Period, which perhaps stands before us and which would constitute a single, world-embracing reality, is beyond our powers of imagination. To anticipate it in phantasy would mean to create it. No one can know what it will bring. . . . If we seek an analogy for our epoch, we find it not in the Axial Period, but rather in another technological age, of which we have no transmitted knowledge: the age of the invention of tools and the use of fire."[67] Jaspers's point is that the second axial age would emerge only after the processes of world unification have sufficiently advanced, as the movement(s) that would characterize the second axial age would emerge out of the tumultuous interaction of the efforts of secular materialists and religious traditionalists to orient the global age. If we were to incorporate a Jasperian notion of the second axial age into the extended version of Bellah's developmental narrative, we might see the current period as a moment of transition in which the dynamics of theoretic religion are reaching their conclusion but the expected new mode of cognitive-religious life has not yet arisen.

Regardless of whether these explorative proposals hold up to further inquiry, the point remains that Bellah's three-stage schema of religious evolution is fecund and profound. Indeed, I would go so far as to claim that we cannot discuss the arc of religious history without giving due consideration to his basic framework.

Despite its many merits, I find that Bellah fails to adequately answer the basic question Why religion? Why has religion been so intimately involved in the historic development of humanity's major cognitive advancements? Why does religion center our energies upon the social structures that enable each cognitive capacity to evolve and mature? Why does religion continue playing this role even after each of its earlier configurations has been disrupted and transformed? Though it might seem simplistic to answer that this all happens because transcendence is real and has been actively stimulating humanity's development throughout history, this response, which is one of the central claims that all the axial religious traditions have historically made, aligns with Bellah's conclusions. Certainly, Bellah is right to emphasize the central roles that biological and cultural evolution play in religious history. Yet his attempt to steer clear of an authentically religious interpretation appears somewhat disingenuous. After showing that distinctly religious visions of reality played a central role in stimulating social and cognitive evolution, is it not reasonable to at least consider the possibility that these visions have exerted the influence they have because they actually align humanity with some higher, transformative spiritual reality?

When evaluating the merits of the developmental narrative framework as a whole, it is important to recognize the ambiguity that inevitably accompanies the use of the term "development." Sometimes "development" is used to describe neutral processes of maturation and growth; a cough develops, and so does a culture of migration. At other times it is used to describe ideal patterns of maturation and growth, as when we speak of human, moral, and spiritual development. Within neutral processes, development is just something that happens; within ideal processes, development constitutes a kind of progress. One of the aims of this chapter has been to consider the insights that both "neutral" and "progressive" developmental narratives provide.

In connection with the more neutral type, I have focused on Bellah's account of how religion stimulates the growth of social complexity and cognitive capacity. Though the cognitive capacities and religious forms he identifies emerge through a process of development, it is not one that necessarily involves moral and spiritual advance. This does not mean, however, that the cognitive and religious developments Bellah presents are optional features of human development. To the contrary. Once, for example, archaic-mythic religion appeared, there was no going back to purely tribal-ritual forms. The same can be said of axial-theoretic religion, and even of the transformations that characterize the contemporary world. This kind of religious development might therefore be described as neutral but irreversible.

I have examined Hegel's and Jaspers's respective accounts of the arc of humanity's moral and spiritual progress in connection with the progressive kind of development. Most thoughtful people no longer find Hegel's narrowly Christo- and Eurocentric view compelling; it is simply too closely tied to the imperialistic logic that modern Europeans used to justify their "civilizing" colonial endeavors. Jaspers's optimistic and inclusive vision of religious progress holds up much better. Of course, Jaspers's spiritual optimism and inclusiveness stem from his underlying convictions about the reality of transcendence. Readers who do not share this conviction might find his framework unconvincing. Yet for those who embrace the ideas that there is a spiritual dimension to human existence and that its latent potentialities are progressively released throughout history, Jaspers's framework should have many attractions. It is not imperialistic, as he does not envision the ideal socio-religious orientation arising in one segment of humanity and then being exported to the rest. It coheres with the historical record. And it provides us with a novel and suggestive framework for interpreting the many otherwise-bewildering religious transformations taking place throughout the world today. I will explore these claims further in the concluding chapter.

Regardless, one of the challenges that anyone who advances a progressive vision of religious history must address is that of "triumphalism" and "supersessionism," which is to say the oft-advanced claim that the historical emergence of one religious community or tradition made all those that came before it irrelevant. Given the long-standing tensions between Jews, Christians, and Muslims

surrounding this theme, the question of supersession can be difficult to consider. However, once we move beyond a preoccupation
with dilemmas of allegiance—Must some religious community accept the authority of this or that historical figure in order to remain
faithful to the covenant of God? Must adherents let go of their former identity and accept a new one?—it becomes possible to evaluate the idea of religious progress in a more objective light.

Clearly, each new moment of religious history is not immediately better than what came before, since new challenges and
pitfalls inevitably appear and the potential for evil only grows as
our capacities expand. Likewise, in our eagerness to embrace the
new, we may abandon patterns of religious life that are worth preserving. Nevertheless, embracing even a moderately "progressive"
vision of religious history does commit us to the claim that some
religious practices and beliefs are more suited for a given period of
history than others. How, then, might we make such distinctions in
practice?

Hick's soteriological ideal can be useful here. Does some pattern of religious practice or belief contribute to the constructive
transformation of humanity's individual and collective affairs? If we
answer yes, then according to Hick's framework, the pattern may
be linked to something true. If we answer no, then it should be either altered or abandoned. And if the answer is "To some extent,"
then we should uncover which features of the practices and beliefs
work and decide how the others can be reoriented and transformed. As mentioned in the previous chapter, this way of conceptualizing religion resembles Imre Lakatos's philosophy of science,
in which the unified field of science is structured by a number of
competing research programs, some of which advance as they progressively generate new insights and discoveries and some of which
degenerate and decline as they protect core commitments that no
longer stimulate scientific growth. It is important to reiterate that
the purpose of advancing this analogy is neither to start arguing
about which religious community is best nor to claim that we now
have an authoritative criterion of religious truth. Rather, I want
simply to present one plausible way of thinking about the characteristics of religious progress, understanding that others can and
should be put forth.

Conclusion

IN THE PRECEDING CHAPTERS, I analyzed the content of the contemporary academic discourse on religion as a series of narrative responses to the perceived failure of secularization theory, developed a typology of the seven major narratives that scholars are advancing today, which I described as the subtraction, renewal, transsecular, postnaturalist, construct, perennial, and developmental narratives, and evaluated each of these narratives by critically engaging three authors who operate within its framework. The purpose of this concluding chapter is to address the question of which, if any, of the seven narratives provides us with the best account of religious history.

As I mentioned in the introduction, I see three ways of pursuing this task. First, we can approach each narrative as a competing research program that must vie against the others until one reigns supreme. Second, we can present each narrative as a kind of methodological heuristic that can be used to analyze distinctive religious phenomena. Or third, we can try integrating the insights of all seven narratives into a meta-narrative whole.

It should be clear to readers who have made it this far that I do not consider the first option persuasive, since each narrative articulates certain important insights that the others do not contain. Subtraction narratives illumine how many features of earlier religious epochs decline as humanity's knowledge and power reach new levels of complexity and scope. Renewal narratives explain that not all subtractions are beneficial and argue that society would benefit by creatively reengaging certain older religious practices and beliefs. Transsecular narratives show that the forces of modernity do not stimulate religion's wholesale marginalization and decline, but rather facilitate its transformation. Postnaturalist narratives trace how modern science disrupted premodern views of nature but now, after many years of overzealous association with naturalism, is beginning to help us consider certain spiritual realities anew. Construct narratives describe how a distinctive concept of "religion in general" developed in the modern West and was then applied to non-Western and premodern peoples. Perennial narratives highlight the common characteristics of diverse systems of religious practice and belief. And finally, developmental narratives explore the various stages through which religion has historically evolved. I find it impossible to embrace one and only one of the seven narratives' perspectives.

What, then, about the second approach to religious history: treating each narrative as a methodological heuristic that can be used to analyze diverse religious phenomena? One way to begin this approach would be to differentiate the processes that each narrative describes from the broader narrative claims that they put forth. Thus, for example, one could acknowledge that intellectual and technological developments can disrupt certain established religious practices and beliefs without also advancing the idea that religion is somehow locked into a generalized process of marginalization and decline.

To get a sense of the fecundity of this approach, consider how the processes described by all seven narratives appear in the Hindu modernist movement that Swami Vivekananda, Rabindranath Tagore, Sri Aurobindo, and Mohandas Gandhi helped launch. These figures all rejected what they saw as superstitious elements of the Hindu tradition (e.g., the caste system) in order to promote intellectual and moral progress (subtraction). Yet they also argued that modern Indians had been too heavily influenced by the West, and thus encouraged Indians to renew their engagement with ancient Hindu teachings (renewal). The religious transformations they pursued were bound up with processes of modernization (transsecular). Recent scientific research shows that many of the metaphysical and cognitive insights they advanced are still relevant today (postnaturalist).[1] Their concept of Hinduism as a world religion was also clearly constructed during the modern period (construct). Many of the ethical ideals they pursued appear in many other religious contexts and settings (perennial). And studying Hindu modernism helps us learn more about the new global stage of religious history into which humanity is currently proceeding (developmental).

It should not be hard to appreciate how this process-based, heuristic approach could be used to analyze a wide variety of religious phenomena. Nevertheless, I would still argue that, on its own, it fails to suitably resolve the challenge of developing a framework for thinking about religion's evolving place in human affairs after the perceived failure of secularization theory. Even if we adopt this kind of sophisticated, multilayered approach some broader narrative framework must still implicitly orient our thoughts. That is, we cannot get away from the task of articulating a more adequate way of thinking about the broader sweep of religious history. And if each of the seven narratives that are currently on offer articulates important insights that the others do not contain, then this more adequate narrative must somehow incorporate elements of them all.

This brings us to the third, synthetic approach, which we can pursue by either creating a new, encompassing eighth narrative framework or by modifying one of the existing frameworks to make room for the best features of the other six. I must confess to not having a clear sense of what such an eighth narrative would be. At least for the time being, I will assume that the strategy of modifying one of the seven existing narratives to more adequately incorporate the others' insights is the most promising approach.

At some point, it will be important to weigh arguments for and against using each of the seven narratives in this way. However, for now let me state outright that I find the developmental narrative best suited to the task. This is because developmental processes are inherently complex, with moments of advancement and decline proceeding simultaneously and with new patterns and ideas taking shape alongside perennial dynamics. A suitably nuanced developmental narrative can easily incorporate the key processes that subtraction, renewal, transsecular, postnaturalist, construct, and perennial narratives describe. The only way to defend this claim is to flesh out such a developmental vision, and I will attempt to do so in the following pages by reorganizing the insights and ideas that the authors considered in previous chapters have advanced. I will therefore only reference content that is newly introduced.

Before proceeding with this task, several cautionary remarks are in order. First, it is important to reiterate the difference between a history of religion and a narrative of religious history. The former seeks to document precisely what has taken place, while the latter aims to provide a persuasive way of approaching the logic of historical events. Histories of religion can be falsified outright, while narratives of religious history, somewhat like Kuhnian paradigms, are more difficult to disrupt because they can cohere with more than one particular historical account. My goal in this concluding chapter is to present a more adequate narrative of religious history than currently exists and not to develop a new history of religion. Certain features of my narrative will therefore need to be modified and revised in subsequent iterations.

Second, recognizing that many may disagree with the narrative presented below, I want to reiterate that the validity of my typology of seven narratives does not depend upon my synthetic narrative's merit. Thus, whether or not readers agree with my take on, say, the axial age, they will be hard pressed to argue that the subtraction, renewal, transsecular, postnaturalist, construct, perennial, and developmental narratives, by whatever name, do not play a central role in the contemporary academic discourse on religion.

Third, in claiming to advance a narrative of religious history that is broadly developmental, I remain acutely aware of the danger of overestimating the reach of my own conceptual schemes. Therefore, instead of trying to articulate a comprehensive theory of religious history, I will focus on advancing our understanding of the various stages of religious history that we can plausibly claim to discern.

Conceptual Framework

I begin by considering the broader conceptual setting in which my proposed narrative proceeds. Clearly, similar narratives of religious history can operate within diverse conceptual frames. As we saw in chapter 7, Hegel's developmental narrative stems from his account of Spirit; Jaspers's, from his more open-ended conception of transcendence; and Bellah's, from his naturalistic understanding of emergent evolution. In a similar vein, though I do not want to bind my narrative to a single conceptual worldview, there is a series of concepts that provide my narrative with robust framing.

My conceptual framework begins from the idea that there is a spiritual reality that transcends human comprehension. This idea leads to the conclusion that conceptions of spiritual reality can differ without being mutually exclusive, as an infinite reality can always be seen in more than one way. Of course, not every concept of transcendence is equally true. But each of the prevalent historical approaches has something important to teach us. The Greek "logos," the Buddhist "emptiness," the Hindu "Brahman," the Abrahamic "God," the Confucian "Heaven," and the Daoist "Way," to name a few, each contributes to our understanding of transcendence. Conversely, the idea that we must choose one of these concepts and reject the others emerges from the false belief that a single concept can encompass what is, by definition, an unencompassable reality.

Although natural science demonstrates that we can understand many of nature's physical laws without referencing transcendence, according to the perspective advanced here, we can appreciate neither the ultimate purpose of the cosmos nor the reality of human life without taking transcendence into view. One persuasive way of synthesizing modern scientific theory with a transcendence-based worldview is through the idea that latent spiritual potencies gradually appear in the natural world through the process of emergent evolution. According to this view, higher degrees of material complexity entail fuller expressions of spiritual life. Thus, insofar as the biological world is more complex than the physical, it displays the new powers of sensation and growth. The human world is more complex still; hence, it displays the powers of rationality and free choice.

These powers of the human spirit enable the process of emergent evolution to continue indefinitely within the social milieu. Thus, when we look back over human history, we find several distinct stages of collective human evolution. We can analyze these stages in terms of the degrees of social complexity and cognitive capacity they display. Recognizing this evolutionary dynamic should lead us to conclude that the profound transformations that have been taking place during the past two centuries are likely to be leading us into an altogether new, distinctly global stage of collective evolution.

Religion has played a central role in each of these stages of collective evolution. Humans' capacity to reflect upon their place in the world—where they came from, where they are going, and what they ought to do—has led to an almost universal consciousness of the reality of transcendence. Humanity has thus yearned from its earliest tribal beginnings to better understand spiritual reality and to learn how to effectively channel the forces it releases into new and revitalized patterns of individual and collective life. Religion can therefore be conceptualized as a system of knowledge and practice that is meant to help humanity achieve these aims, albeit in a manner commensurate with the contemporary levels of social complexity and cognitive capacity.

History also demonstrates the corruptibility of religious endeavors. Examples come readily to mind. Yet it is important to see that—again, according to the view being put forth here—these corruptions do not emanate from religion as such, but rather from several pernicious fallacies of thought, among the most destructive of which are the tendencies to see more agency in the world than really exists (superstition) and to overestimate the scope of our own practices and beliefs (dogmatism). I emphasize these two fallacious tendencies in particular because they directly undermine the ideal of "spiritual objectivity" that can be plausibly said to make religion work.

Generally speaking, objectivity requires us to move beyond our immediate perceptions in order to acquire a more accurate understanding of reality. The ideal of objectivity is thus the lifeblood of good scientific, ethical, and even religious inquiry. In the context of religion, objectivity involves a constant effort to orient our lives around the spiritual promptings and ideals that emanate from transcendence, as well as an appreciation of our inability to contain divinity within any single conceptual scheme. Superstition undermines our capacity to distinguish true spiritual perceptions from false ones, while dogmatism leads us to confuse one particular conceptual schema with the ultimate truth. Superstition and dogmatism thus tend, in the long term, to corrupt religious endeavors by producing ignorant, misguided, prideful, and combatively closed habits of practice and thought. However, it is not always clear how commitment to spiritual objectivity would lead one to respond to instances of superstition, dogmatism, or even other forms of corruption taking root in one's religious milieu. In some instances, the right course may be to rededicate oneself to the core principles of one's religious tradition. In other instances, it may be necessary to utilize outside perspectives and resources to critique and reorient one's tradition. And in other instances still, the only course may be to abandon one's community or tradition outright and search for another. The difficulty comes in being able to discern which of these strategies constitutes the most truthful and appropriate response.

My goal in briefly describing the elements of this conceptual framework is not to convince all readers that it is true, but rather to articulate the basic features of a reasonable transcendence-based worldview that fits the basic features of the narrative of religious history presented below. To help readers focus on this narrative instead of quibbling about metaphysics, I will avoid discussing transcendence-based dynamics or forces. My purpose in doing so is not to kowtow to overzealous secular norms, but to facilitate meaningful engagement with the central ideas I want to advance.

Tribal Religion

Although paucity of historical records makes it difficult to specify what life was like during the longest, tribal phase of religious history, we do have enough data to suggest that certain general features were present. I will mention four in particular:

(1) There was little, if any, differentiation between religion and society. Every aspect of individual and collective life was pervaded by reference to and interaction with spiritual entities and forces. This lack of differentiation may appear to problematize any effort to speak of "tribal religion," but

we can bypass this dilemma by acknowledging that we use the term to help analyze certain facets of early tribal life.

(2) Tribal religion was structured by a complex set of ritual observances. Prior to the possession of a complex narrative language and systems of external symbolic storage like writing, people could generate and disseminate knowledge only by incorporating it into a set of indefinitely preserved rituals. One of the primary achievements of tribal religion was thus to help launch the very process of cultural evolution.

(3) The goal of spiritual transformation does not seem to be a major part of tribal religion. Energies were alternatively directed toward perpetually realigning tribal life with an eternal sacred order. The idea of transforming individual and collective life to reflect a higher spiritual ideal appears to have come more into focus during the axial age.

(4) Tribal religion was pervaded by an overactive tendency to detect agency in the world. Gods, spirits, and demons were observed in all aspects of life and were credited with causing most events. Nevertheless, we can see the tribal proliferation of spiritual entities as the fruit of an authentic attempt to grapple with divine infinitude.

Archaic Religion

Tribal religion succeeded in stabilizing human life during the longest period of human history. However, the accumulation of knowledge and cultural complexity eventually led humanity into what is often described as an archaic stage. This new period began with the emergence of chiefdoms, the likes of which we find in abundance in the Polynesian Islands. It reached maturity in the great archaic empires (e.g., those of the Egyptian pharaohs, the Aztecs, the Mesopotamians, the Yoruba, the Shang and Zhou Chinese) that were ruled by divine kings. Each divine king saw himself as the intermediary between gods and people and performed rituals on behalf of his subjects, if not the entire human race. The masses continued to perform their own rituals in local settings but began to perceive themselves as part of a wider mythological framework with the divine king at its center. Thus, whereas collective ritual provided the framework for tribal life, mythology gave unity and coherence to archaic civilizations.

Archaic religion was characterized by a growing sense of universality. Each divine king felt that he maintained the cosmic order and therefore sought to extend and enrich his domain in perpetuity. This, in turn, stimulated expansionist military campaigns, efforts to build monumental structures (e.g., the Egyptian pyramids and Aztec temples), programs to centrally coordinate the empire's affairs, and an early explosion of mathematical, astronomical, technological, and theological insights. One major theological accomplishment of this period was the development of a systematic vision of a divine pantheon with one occupying a position of supreme authority.

The gulf that existed between the masses and divine kings allows us to begin speaking of religion as a distinct feature of human affairs. Certainly, interaction with spiritual entities and forces remained a regular feature of individual and collective life. But there was a special kind of ritual that only the divine king could perform on behalf of his subjects. Furthermore, it was during this period that "religious specialists" began assisting the divine king with his ritual duties, systematizing religious practice and belief, and pursuing new areas of intellectual endeavor.

Although the archaic period of religious history profoundly stimulated the advancement of human culture, conflict, violence, and oppression were common tendencies. The divine king's desire to constantly expand his empire created a cycle of "sacred" warfare and cultures of slavery and oppression. In this regard, consider the Israelites' enslavement by the Egyptians and the Aztecs' practice of sacrificing captured peoples before the altar of their gods. Such destructive tendencies led many central axial figures to seek to liberate humanity from an archaic order that had become unjust, oppressive, and corrupt.

The Axial Age

Broadly considered, the axial age (here including the axial renaissance movements) stretched from approximately 800 BCE to the

beginning of the modern period, circa 1500 CE. I therefore extend it
in this synthetic narrative to encompass the emergence and development of Upanishadic Hinduism, Buddhism, Judaism, Zoroastrianism,
Greek philosophy, Confucianism, Daoism, Christianity, and Islam.
Given the vast complexity and scope of this period, it is helpful to
differentiate two subsidiary phases: (1) the classical axial period,
which involved the founding of most of the major religious lineages
that currently exist in the world; and (2) the medieval axial period,
which included the development of Christianity, Islam, Mahayana
Buddhism, neo-Confucianism, and the "classical" strains of Hindu
practice and thought (e.g., Bhakti, Puranic Hinduism, and Vedanta).[2]
Both phases exhibited common characteristics, but the medieval axial
period was distinguished by the tendency to synthesize elements of
the classical axial movements. It is for this reason that some have re-
ferred to the latter phase as an "axial renaissance."

Although each of the classical axial movements displayed different cultural and conceptual characteristics, they all advanced the
idea of a good beyond human flourishing. A key feature of this notion was the claim that people should sacrifice worldly advantages
in order to grow closer to the transcendent good, and groups of
particularly devout believers abandoned society and joined together
in new kinds of communities (e.g., monasteries, sanghas, academies)
in order to follow such a sacrificial path. This constituted a radical
departure from the tribal vision of sacred ritual and the archaic notion of divine kingship, both of which considered active and faithful
involvement in normal social life to be a sacred responsibility. That
said, strong patterns of complementarity did arise between the new
axial renunciates and the masses, whose religious life, it is often argued, remained inscribed within archaic norms and focused on the
tasks of human flourishing. The masses materially supported the
renunciates, while the renunciates helped the masses progress via
prayer, vicarious merit, education, and wise counsel. Because of the
support of the masses, renunciates were able to devote long hours
to study and thought, which helps explain why philosophy, science,
and theology arose during the classical axial period.

Imbalances and oppressive tendencies appeared within the pattern of axial complementarity, three of which warrant special attention. First, although the tremendous cognitive energy deployed by

axial renunciates stimulated remarkable intellectual advance, these renunciates often fell prey to the dogmatic fallacy of confusing their own theoretical constructions with reality itself. This was a particular struggle for the hypertheoretical Greeks and their later Abrahamic interpreters. Second, as religious specialists sought to translate their founders' teachings into a coherent pattern for community life, they often elaborated legal doctrine with abstract specificity and without attending to present social concerns. This pattern of legalism was particularly evident during the later phases of medieval Islam. And third, the axial ideal of renunciation often stimulated immoderate patterns of otherworldly asceticism, with Gnosticism being the most prominent example in the West.

Although the medieval phase of the axial age involved significant religious developments throughout the world, the two most important globally were Christianity and Islam. In addition to the fact that these two traditions today claim the allegiance of some 55 percent of the world's population, their ongoing interactions brought humanity to the threshold of modernity. Christianity and Islam were both distinguished by how they brought together facets of the classical axial movements; Christianity took shape as a blend of Jewish, Greek, and Roman influences, while Islam drew on Zoroastrianism, Hinduism, and Chinese thought in addition, not to mention Christianity itself. This is not to say that Christianity and Islam were merely syncretic movements that offered nothing new. To the contrary, it was only because of their novel practices and beliefs that they were able to synthesize the preceding axial movements in such far-reaching and effective ways.[3] In what follows, then, I will briefly describe the histories of Christianity and Islam and then offer some reflections about their historic interaction.

During the first three centuries of Christian history, the Christian community worked to establish a vibrant pattern of collective life. In hindsight, we can see that many features of these early Christian dynamics gave the community a selective advantage over other contemporaneous religious movements. Early Christians consciously disregarded ethnic, linguistic, religious, and socioeconomic differences and sought to bring all people together into a single religious community, making Christianity attractive to those who were neither Roman citizens nor members of the Jewish community. Likewise, many women were attracted to Christianity because it allowed them to play a far more prominent role in religious life than either Judaism or the Roman religion allowed. And because of early Christians' commitment to caring for the sick, particularly during periods of plague, and their willingness to accept intermarriage, fewer Christians died and more were born than in other communities during the period. It is not difficult to see how Christianity went from being a small Jewish sect to a major force within the Roman Empire in three centuries.

A new phase of Christian history began in the fourth century when the emperor Constantine converted and began working to establish a Christian civilization. Toward this end, the church became increasingly involved in economic, political, and military affairs and sought to gain greater influence among aristocrats, princes, and kings. The assumption seemed to be that the masses would follow the leaders into the Christian fold, a kind of trickle-down theory of conversion. Christian monastic life also began to take shape during the fourth century, with monastics dedicating themselves to the classical axial goal of renouncing the world and vigorously pursuing the transcendent good. A tension thus appeared in Christianity during this time, with one facet of the church concentrating more on influencing elite society and another on pursuing spiritual transformation in isolation from the world.

These poles coalesced during the eleventh century within a widespread effort to bring monastic virtue back to church leadership and the public domain. Numerous church reform movements arose during this period, and mendicant friars sought to transform the new urban public through vigorous preaching campaigns and public displays of monastic-style renunciation. These efforts came to a head five centuries later in the Protestant Reformation and awoke a series of cross-pressures that have played a fundamental role in the modern West ever since. However, to understand the origin of these cross-pressures, we must also acknowledge the influence of medieval Islam.

During the ministry of Muhammad (609–32), Islam grew from being a monotheistic upstart movement among the tribes of Mecca to the dominant force in the Arabian Peninsula. Within a few decades after Muhammad's death, Islam had succeeded in incorporating many of the Asian and African territories of the former Alexandrian Empire. In 762, the Abbasid caliph al-Mansur launched a great effort to systematically translate the entire Greek corpus into Arabic. This gave Islamic scholars a rich harvest of knowledge upon which to build. They succeeded in revising and extending nearly every aspect of Greek knowledge in the following centuries and made breathtaking achievements in mathematics, astronomy, optics, sociology, history, and medicine. Nevertheless, a distinct tension emerged within Islamic culture during these years. On the one hand, some thinkers were so carried away by their appreciation of Greek thought that they adopted its conceptual framework wholesale. On the other hand, noting the significant differences between Greek thought and Qur'anic teaching, Islamic jurists began belittling the value of science and philosophy.

The best Islamic thinkers used this tension to advance ground-breaking insights into the evolutionary nature of existence, focusing in particular on the phenomena of history, spiritual development, and biological life. But Islamic society as a whole failed to follow this course, falling instead into a series of explicit conflicts between rationalist and legalist interpretations of Islam. Because Islamic rationalism was more grounded in Greek philosophy than Qur'anic verse and less accessible to the masses of believers, the jurists generally prevailed in the public sphere. But the rational and explorative impulse would not be entirely quelled, and it appeared again in Sufi mysticism. Notwithstanding the Sufi mystics' profound contributions to poetry and the devotional life of Islamic peoples, they gave undue consideration to abstract metaphysical debates and paid little attention to pressing social concerns. Islamic society therefore remained in the hands of the legalists and gradually fell into intellectual decline. Fortunately, Islamic and Greek learning had been largely transmitted to Europe by this time.[4] This process of knowledge dissemination played a crucial role in stimulating the Renaissance, and advanced Islamic discoveries provided Europeans with a basis upon which to pursue many lines of inquiry that later became hallmarks of the Scientific Revolution.

In Europe, the interaction of this new and evidently non-Christian knowledge with a growing desire to reform both church and public affairs awoke many of the forces that shaped the subsequent development of the modern West. The efforts of certain Christian thinkers to belittle the new learning because of its non-Christian origin and to bolster orthodox conviction were significant in this regard, for they helped consolidate the idea that science and religion inherently contradict each other. On the other hand, numerous Christian thinkers embraced the new learning and worked to incorporate it into a Christian worldview. It is largely because of their efforts that the Scientific Revolution took place. However, the institutional prestige of the critics added increased weight to the burgeoning narrative of science-religion conflict.[5]

Modernity I: Global Stirrings and Western Beginnings

Although the period of modernity is much broader and more complex than what we see taking place in the West, Western developments have exerted a wildly disproportionate influence upon the modern world and will likely continue to do so for some time. To better understand the link between modernity's global horizon and its Western beginnings, then, it is important to frame the period in terms of the preceding axial developments.

Levels of social complexity were particularly high in late medieval China, India, Europe, Japan, and the Islamic world. It was hypothetically possible for any one of these civilizations to have made the breakthrough into modernity. But that breakthrough occurred in Europe and then, via the global expansion of Europe's cultural, political, economic, and military influence, helped stimulate the emergence of modernity throughout the world. The claim here is not that modernity was invented in Europe and exported elsewhere, but that Europe helped stimulate the process of global ferment that subsequently brought (and is still bringing) the rest of humanity into the modern age. Certainly, many of these global changes carried within them a massive stamp of Western cultural influence. But this influence was not hegemonic, as each axial civilization gradually developed distinctive modern characteristics by drawing upon its own cultural resources in order to respond to

Western pressures. We can therefore say that the modern period has thus far been characterized by the gradual emergence of multiple modern configurations under the catalyzing influence of an ascendant modern West.

This dynamic is on display in the historical development of a general concept of religion. During the early modern period, European Christians saw different religious configurations as just so many perversions of orthodox Christian teaching.[6] This framework came under increasing pressure when Europeans encountered far-flung and ancient religious traditions that could not have derived from Christianity and that also showed remarkable levels of moral and intellectual sophistication. Combined with the so-called Wars of Religion, these new perspectives made the problem of religious diversity loom large in the early modern European mind. The solution that arose was to see all Christian denominations and non-Christian traditions as separate instances of religion, each with its own set of practices and beliefs that contradicted those espoused by others. To prevent such differences from generating conflict, many Enlightenment thinkers concluded that religion's public influence should be legally curtailed and the rights of individuals to choose their own religion guaranteed. Western scholars used this vision of religion to systematically study the different cultures and peoples of the world, while policymakers used it to formulate numerous domestic and international laws.

However, non-Western peoples did not simply accept modern Western concepts of religion, but rather developed distinctive concepts of religion by engaging in cultural negotiations with the West. The Japanese example is particularly instructive. The Japanese developed a general concept of religion under Western duress, but in a way that let them present Christianity and Buddhism as religions while identifying another group of Japanese practices and beliefs that bore explicit reference to the divine, Shinto, as a nonreligious cultural tradition. Additionally, the Japanese did not perceive any conflict between science and spiritual belief. They also maintained that not all religions involve belief in God (e.g., Buddhism and Confucianism), a claim that later exerted a profound influence upon the Western understanding of religion.

Despite these constructive dynamics, it seems reasonable to suggest that religion has been one of the great discoveries of the modern period, as it was only through this concept that we learned to examine and compare those features of human culture and civilization that explicitly reference the divine. This ability has subsequently helped us see that religion is a nearly universal feature of human life and that certain truths, values, and existential structures perennially occur in different contexts and settings. Scholarly accounts of religion have long been Christo- and Western-centric. Yet understanding of the concept has steadily improved through systematic application, criticism, and revision.

We can therefore see that the modern development of a general concept of religion took place via the interplay of Western illusions and expansionist political agendas, the cultural insights and negotiations of non-Western peoples, and profound discoveries about the world. Similar dynamics appear in countless other modern settings as well, as these patterns of interaction characterize the modern period as a whole.

Having discussed the phenomenon of multiple modernities, I want now to consider the internal development of the modern West. As mentioned above, medieval Christianity was increasingly animated by the desire to bring monastic-style virtue back into church leadership and the public sphere. The most profound and far-reaching expression of this desire was the Protestant Reformation. Though the Protestant Reformation yielded many results, the introduction of dualistic tendencies into modern Western culture was one of the most significant. The presence of spiritual forces in nature was rejected and replaced by a framework in which God stood over and above a lifeless physical domain. The idea that the church mediated humanity's relationship with God was supplanted by the notion that a direct connection existed between God and humanity. And the belief in people's potential to transform themselves by acquiring virtuous dispositions was replaced by the idea that human nature is fixed and fallen and can only be transformed by divine intervention.

The emergence of these new dualistic notions contributed to the disruption of the "virtue tradition" of moral inquiry that had long influenced Christian (and Jewish and Islamic) civilization.

The idea had been that human beings possessed latent spiritual potential that could be individually and collectively brought forth by their cultivation of virtuous dispositions. This meant that human development was guided by an inborn moral purpose that had been given to us and shaped by God. The Protestant Reformation helped undermine this framework by presenting humans as having a fixed and fallen nature that could only be redeemed through salvation. The Deists later inverted this Protestant perspective by claiming that God had designed human self-interest so that its proper coordination would generate the ideal society. Either way, higher moral purpose was no longer considered an inborn part of human nature. This made notions of moral objectivity difficult to maintain and contributed to the emergence of the cycle of conflict—different groups trying to force their perspectives upon others through legal and ideological means—that characterizes much contemporary moral discourse.

Modern dualism led many progressive Europeans to embrace naturalistic and secular beliefs by inadvertently consolidating the idea that religion contradicts modern science and modern norms of governance and public discourse. The perception of conflict between science and religion began arising during the late medieval period when certain dogmatic Catholic thinkers sought to discredit the new learning and consolidate their orthodox perspectives. The conflict diminished somewhat when Protestants embraced a dualistic framework that cohered with the new mechanistic science. However, the development of Darwinian theory undermined this momentary coherence by bringing the supposedly incorruptible phenomena of mind and life back into the spiritless natural world. Many Protestant thinkers began opposing Darwinian theory as a result, which cemented the idea that science and religion are somehow fundamentally at odds. The historical reality is far more complex than this account suggests.[7] But the point remains that by helping to consolidate the idea of an inherent conflict between science and religion, modern dualism led many Westerners to embrace naturalism.

The disruption of the virtue tradition also created a new polarity between those who sought to root morality in salvation and those who felt that social progress came from properly coordinated self-interest. Following the Wars of Religion, many progressive Europeans argued that religion could not ground a peaceful social order, as there was no rational or empirical way to decide between different beliefs. Accordingly, they claimed that modern forms of governance and public discourse should concentrate on coordinating self-interest and leave individuals free to believe what they wanted in the private domain. When combined with the rising tide of naturalism, this new political vision helped crystallize the idea that religion would gradually lose influence in the modern world or even disappear. For if religion contradicts modern science and cannot legitimately inhabit the modern public sphere, the continued development of modern science and the public sphere should stimulate religion's general decline. Here is where the subtraction narrative appears, and hence the theory of secularization.

Of course, the exclusive humanism of naturalism and secularism does not represent the entirety of the modern West. There have always been Christians who claimed that their communities' efforts to enact God's teachings and will stimulated the best features of the modern Western world and continue sustaining them today. Many advocates of this perspective have conservative convictions and recommend solving contemporary problems by renewing religion and public virtue. Others dedicate themselves to progressive processes of social change, working, for example, to abolish slavery, to promote racial and gender equality, and to right the crippling economic inequality that plagues the contemporary world. Regardless, the framework of civil religion constitutes a major force in the modern West.

Another pair of influential modern forces arose from the view that both civil religion and humanism that excludes religion obfuscate the transformative energies and emotions that lie deep within human life. The main debate among such expressivists is whether or not these inner realities connect in some way with transcendence. Expressivists pursuing the first and most intellectually prominent strand take the antireligious route, arguing that we can live more courageously, nobly, and profoundly when we embrace our lack of cosmic purpose and work instead to channel our darker energies and existential needs. Figures like Friedrich Nietzsche and Jean-Paul Sartre exemplify this conviction, as do Marxists who recommend overthrowing capitalism and religion in order to establish a radically egalitarian order.

The less prominent strand of expressivist thought explicitly acknowledges the spiritual dimensions of existence but elevates the individual's spirituality above any kind of organized religion. These spiritual expressivists tend to prize mystical experiences and to believe that spirituality promotes health and well-being. They also often embrace aspects of non-Western religious practice and thought on the grounds that these traditions are somehow less authoritarian and more in touch with the ebb and flow of spiritual life than their Western counterparts. Modern science occupies an ambiguous position within this framework, as the mechanistic worldview that came to prominence during the Enlightenment is considered a great barrier to spiritual progress, while recent developments in physics and psychology are often heralded as profound confirmations of spiritual truth. The idea of being spiritual but not religious comes from this cultural trajectory, as does the growing prominence of the perennial narrative framework.

Modernity II: The Global Age

To move beyond modernity's Western beginnings and examine the current period of globalization, we must examine the differences between European and American modernity and consider what effect their respective globalization has had upon the world. The basic suggestion I want to make here is that the globalization of European-style modernity stimulated an elite-centered process of secularization, while the subsequent globalization of American-style modernity helped disrupt and undermine this dynamic.

When considering the distinguishing features of European modernity, a key point to mention is the prominence of the ideal of national self-determination. During the early modern period, the idea arose that a number of different peoples populated Europe, each with a common language, history, and culture and each with the right and responsibility to govern themselves in the form of a nation-state. All other identities, values, and beliefs were to be subservient to the interests of the nation-state, particularly those concerning religion. Many European countries therefore established a national church that was regulated and supported by the state and that saw its mandate as contributing to the national good. Religion thus became a kind of public service that European states provided for their citizens. This new state-religion configuration was a far cry from the civilization-building powers that were released during the axial age. It stifled the culture of initiative, innovation, and grassroots engagement that sustains a vibrant collective religious life and therefore contributed to the gradual dwindling of religious commitment among Europeans. However, this dwindling was also stimulated by the fact that the nation-state was made the object of quasi-religious veneration, which channeled the religious impulses of Europeans into destructive nationalistic fervor. This trajectory of modernity became most pronounced during the First and Second World Wars.

The postwar establishment of a global system of nation-states helped spread European-style secularization throughout the world. Many postcolonial leaders had been educated in the West and sought explicitly to regulate and limit religion's role in their newly constituted lands. Newly liberated publics were often so enthralled by modern Western civilization that they warmly embraced visions of secular progress. This dynamic peaked during the decades following the Second World War and led many postwar scholars to claim that secularization theory had been empirically confirmed. However, by the 1980s religion's public influence began resurging in almost every region of the world. To appreciate why this resurgence took place and why it is still occurring today, we need to understand the role religion has played in the United States and then to consider how the globalization of American culture has affected the world.

Whereas in Europe religious favoritism and regulation were the norm, the U.S. government has long endorsed a more robust practice of religious freedom. This hands-off approach created a unique set of free-market conditions. The effects have been profound. A culture of religious innovation gradually appeared, whereby different religious organizations competed with one another for membership and funds. A dizzying variety of religious forms arose, offering an unprecedented range of options for a new kind of religious consumer. Individuals and communities generally felt a heightened sense of ownership over their religious commit-ments and dedicated significant time and resources to making sure that their organizations flourished and spread. Non-Christian reli-gions fared well in American culture, succeeding both in mobiliz-ing their traditional communal base and in attracting new believers. The novel and influential notion of being spiritual but not religious crystallized within American public life and became a significant cultural force. American evangelical Christians in par-ticular showed remarkable fervor in spreading their faith, leading to the rapid spread of evangelical and charismatic movements throughout the world. The point here is not that American reli-gious life is somehow ideal, but rather that American modernity supports a far richer and more dynamic religious life than the European model, despite the fact that the two regions display equal levels of technological, economic, and political sophistication.

The globalization of American culture has tended to disrupt global processes of European-style secularization and to help reli-gious actors acquire a more prominent role in public settings than they had under either colonial or early postcolonial rule. This dynamic can be attributed partially to the fact that the cultural conditions that stimulated European secularization never took global root. Thus, as European influence dwindled, the enduring religious dispositions of the masses found greater and more vari-able expression. The massive cultural influence of the United States has helped stimulate this process by influencing many to adopt American attitudes of individuality, competition, and choice. At the same time, many movements within the so-called global re-surgence of religion have tried to utilize diverse axial resources to halt the rising tide of inequality and cultural disintegration that the globalization of American culture has brought in its wake. Some of these movements have been benevolent, while others have been fanatical and destructive. We can see that the global resurgence of religion simultaneously involves the disruption of European secu-lar ideologies, the spread of a more free-market brand of religios-ity, and the emergence of efforts to alter the dynamics of inequality and cultural disintegration that Americanization arguably has spread throughout the world. It should be no surprise, then, that the decade in which religion's global resurgence began to take place (the 1980s) was the same in which the United States became the undisputed cultural, political, economic, and military leader of the world.

Again, by emphasizing the global influence of European and American modernity, I am not denying the influence that non-Western modernities have had upon processes of globalization; one need only consider the growing global profile of South and East Asian societies to see such influence at work today. My purpose has rather been to help clarify how certain Western-led globalizing forces have affected the religious life of humankind.

Future Trajectories

Although some consider the attempt to speculate about the future of religion unproductive and naïve, given the contingency and uncertainty that characterize human affairs, I would argue that we can tentatively highlight certain general trajectories without going too far astray. I will mention here six that seem particularly significant:

First, in the coming years, religion will probably continue to be a major force in world affairs. This trajectory will be stimulated by the processes of globalization, which disrupt the national imaginaries that long nourished secularism, as well as by a growing sense that secularist projects have failed to deliver their promised social goods. Beyond the horrors that aggressively secularized states (e.g., Stalinist Russia and Nazi Germany) have unleashed upon the world, the contemporary slide of many liberal-democratic states into oligarchy, rampant inequality, prejudice, xenophobia, and political gridlock helps consolidate this sense of secularism's failure. Of course, the role of religion in modern societies will continue to evolve. Spiritual ideologies that explicitly differentiate themselves from religion will likely gain traction, as will new forms of religious conservatism and fundamentalism that seek to lead humanity back to some idealized religious past. Regardless, religion's social and political importance should continue.

Second, the continued spread of capitalism and modern technology will create more free-market religious conditions in many regions. Although the resultant dynamics will differ in certain ways from those that characterize the contemporary United States, more pluralized models of religious life, in which an ever-growing variety of religious groups vie with one another (and nonreligious organizations) for believers, public influence, and funds, are likely to emerge. At the same time, however, these new market conditions will enable the spread of competing naturalist and consumerist ideals.

Third, many religious actors will continue trying to halt or transform the rising tide of global inequality and cultural decay. Some will do so by trying to forcefully facilitate some kind of orthodox religious renewal, while others will engage in more benevolent and long-term efforts to preserve the best elements of the current world order while overcoming its many destructive and oppressive features. In either case, we can expect that many from among both sets of actors will draw upon the resources of one or several axial traditions in their efforts to challenge and transform contemporary social dynamics.

Fourth, processes of globalization will likely continue to consolidate the growing conviction that religion is a common sphere of human endeavor. Such a development will help stimulate the gradual emergence of a new global conversation on the role of religion in society, with particular emphasis being given to the question of how religion's many constructive powers can be effectively encouraged while at the same time discouraging the diverse expressions of fanaticism, superstition, and oppression that we see around us in the world today.

Fifth, it seems plausible to expect that intellectual elites will increasingly appreciate how certain religious concepts are at least coherent with the natural-scientific framework and may even offer certain explanatory advantages over their naturalistic counterparts. This shift would be stimulated by developments in both the natural and the social sciences, as well as by ongoing philosophical discussion of the explanatory and existential difficulties that naturalistic worldviews face.

Sixth, though I am moving into highly speculative terrain, I find it reasonable to conclude that something like a second axial age will eventually emerge. I agree with Jaspers that ongoing processes of material and social globalization are setting the stage for the kind of foundational spiritual transformation that we witnessed during the classical axial period. Though we cannot now know how precisely such a second axial age will unfold, it seems clear that it will involve the entire planet and probably will not display the same kind of internal diversity as the movements of the first axial age. Additionally, just as the movements of the first axial age gradually transformed and replaced the preceding archaic and tribal orders, the movement(s) of the second axial age would likely transform and replace the current world order. Capitalism, democracy, and other such forces thus should not be considered the final stage of human evolution, but rather as forces that are creating the conditions under which a distinctly new pattern of collective life can begin to emerge.

In offering such an optimistic view of humanity's collective future, I acknowledge that phenomena such as climate change, nuclear war, and the development of artificial intelligence threaten us with the distinct possibility of annihilation. Indeed, some environmentalists have become so certain of humanity's impending demise that they have decided to accept their fate and find what joy they can during the quickly dwindling remainder of their time on earth.[8] Obviously, if such apocalyptic scenarios play out, the so-called second axial age would not arrive, or at least would be very short-lived. Nevertheless, I do believe that the requisite changes can be made, though not by human technological and political ingenuity alone. Rather, a profound spiritual transformation is needed, the likes of which arose during the first axial age. I would even go so far as to suggest that a second axial age will likely emerge as one or more religiously inspired movements arise to help humanity overcome its looming existential threats. Religious innovations have played a central role in helping humanity address profound social crises during every previous period of history; why, then, should they not do the same again today?

Notes

Introduction

1. Casanova, *Public Religions in the Modern World*, 17; Toft, Philpott, and Shah, *God's Century*, 1; Berger, cited in Toft, Philpott, and Shah, *God's Century*, 71–72.
2. See Berger, Davie, and Fokas, *Religious America, Secular Europe?*; Finke and Stark, *The Churching of America, 1776–2005*; Philpott, "Has the Study of Global Politics Found Religion?," 191.
3. Asad, *Formations of the Secular*, 1.
4. Charles Taylor first used the terms "subtraction narrative" and "subtraction story." See Taylor, *A Secular Age*, 588.
5. Bruce, *Fundamentalism*, 12–13.
6. All of the subsequent narrative frameworks also seek to move beyond the dialect of subtraction and renewal narratives in their own way.
7. Because of the connection between this narrative and the ideas advanced by both subtraction and renewal narratives, I choose to use the term "transsecular" instead of "transsubtraction."
8. I refer here respectively to Taylor's *A Secular Age* and Eisenstadt's "Multiple Modernities."
9. Fuller, *Spiritual, but Not Religious*.
10. When considering other attempts to frame the academic study of religion as a whole, we find three prevalent approaches. The first, a tradition-based approach, exemplified by Huston Smith's *The World's Religions*, analyzes and compares diverse religious traditions. The second, a theorist-based approach, considers the views of prominent theorists of religion, such as Max Weber and Émile Durkheim. Daniel Pals's *Nine Theories of Religion* utilizes this approach. And the third, a cultural-thematic approach, engages religion as a case study for considering broader social-critical themes, such as power, gender, ritual, and belief.

Consider, in this regard, Malory Nye's *Religion: The Basics*. Though each of these approaches has its merits, I find that analyzing the narrative commitments that undergird the various strands of the contemporary academic discourse on religion provides a more coherent and encompassing perspective.

11. Gorski et al., "The Post-Secular in Question."
12. Barbato, "Conceptions of the Self for Post-Secular Emancipation"; Barbato, "Postsecular Revolution."
13. Wrathall and Lambeth, "Heidegger's Last God"; Asad, *Genealogies of Religion*; Asad, *Formations of the Secular*.
14. Varela, Thompson, and Rosch, *The Embodied Mind*.
15. Mellor and Shilling, *Sociology of the Sacred*; Seligman, *Possessing Spirits and Healing Selves*.
16. Flanagan, *The Bodhisattva's Brain*; Nikkel, *Radical Embodiment*.
17. Mircea Eliade described this pattern of belief in his *The Myth of the Eternal Return*.
18. See T. Lewis, *Why Philosophy Matters for the Study of Religion*; Schilbrack, *Philosophy and the Study of Religions*.

Chapter One. The Subtraction Narrative

1. Comte, *The Positive Philosophy of Auguste Comte*, 186, 202, 231, 550–53.
2. Dennett, *Breaking the Spell*, 15.
3. Ibid., 68.
4. Ibid., 126.
5. Skinner, "'Superstition' in the Pigeon."
6. Dennett, *Breaking the Spell*, 118.
7. Ibid., 136, 142.
8. Dennett, *Darwin's Dangerous Idea*, 185.
9. Ibid., 184–85.
10. For critiques of Skinner's methodology and conclusions, see Staddon and Simmelhag, "The 'Superstition' Experiment"; Timberlake and Lucas, "The Basis of Superstitious Behavior."
11. Midgley, *Evolution as a Religion*, 6.
12. Dennett, *Breaking the Spell*, 199.
13. Bellah, *Religion in Human Evolution*.
14. Relevant works by Dewey include *Liberalism and Social Action; Democracy and Education; Art as Experience; Experience and Nature*.
15. Dewey, *The Quest for Certainty*; Dewey, *Reconstruction in Philosophy*.
16. Dewey, *A Common Faith*, 25.
17. Dewey, *The Quest for Certainty*, 13.
18. Ibid., 52.
19. Dewey explains that our "beliefs about values are pretty much in the position in which beliefs about nature were before the scientific revolution."

This gives us an idea of the magnitude of change that he believes is necessary for religion to find its proper place in society, as well as of the great benefits that he thinks will flow from this transformation. Ibid., 104.

20. Gandhi, *An Autobiography*.

21. From a brief glance at various Bahá'í sources, we can see that they are quite explicit about the need to pursue individual and collective spiritual transformation in an increasingly scientific manner. "Bahá'u'lláh has come to free humanity from this long bondage, and the closing decades of the twentieth century were devoted by the community of His followers to creative experimentation with the means by which His objective can be realized. The prosecution of the Divine Plan entails no less than the involvement of the entire body of humankind in the work of its own spiritual, social and intellectual development." Likewise, Shoghi Effendi says, "The Revelation proclaimed by Bahá'u'lláh, His followers believe, is divine in origin, all-embracing in scope, broad in its outlook, *scientific in its method*, humanitarian in its principles and dynamic in the influence it exerts on the hearts and minds of men." See Universal House of Justice, *Turning Point*, 110; Effendi and Universal House of Justice, *Science and Technology* (emphasis added).

22. Recent studies suggest that the Bahá'í Faith has proportionately been the fastest growing religion over the previous century. Johnson and Grim, *The World's Religions in Figures*, 59–62.

23. For a more detailed articulation of these features of the Bahá'í community pattern of inquiry, see Lample, *Revelation and Social Reality*.

24. Alexander, *The Dark Side of Modernity*; Gauchet, *The Disenchantment of the World*; Habermas, *The Structural Transformation of the Public Sphere*; Jaspers, *The Origin and Goal of History*; Nagel, *Secular Philosophy and the Religious Temperament*.

25. Taylor, *A Secular Age*, 652.

26. Gauchet, *The Disenchantment of the World*, 9, 10, 4.

27. Ibid., 11.

28. Ibid., 27, 29.

29. Ibid., 6.

30. Ibid., 127.

31. Ibid., 153, 137.

32. Ibid., 4. The first French version of *The Disenchantment of the World* was published in 1985.

33. Ibid., 21.

34. Berger, "The Desecularization of the World"; Philpott, "Has the Study of Global Politics Found Religion?"; Stark and Bainbridge, *A Theory of Religion*; Toft, Philpott, and Shah, *God's Century*.

35. Casanova, "Cosmopolitanism, the Clash of Civilizations and Multiple Modernities"; Eisenstadt, "Multiple Modernities"; Thomas, "Taking

Religious and Cultural Pluralism Seriously"; Thomassen, "Anthropology, Multiple Modernities and the Axial Age Debate."

36. Davie, "Religion in 21st-Century Europe."
37. Norris and Inglehart, *Sacred and Secular.*
38. Berger, "The Desecularization of the World," 10–11.

Chapter Two. The Renewal Narrative

1. Bruce, *Fundamentalism*, 12–13.
2. MacIntyre, *After Virtue*, 1–5.
3. Ibid., 6–10.
4. Ibid., 25.
5. Ibid., 191. MacIntyre is here describing Weber's thought.
6. MacIntyre, *Whose Justice? Which Rationality?*, 163.
7. MacIntyre, *After Virtue*, 263.
8. Salvatore, *The Public Sphere.*
9. MacIntyre, *After Virtue*, 263.
10. Stout, *Democracy and Tradition*, 123.
11. Taylor, "A Catholic Modernity?," 36–37.
12. Heidegger, *The Question Concerning Technology and Other Essays*, 55.
13. Wrathall and Lambeth, "Heidegger's Last God," 167.
14. Young, *Heidegger's Later Philosophy*, 22.
15. Wrathall and Lambeth, "Heidegger's Last God," 174.
16. Heidegger, "Plato's Doctrine of Truth," 164.
17. Ibid., 178–79.
18. Wrathall, *Heidegger and Unconcealment*, 218–21. Heidegger examines the contributions of many other philosophers, including Aristotle, Augustine, Leibniz, Spinoza, Kant, and Hegel. Yet the point remains that he does take the four thinkers mentioned as paragons of their respective epochs. After explaining how "*meta-physics begins* with Plato's interpretation of Being as *idea*," Heidegger makes the following remarks: "For medieval Scholasticism, Thomas Aquinas' thesis holds good: 'Truth is properly encountered in the human or in the divine intellect.' The intellect is where truth has its essential locus.... At the beginning of modern times Descartes sharpens the previous thesis by saying: 'Truth or falsehood in the proper sense can be nowhere else but in the intellect alone.' And in the age when the modern era enters its fulfillment Nietzsche sharpens the previous thesis still further when he says, '*Truth is the kind of error* without which a certain kind of living could not live. In the final analysis, the value for *life* is what is decisive.'" Heidegger, "Plato's Doctrine of Truth," 178–79.
19. Nietzsche, *Thus Spoke Zarathustra*, 57.
20. Nietzsche, *The Gay Science*, 120 (emphasis added). For a discussion of the religious dimensions of Nietzsche's thought, see Young, *Nietzsche's Philosophy of Religion*; Benson, *Pious Nietzsche.*

21. Wrathall, *Heidegger and Unconcealment*, 241.

22. Heidegger, *The Question Concerning Technology and Other Essays*, 28.

23. This is also why Heidegger considers the poetry of Friedrich Hölderlin so essential; Hölderlin strives to re-create the world of early Greece in order to help stimulate a renaissance of German culture and spirituality. Safranski, *Martin Heidegger*, 282.

24. Wrathall and Lambeth, "Heidegger's Last God," 181.

25. Indeed, it is hard not to think, when reading the late Heidegger, of Nietzsche's apt diagnosis of the early Greek romanticism that plagues German philosophy: "German philosophy as a whole . . . is the most fundamental form of *romanticism* and homesickness there has ever been: the longing for the best that ever existed. One is no longer at home anywhere; at last one longs back for that place in which alone one can be at home, because it is the only place in which one would want to be at home: the *Greek* world. . . . One wants to go back, through the Church Fathers to the Greeks . . . above all the pre-Socratics—the most deeply buried of all Greek temples!" Nietzsche, *The Will to Power*, 225.

26. Dreyfus and Kelly, "Saving the Sacred from the Axial Revolution."

27. Rorty, *Essays on Heidegger and Others*, 49.

28. Sorkin, *The Religious Enlightenment*.

29. Taylor, *A Secular Age*.

30. Whitehead, *Process and Reality*, 31.

31. Safranski, *Martin Heidegger*, 277.

32. Cited in Wolin, "National Socialism, World Jewry, and the History of Being."

33. Cited ibid.

34. Di Cesare, "Heidegger—'Jews Self-Destructed.'"

35. Faye, *Heidegger*.

36. Sevea, *The Political Philosophy of Muhammad Iqbal*; Shariati and Khamene'i, *Iqbal*; Mir, *Iqbal*; Schimmel, *Gabriel's Wing*; Iqbal, *The Reconstruction of Religious Thought in Islam*.

37. Iqbal, *The Reconstruction of Religious Thought in Islam*, 6.

38. Arberry, *The Koran*, 183. Emphasis added.

39. Iqbal, *Thoughts and Reflections of Iqbal*.

40. Iqbal, *The Reconstruction of Religious Thought in Islam*, 124.

41. For a contemporary discussion of the legacy of Islamic polemics in Western thought, see Quinn, *The Sum of All Heresies*.

42. Iqbal, *The Reconstruction of Religious Thought in Islam*, 99.

43. Ibid., 102–3.

44. Ibid., 101.

45. Arberry, *The Koran*, 197.

46. Ibid., 62.

47. Ibid., 343.

48. Al-Biruni also developed fieldwork-based anthropology.

49. Ibn Khaldūn advanced these insights in his epochal *Muqaddimah*. For Iqbal's discussion of Rumi's evolutionary thought, see *The Reconstruction of Religious Thought in Islam*, 147–48.
50. Iqbal, *The Reconstruction of Religious Thought in Islam*, 74–75. For contemporary studies of Iqbal's political thought, see Majeed, *Muhammad Iqbal*; Sevea, *The Political Philosophy of Muhammad Iqbal*.
51. Iqbal, *The Reconstruction of Religious Thought in Islam*, 120–38.
52. Ibid., 119–20, 6.
53. Ibid., 6, 26.
54. Ibid., 12.
55. Ibid., 123.
56. Dallal, *Islam, Science, and the Challenge of History*; Belting, *Florence and Baghdad*; Saliba, *Islamic Science and the Making of the European Renaissance*; Lowney, *A Vanished World*; Menocal, *The Ornament of the World*; Salvatore, *The Public Sphere*.
57. Siedentop, *Inventing the Individual*, 3.
58. Taylor, *A Secular Age*, 155.
59. See Bellah et al., *Habits of the Heart*.
60. Iqbal, *Thoughts and Reflections of Iqbal*, 120.

Chapter Three. The Transsecular Narrative

1. Taylor, *A Secular Age*.
2. Taylor, "What Was the Axial Revolution?," 37.
3. Ibid., 38.
4. Taylor, *A Secular Age*, 516, 71.
5. Taylor does not explicitly use this phrase, "conservative civil religion," though it describes his account of this position well. See ibid., 414, 528.
6. Ibid., 371–74.
7. Ibid., 637. Counter-Enlightenment thought reached the public after the two world wars undermined the moral authority of both exclusive humanism and civil religion. After European powers spent the wars claiming to represent Christian and/or enlightened civilization as they slaughtered one another in droves, it was only natural to feel that they had somehow lost touch with modern humanity. It is therefore not surprising that the 1960s witnessed the emergence of immanent movements (e.g., radical politics and subversive art) and spiritually oriented movements (e.g., New Ageism, interest in non-Western religion, and a spiritualized festive culture) that drew quite centrally on Counter-Enlightenment thought. Ibid., 377.
8. Ibid., 545.
9. Ibid., 507, 513.
10. Ibid., 770.
11. Ibid., 300, 423.

12. Ibid., 727.

13. Ibid., 631, 652.

14. See Josephson, *The Invention of Religion in Japan*; Saliba, *Islamic Science and the Making of the European Renaissance*; Stroumsa, *A New Science*; van der Veer, *Imperial Encounters*; Weatherford, *Genghis Khan and the Making of the Modern World*.

15. Van der Veer, *The Modern Spirit of Asia*.

16. Taylor's methodology nevertheless provides us with resources to engage and interpret other axial age trajectories. For an account of the current discourse on the diverse movements of the axial age, see Boy and Torpey, "Inventing the Axial Age"; Eisenstadt, "Multiple Modernities in an Age of Globalization"; Eisenstadt, "The Reconstruction of Religious Arenas in the Framework of 'Multiple Modernities'"; Thomassen, "Anthropology, Multiple Modernities and the Axial Age Debate."

17. See Stark and Bainbridge, *A Theory of Religion*, 25–54, 279–314.

18. Stark, *The Triumph of Christianity*, 363–64.

19. Ibid., 13–14, 38–43, 57–59.

20. Ibid., 81–83. The size of the Jewish community at the time of Christianity's emergence is often underappreciated. For example, Stark estimates that there were around nine million Jews living in the Roman Empire (10–15 percent of the empire's total population) and another seven million inhabiting other regions of the Near East. Ibid., 33, 79.

21. Ibid., 118, 136, 157. For all its vigor and active evangelization, Christianity did not grow at an explosive rate. In fact, Stark explains that a 3.4 percent growth rate explains the known data. If such a rate held steady for the first three hundred or so years, Stark estimates that there would have been 1,397 Christians in the Roman Empire in year 50; 7,434 in year 100; 39,560 in year 150; 210,516 in year 200; 1,120,246 in year 250; 5,961,290 in year 300; 8,904,032 in year 312, when Constantine converted; and 31,722,489 in year 350, just over a decade after his death. Ibid., 157.

22. Ibid., 174, 196.

23. Ibid., 306.

24. Stark's distinction between the Church of Power and the Church of Piety and his contention that the Church of Piety arose in the eleventh century to reform the Catholic Church by enlisting public support meshes with Taylor's narration of Christian reform.

25. Ibid., 309.

26. Ibid., 307, 321, 331.

27. Ibid., 354.

28. Ibid., 355.

29. See Bruce, *Secularization*, 146–47.

30. Stark, *The Triumph of Christianity*, 359–60, 363.

31. Ibid., 397–406; 377.

32. Cited ibid., 379, 376.
33. Ibid., 376, 382.
34. Indeed, though Stark uses the index of religious freedom to support his claim that modern European societies are secularized because they are not religiously free, he fails entirely to explain why Islamic countries with very low levels of religious freedom still remain highly religious.
35. Finke and Stark, *The Churching of America, 1776–2005.*
36. Conditions in Ghana and India are very different from those in the United States, but we still encounter significant religious diversity and independence from state apparatus.
37. A similar set of fallacies was propagated by neoliberal economists who thought that the idea of a self-regulating free market could explain every historical instance of economic prosperity or decline. The simplicity of this idea was alluring, and it gripped public policy and economic practice throughout the world. Although economists have subsequently recognized that the market does display certain self-regulating patterns, they have also almost universally acknowledged that applying this principle to the entire economy is false and destructive. Something similar can be said of Stark's theory of free religious markets. For a compelling account of the logic and history of neoliberalism, see Harvey, *A Brief History of Neoliberalism.*
38. Stout, *Democracy and Tradition*, 93, 97, 93.
39. For Stout's critique of such "secularist" perspectives, see ibid., 63–91.
40. Ibid., 26–27. For Stout's critique of such traditionalist perspectives, see ibid., 92–139. I find that Stout's arguments do not take adequate account of Rawls's subsequent reflections on religion in *Political Liberalism.*
41. Stout, *Democracy and Tradition*, 12.
42. Stout, *Blessed Are the Organized*, 57.
43. Stout, *Democracy and Tradition*, 23; Stout, *Blessed Are the Organized*, xv.
44. Stout, *Blessed Are the Organized*, 245, 255.
45. Stout, *Democracy and Tradition*, 23. Stout claims that Emerson believed that democracy can only emerge once each citizen begins striving to "achieve a higher form of goodness or excellence," for the individual struggle for moral and spiritual excellence helps democratic citizens combat the tendency to embrace public orthodoxy, whether of a secular or a religious nature. For Emerson, then, democracy and the independent investigation of moral and spiritual truth go hand in hand. Ibid., 29, 40.
46. Ibid., 70.
47. Lincoln, "Second Inaugural Address."
48. King, "I Have a Dream . . ."
49. Stout, *Democracy and Tradition*, 123–24, 85.
50. Stout, *Blessed Are the Organized*, 287, 226, 287.
51. MacIntyre, *After Virtue*, 263.

52. Micklethwait and Wooldridge, *God Is Back*, 9–25.

53. See Eisenstadt, "The Reconstruction of Religious Arenas in the Framework of 'Multiple Modernities.'"

Chapter Four. The Postnaturalist Narrative

1. Even such a definition of "naturalism" requires further specification. Hence, we have terms like "reductive naturalism," "emergent naturalism," "supervenience physicalism," "eliminativism," "token physicalism," and the like. Furthermore, there are many forms of naturalism that do not identify themselves with the concepts and methods of natural science (e.g., the naturalism of John McDowell). For a fuller discussion of the various ways that the term "naturalism" is used today, see Munro, "Meanings of 'Naturalism' in Philosophy and Aesthetics."

2. Nagel, *Secular Philosophy and the Religious Temperament*, 42.

3. Ferguson, "The Heretic."

4. Steven Pinker, Twitter post, October 16, 2012, 4:36 p.m., https://twitter.com/sapinker/status/258350644979695616; Leiter and Weisberg, "Do You Only Have a Brain?"

5. Nagel, *Secular Philosophy and the Religious Temperament*, 43, 25.

6. Nagel, *The View from Nowhere*, 7–8.

7. Nagel, *Secular Philosophy and the Religious Temperament*, 3, 6.

8. One might even argue that the scientific impulse to understand the world is derived from our religious impulse to align ourselves with the cosmic order. This point is developed by William Desmond in *Desire, Dialectic, and Otherness*.

9. Nagel, *Secular Philosophy and the Religious Temperament*, 5.

10. Charles Taylor helpfully offers an amplified description of this line of thought in *A Secular Age*, 366–68.

11. Nagel, *Secular Philosophy and the Religious Temperament*, 9.

12. Ibid., 10–11.

13. Ibid., 12–14. Nagel draws upon John Richardson's work for this reading of Nietzsche. See Richardson, *Nietzsche's New Darwinism*. Nagel's purpose in critiquing Darwinianism is not to debunk the theory of evolution, but rather its absolutization. As he says, "Darwin's theory of evolution on its own does not have this consequence, because Darwin recognized that it did not explain the origin of life—only the origin of species through natural selection once life and biological heredity were in existence." See Nagel, *Secular Philosophy and the Religious Temperament*, 15.

14. Ibid., 16–17. It is interesting to note that the arguments of *Mind and Cosmos* do not significantly depart from the arguments Nagel presented in earlier works. Instead of being an ill-aimed shot in the dark from a "once-great thinker," *Mind and Cosmos* is the next logical step in the widely celebrated sequence of thought that Nagel had long been developing.

15. Nagel, "A Philosopher Defends Religion"; Nagel, *Mind and Cosmos*, 94.

16. Nagel, *The Last Word*.

17. Toft, Philpott, and Shah, *God's Century*.

18. C. S. Lewis, *Mere Christianity*, 136–37.

19. Jonas, *The Phenomenon of Life*, 7.

20. Ibid., 12.

21. Ibid., 218–21.

22. Ibid., 43.

23. Ibid., 233.

24. Ibid., 277.

25. Ibid., 232.

26. Marion, *Being Given*, 7.

27. For a more recent attempt to bridge existential phenomenology and natural science, see Thompson, *Mind in Life*.

28. For a more in-depth account of Jonas's views on this theme, see Jonas, *The Gnostic Religion*.

29. See Blumenberg, *The Legitimacy of the Modern Age*; Löwith, *Meaning in History*.

30. Whitehead's books include *A Treatise on Universal Algebra, with Applications; The Axioms of Projective Geometry*; "On Mathematical Concepts of the Material World"; *The Axioms of Descriptive Geometry; An Introduction to Mathematics; Principia Mathematica* (cowritten with Bertrand Russell); *An Enquiry Concerning the Principles of Natural Knowledge; The Concept of Nature; The Principle of Relativity, with Application to Physical Science; The Aims of Education and Other Essays; Science and the Modern World; Modes of Thought; Symbolism, Its Meaning and Effect; Religion in the Making; Process and Reality; Adventures of Ideas*.

31. Whitehead, *Religion in the Making*, front of jacket.

32. Whitehead, *Science and the Modern World*, 3, 5. Whitehead acknowledges that individuals like Aristotle clearly manifested the scientific mindset during an earlier age, but claims that it has never before animated a civilization at large.

33. Ibid., 181–82.

34. Ibid., 5, 10–11.

35. Ibid., 39, 15, 43.

36. Ibid., 27–29, 31, 33.

37. Ibid., 46–48.

38. Ibid., 54.

39. Ibid., 51.

40. Ibid., 58–59.

41. Ibid., 185.

42. Gould, *Rocks of Ages*.

43. Whitehead, *Science and the Modern World*, 34.

44. Whitehead, *Religion in the Making*, 189.

45. Gaukroger, *The Emergence of a Scientific Culture*, 3, 21, v.
46. Dewey, *The Quest for Certainty*, 13; Taylor, *A Secular Age*, 652.
47. See Polkinghorne, *Belief in God in an Age of Science*; Polkinghorne, *Science and Providence*; Polkinghorne, *Quantum Physics and Theology*; Stapp, *Mindful Universe*; Stapp, *Mind, Matter and Quantum Mechanics*; Ward, *More Than Matter?*; Bohm, *Wholeness and the Implicate Order*; Peat, *Infinite Potential*.
48. Whitehead, *Process and Reality*, xiv, 14.
49. Hick, *An Interpretation of Religion*, 73.
50. For a good discussion of this kind of religious epistemology, see Moser, *The Evidence for God*.
51. In fact, I would argue that scientific thinkers in the West would be much more willing to consider the viability of spiritual perspectives if they had not been so thoroughly put off by the aggressive and narrow-minded fundamentalism that often issues from religious circles.
52. This is a curious tendency, given that most of the world's major systems of religious thought explicitly encourage people to organize their lives around a universal spiritual reality. Furthermore, situated as we are in an increasingly global society, all the world's religions are today being forced to inhabit a common field of action.

Chapter Five. The Construct Narrative

1. Asad, *Formations of the Secular*, 256, 13–14.
2. Asad, *Genealogies of Religion*, 138–40.
3. Ibid., 117–19.
4. Asad, *Formations of the Secular*, 199; Asad, *Genealogies of Religion*, 207.
5. Cited in Asad, *Genealogies of Religion*, 29. This point is strengthened when we take note of Geertz's claim that "religious symbols are a means of coming positively to terms with" the subjective experiences of "ignorance, pain, and injustice." Ibid., 46.
6. Ibid., 57–58.
7. "What is interesting, I think, is not merely that some forms of suffering were to be taken more seriously than others, but that 'inhuman' suffering as opposed to 'necessary' and 'inevitable' suffering was regarded [by the modern project] as being essentially *gratuitous*, and therefore legally punishable. Pain endured in the movement toward becoming 'fully human,' on the other hand, was necessary, in the sense that there were social or moral reasons why it had to be suffered." Asad, *Formations of the Secular*, 113.
8. Asad, *Genealogies of Religion*, 233.
9. See Casanova, "Cosmopolitanism, the Clash of Civilizations and Multiple Modernities"; Eisenstadt, "Multiple Modernities in an Age of Globalization"; *Comparative Civilizations and Multiple Modernities*; "Multiple Modernities."

10. Preston, *Sword of the Spirit, Shield of Faith.*
11. Taylor, *The Ethics of Authenticity.*
12. Stroumsa, *A New Science,* viii–ix.
13. Ibid., 2, 5, 7.
14. Ibid., 19.
15. Ibid., 147–48.
16. Ibid., 54, 59.
17. Ibid., 124.
18. Ibid., 77–79. Some used this strategy to make sense of the Native Americans' existence, presenting them as descendants of the Ten Tribes of Israel. Great efforts were exerted to show exactly what route these tribes had taken from the Holy Land to the New World. Others used the myth of the Flood to make sense of the existence of flood narratives throughout the world, to search the exact location of the Garden of Eden, or to make sense of the similarities between Christianity and other religions. Ibid., 78.
19. Ibid., 83, 89.
20. Ibid., 97.
21. From here, it is not hard to imagine how the combination of a secularized developmental narrative with the degenerative thrust of the renewal narrative and a "perennialization" of the natural-scientific framework allows for the subtraction narrative to emerge. Society improves and religion declines, the thought goes, as we gradually discover the eternal natural-scientific truth. Transsecular, postnaturalist, and construct narratives were only able to emerge after the subtraction narrative had taken shape, as they all carry within them a critique of this narrative framework.
22. See Nongbri, *Before Religion.*
23. Josephson, *The Invention of Religion in Japan,* 257.
24. Ibid., 3, 5.
25. Ibid., 25.
26. Ibid., 40, 58, 38.
27. Ibid., 73.
28. Cited ibid., 80.
29. Cited ibid., 89.
30. The last term, *fumie* (religious emblems), refers to the practice of trampling on Christian icons that had been previously demanded of Dutch merchants who wished to trade with Japan in order to demonstrate their distance from Christianity. Though the treaty's English translation states that this practice has been abolished, the Japanese version specifies "in Nagasaki," which is where the American settlement had been established. Ibid., 90–91.
31. Ibid., 94, 99. Most of the gods that would later constitute the Shinto pantheon "were imported from China, Korea, and, indirectly, from India."

Even the imperial cult, which grounded Shinto practice and metaphysics, was originally situated in a Buddhist context. If things had gone somewhat differently, Josephson explains, "we might now regard Shinto as a form of Buddhism, Hinduism, Daoism, Confucianism, or something else entirely." Ibid., 100–101.

32. Ibid., 109, 104.

33. Ibid., 121, 109–10, 112–13.

34. Ibid., 132.

35. Said, *Orientalism;* Josephson, *The Invention of Religion in Japan,* 193–94, 221.

36. Van der Veer, *The Modern Spirit of Asia.*

37. Josephson, *The Invention of Religion in Japan,* 163.

38. See Gregory, *The Unintended Reformation.* It is, nevertheless, interesting to note certain similarities between Shintoism and the Protestant Reformation. Both movements were motivated by the belief that their respective civilizations were experiencing moral degradation and worldly decline and that they must abandon current habits and reestablish older ways of life in order to restore their civilization to its previous glory. While we can still posit a causal connection between the Protestant Reformation and the differentiation of religion from other spheres of endeavor, Josephson helps us see that other movements can stimulate a similar process of cultural transformation, albeit with different ultimate results.

39. Josephson, *The Invention of Religion in Japan,* 162. This line of thought also demonstrates that "religion" is not as static a concept in the world today as Asad suggests, but rather one that has evolved differently in different settings and will continue to do so as more cultures and peoples join in the conversation.

40. "There is general agreement among historians of the history of religions that Islamicate civilization produced the greatest pre-modern historical studies of world religions. Indeed, Western scholarly approbation of this literature has been sustained and enthusiastic, based on the observation that historical science was pioneered by Muslims. Considering the extent to which the Muslim contribution has been neglected, this point can bear reiteration. . . . But the history of religions waited until the nineteenth century for any other historian to take the religions of others as seriously as Shahrastani did." Wasserstrom, "Islamicate History of Religions?," 408.

41. This is a point with far-reaching implications, as it requires us to wrestle with the challenge of interpreting how different cultures and peoples throughout the world locate themselves within one of the subspecies of "religion." Regardless of the conclusions we may draw, it should be clear that the construction of a general concept of religion has played a tremendous role in shaping the modern world.

42. Cited in Asad, *Genealogies of Religion*, 29.
43. Nongbri, *Before Religion*, 18.

Chapter Six. The Perennial Narrative

1. Schmitt, "Perennial Philosophy"; Blavatsky, *The Secret Doctrine*; Adiswarananda, *Vivekananda, World Teacher*; Coomaraswamy, *The Essential Ananda K. Coomaraswamy*; Schuon, *The Transcendent Unity of Religions*; H. Smith, *Forgotten Truth*; Campbell, *The Hero with a Thousand Faces*; Hick, *An Interpretation of Religion*; Otto, *The Idea of the Holy*; Kierkegaard, *The Concept of Anxiety*; Michalski, *The Flame of Eternity*; Hagan, *Buddhism Plain and Simple*; Ibn Khaldûn, *The Muqaddimah*; Toynbee, *A Study of History*.

2. Huxley's *Brave New World* and *Point Counter Point* are respectively ranked by the Modern Library as the fifth and forty-fourth best English-language novels of the twentieth century. See "100 Best Novels," *Modern Library* (Random House, 1988), http://www.modernlibrary.com/top-100/100-best-novels/; Huxley, *The Perennial Philosophy*.

3. Toksvig, "Aldous Huxley's Prescriptions for Spiritual Myopia."

4. Huxley, *The Perennial Philosophy*, 16, 43, 112, front matter.

5. T. Nagel, *The View from Nowhere*, 8.

6. Huxley, *The Perennial Philosophy*, 48–49, 191, 55.

7. Cited ibid., 49–50.

8. Ibid., 251–52.

9. Ibid., 211, 125.

10. Huxley, *Island*. In this pessimistic aspect, Huxley's perennial narrative thus comes close to MacIntyre's renewal narrative.

11. For a description of Huxley's mescaline-fueled investigations of the occult, see Huxley, *The Doors of Perception*. While I do not reject the possibility of drug-induced transpersonal experiences and acknowledge that the scientific investigation of these phenomena is worthwhile, I do feel that more scrutiny is needed than Huxley musters. Still, Huxley's personal experiments did lead him to a fascinating theory of mind: "The suggestion is that the function of the brain and nervous system and sense organs is in the main *eliminative* and not productive. . . . According to such a theory, each of us is potentially Mind at Large. But in so far as we are animals, our business is at all costs to survive. To make biological survival possible, Mind at Large has to be funneled through the reducing valve of the brain and nervous system. . . . Certain persons, however, seem to be born with a kind of bypass that circumvents the reducing valve. In others temporary by-passes may be acquired either spontaneously, or as the result of deliberate 'spiritual exercises,' or through hypnosis, or by means of drugs." Ibid., 15.

12. Schleiermacher, *On Religion*, 37–39. For a further discussion of the history of this approach to religious experience, see Proudfoot, *Religious Experience*.

13. Huxley, *The Perennial Philosophy*, 183, 238–39, 48, 239–30.
14. R. Johnson, *Gandhi's Experiments with Truth*, 71.
15. Cited in Karlberg, "Constructive Resilience," 236.
16. For a good analysis of the diverse appearance of the Golden Rule in world religions, see Neusner and Chilton, *The Golden Rule*. For an account of the deep conceptual overlap of the great religious-philosophical traditions of the world, see Collins, *The Sociology of Philosophies*.
17. Hick, *An Interpretation of Religion*, 71.
18. Hick submits the ontological argument, argument from design, argument from human existence, argument from the universality of religious experience, and several others to a similar critique.
19. Ibid., 162.
20. Cited ibid., 237.
21. Ibid., 236–37, 175.
22. Ibid., 245.
23. Ibid., 164, 64, 32–33, 240.
24. Ibid., 40.
25. Ibid., 328–31.
26. Lakatos, *The Methodology of Scientific Research Programmes*.
27. Otto, *The Idea of the Holy*, 2.
28. Marion, *Being Given*.
29. Otto, *The Idea of the Holy*, 12–13.
30. Ibid., 64.
31. Ibid., 132–34.
32. Ibid., 75, 80, 95, 83–84, 56.
33. Bellah, *Religion in Human Evolution*, 117–74.
34. Nevertheless, the fact that Otto's work could technically fall within either the perennial or developmental narrative framework illustrates that the seven narrative frameworks considered in this work do not constitute hard and fast categories, but can overlap and influence one another in significant ways.
35. For further attempts to evaluate and ground Marion's claims in the broader tradition of religious thought, see Farmer, *A Genealogy of Marion's Philosophy of Religion*; Carlson, *Indiscretion*.

Chapter Seven. The Developmental Narrative

1. Stroumsa, *A New Science*.
2. In what follows, I draw primarily from the one-volume edition of Hegel's 1827 *Lectures on the Philosophy of Religion*, which is by no means his final word. He provided two substantively different accounts of religious history before 1827 and would articulate another just four years later. Furthermore, the text of the 1827 *Lectures* is not authoritative, for it was established by combining Hegel's lecture notes with several students'

written records of his spoken word. See Hodgson, "Editorial Introduction," 7. Nevertheless, the 1827 one-volume edition of Hegel's *Lectures* presents the most extensive, coherent, and complete record of Hegel's vision of world religion.

3. For an extensive analysis and defense of Kant's "critical" philosophy, see Allison, *Kant's Transcendental Idealism.*

4. This reading of Kant's theory of the transcendental imagination is informed by Heidegger's *Phenomenological Interpretations of Kant's "Critique of Pure Reason."*

5. We can even extend our understanding of the world by using reason to unfold the implications of these concepts—for example, in philosophy or mathematics. For a further account of Kant's theory of a priori concepts, see Thomasson, "Categories."

6. Examples of analytic interpretations of Hegel include Pippin's *Hegel's Idealism* and Pinkard's *Hegel's Phenomenology* and *Hegel's Naturalism.* Examples of "Continental" interpretations of Hegel include O'Regan's *The Heterodox Hegel*, Desmond's *Hegel's God*, and Hodgson's *Hegel and Christian Theology.*

7. In this regard, I disagree with Hodgson's efforts to present Hegel as an orthodox Christian theologian. Indeed, after Glenn Magee in *Hegel and the Hermetic Tradition* exhaustively demonstrated Hegel's deep involvement in hermetic mysticism, I find it hard to understand how anyone could plausibly make this claim.

8. Hegel, *Lectures on the Philosophy of Religion, One-Volume Edition*, 205.

9. Ibid., 225, 220, 229–35.

10. Ibid., 236–37, 244–45.

11. Ibid., 251, 254–56.

12. Ibid., 276, 273.

13. Ibid., 300–302.

14. Ibid., 313–15.

15. Ibid., 332–33, 344–45.

16. Ibid., 257, 364–67.

17. Ibid., 372, 384, 377.

18. Ibid., 434, 455, 473, 481–83

19. Ibid., 486. In his 1824 *Lectures*, he credits Islam. G. W. F. Hegel, *Lectures on the Philosophy of Religion*, vol. 3, pp. 243–49.

20. T. Lewis, *Religion, Modernity, and Politics in Hegel*, 227.

21. Magee, *Hegel and the Hermetic Tradition.*

22. Hodgson, *Hegel and Christian Theology*; T. Lewis, *Religion, Modernity, and Politics in Hegel.*

23. See Stark's *Discovering God; The Triumph of Christianity; How the West Won.*

24. Gauchet, *The Disenchantment of the World*, 4.

25. Comte, *The Positive Philosophy of Auguste Comte*; Feuerbach, *The Essence of Christianity*; Weber, *The Protestant Ethic and the Spirit of Capitalism.*

26. Pew Research Center, "U.S. Public Becoming Less Religious."

27. Hunter, *To Change the World*; Putnam and Campbell, *American Grace*.

28. Desmond, *God and the Between*. It is important to mention here that Desmond himself would not use the word "dialectical" to describe his own approach, which he labels "metaxological." However, for readers who are not privy to debates about the nature and limitations of Hegel's dialectic, I associate the word with Desmond to signify that his approach falls within the broad area of philosophical concern.

29. Kirkbright, *Karl Jaspers*, 148–51.

30. Popper, *The Open Society and Its Enemies*; Horkheimer and Adorno, *Dialectic of Enlightenment*.

31. Jaspers, *The Origin and Goal of History*, 2.

32. Jaspers developed his axial age thesis by extending and refining insights that had already been advanced by brothers Alfred and Max Weber. Alfred Weber had argued in 1935 that ancient China, India, and Greece stimulated a "synchronistic world age" by independently developing the practice of "universally-oriented religious and philosophical seeking." Similarly, Max Weber had highlighted the significance of the simultaneous appearance of the Hebrew prophets, the Hindu sages, the Buddha, Zoroaster, and the Greek philosophers in the first millennium BCE. Jaspers disagreed with key features of both Webers' formulations; he rejected Alfred's efforts to explain these sociospiritual developments in terms of underlying material dynamics and contested Max's attempt to use the notion of a prophetic age in order to bolster a narrative of Christian and Western exceptionalism. However, he did adopt their general account of a synchronistic period of global sociospiritual transformation during the first millennium BCE and claimed that this period provided the foundations for the modern world. It is important for us to recognize that, for Jaspers, modernity is not something that happens in the West and is exported to the rest of humanity. To the contrary, he considered modernity to be a process of global ferment that was only just beginning and that would, in time, create a world order that was entirely different from the one that we associate with modernity today. See Joas, "The Axial Age Debate as Religious Discourse," 7–9; Boy and Torpey, "Inventing the Axial Age," 244–45.

33. This is a historically inaccurate claim, because it overlooks the wide variety of other ancient civilizations that also arose throughout the world. See Trigger, *Understanding Early Civilizations*.

34. Jaspers, *The Origin and Goal of History*, 44–45.

35. Ibid., 4.

36. Ibid., 2.

37. Ibid., 5–7.

38. Ibid., 55–56.

39. Ibid., 23.

40. Ibid., 87.

41. Ibid., 84–86.
42. Ibid., 95–97.
43. Indeed, even in the 1950s he clearly saw that the age of "the unity of the earth has arrived" and that "all the crucial problems have [irreversibly] become world problems." Ibid., 127.
44. Ibid., 224.
45. Ibid., 227, 97.
46. Berger, "The Desecularization of the World"; Karpov, "Desecularization"; Toft, Philpott, and Shah, *God's Century*; Habermas, "Secularism's Crisis of Faith"; Habermas, *An Awareness of What Is Missing*; May et al., "The Religious as Political and the Political as Religious"; Wilson and Steger, "Religious Globalisms in the Post-Secular Age"; Hick, *An Interpretation of Religion*, 40.
47. Provan, *Convenient Myths*; Bellah, "What Is Axial about the Axial Age?"; Taylor, "What Was the Axial Revolution?"; Thomassen, "Anthropology, Multiple Modernities and the Axial Age Debate."
48. Arnason, Eisenstadt, and Wittrock, *Axial Civilizations and World History*, 2. See also Eisenstadt, *The Origins and Diversity of Axial Age Civilizations*.
49. Taylor, "What Was the Axial Revolution?," 30.
50. Boy and Torpey, "Inventing the Axial Age." Nevertheless, I find that there is still value in having a term to describe the deeply resonant movements that Jaspers identifies. In this regard, I would like to suggest that, as long as we remain aware of the fact that the "axial age" is not the singular axis of history, but rather one period of profound "axiality" among others, then there is no problem with continuing to use the term. Indeed, it is also appropriate to continue to describe movements like Christianity and Islam as "axial renaissance" endeavors, because such movements did seek to reclarify and reenact many of the insights that the earlier axial movements pursued. Nevertheless, I would still envision the axial age and axial renaissance concepts eventually giving way to more accurate and descriptive conceptual terms.
51. Voegelin, *Order and History*, vol. 4, p. 49.
52. Eisenstadt, "The Reconstruction of Religious Arenas in the Framework of 'Multiple Modernities,'" 592.
53. Ibid.
54. Jaspers, *The Origin and Goal of History*, 58–59.
55. Donald, *Origins of the Modern Mind*; Donald, *A Mind So Rare*.
56. Developmental processes thus animate not only the emergence of new cognitive capacities, but also their internal development. Donald, *A Mind So Rare*.
57. Bellah, *Religion in Human Evolution*, 131, 125.
58. Ibid., 139, 183, 215.
59. Ibid., 13.
60. Taylor, "What Was the Axial Revolution?," 37.

61. Gaukroger, *The Emergence of a Scientific Culture*; Saliba, *Islamic Science and the Making of the European Renaissance*; Sorkin, *The Religious Enlightenment*; Siedentop, *Inventing the Individual*; Stroumsa, *A New Science*; Eisenstein, *The Printing Revolution in Early Modern Europe*; Weber, *The Protestant Ethic and the Spirit of Capitalism*; Josephson, *The Invention of Religion in Japan*; van der Veer, *The Modern Spirit of Asia*; Starr, *Lost Enlightenment*.

62. *Merriam-Webster Online* (2014), s.v. "research," http://www.merriam-webster.com/dictionary/research.

63. Cannadine, "Review: 'The Transformation of the World.'"

64. Osterhammel, *The Transformation of the World*, 873.

65. Bellah, *Religion in Human Evolution*, xix.

66. Richard Madsen, in "The Future of Transcendence," also makes this problematic assumption in his attempt to outline a sociology of the second axial age.

67. Jaspers, *The Origin and Goal of History*, 96–97.

Conclusion

1. See Siderits, Thompson, and Zahavi, *Self, No Self?*.

2. Clearly, use of such broad categories is bound to run into difficulties given the infinite complexity of actual historical facts. Nevertheless, when kept at the appropriate level of generality, the terms allow us to develop a great deal of insight into this phase of religious history.

3. We see a similar process of synthesis in the medieval movements of Mahayana Buddhism, Neo-Confucianism, and classical Hinduism.

4. My analyses do not give sufficient attention to the part that the diffusion of Chinese and Indian thought, often via channels opened by the Mongolian Empire, played in this process. See Saunders, *The History of the Mongol Conquests*; Weatherford, *Genghis Khan and the Making of the Modern World*.

5. One point to mention is that the evolutionary perspectives articulated by the likes of Ibn Miskawayh, al-Biruni, Ibn Khaldūn, and Rumi during the Golden Age of Islam were not widely available during this period of European thought. Although it is unlikely that Christian thinkers would have embraced these perspectives even if they had been available, it is interesting to note that with such an evolutionary framework there would have been little difficulty in presenting modern scientific discoveries and enduring religious insights as facets of a coherent whole.

6. Similar interpretive frameworks had arisen in most regions of the world as well.

7. See Harrison, *The Territories of Science and Religion*.

8. Kingsnorth and Hine, "Uncivilization"; D. Smith, "It's the End of the World as We Know It . . . and He Feels Fine."

Bibliography

Adiswarananda, Swami. *Vivekananda, World Teacher: His Teachings on the Spiritual Unity of Humankind.* Woodstock, VT: Skylight Paths, 2006.

Alexander, Jeffrey C. *The Dark Side of Modernity.* Cambridge, UK: Polity, 2013.

Allison, Henry E. *Kant's Transcendental Idealism: An Interpretation and Defense.* New Haven, CT: Yale University Press, 2004.

Arberry, A. J., ed. *The Koran: Interpreted.* New York: Touchstone, 1996.

Arnason, Johann P., S. N. Eisenstadt, and Björn Wittrock, eds. *Axial Civilizations and World History.* Leiden, The Netherlands: Brill, 2005.

Asad, Talal. *Formations of the Secular: Christianity, Islam, Modernity.* Stanford, CA: Stanford University Press, 2003.

——. *Genealogies of Religion: Discipline and Reasons of Power in Christianity and Islam.* Baltimore, MD: Johns Hopkins University Press, 1993.

Barbato, Mariano. "Conceptions of the Self for Post-Secular Emancipation: Towards a Pilgrim's Guide to Global Justice." *Millennium—Journal of International Studies* 39, no. 2 (November 29, 2010): 547–64.

——. "Postsecular Revolution: Religion after the End of History." *Review of International Studies* 38, no. 5 (January 2, 2013): 1079–97.

Bellah, Robert. *Religion in Human Evolution: From the Paleolithic to the Axial Age.* Cambridge, MA: Belknap Press of Harvard University Press, 2011.

——. "What Is Axial about the Axial Age?" *European Journal of Sociology* 46, no. 1 (2005): 69–89.

Bellah, Robert, and Hans Joas, eds. *The Axial Age and Its Consequences.* Cambridge, MA: Belknap Press of Harvard University Press, 2012.

Bellah, Robert, Richard Madsen, William M. Sullivan, Ann Swidler, and Steven M. Tipton. *Habits of the Heart: Individualism and Commitment in American Life.* Berkeley, CA: University of California Press, 2007.

Belting, Hans. *Florence and Baghdad: Renaissance Art and Arab Science.* Edited by Deborah Lucas Schneider. Cambridge, MA: Belknap Press of Harvard University Press, 2011.

Benson, Bruce Ellis. *Pious Nietzsche: Decadence and Dionysian Faith.* Bloomington, IN: Indiana University Press, 2008.

Berger, Peter. "The Desecularization of the World: A Global Overview." In *The Desecularization of the World: Resurgent Religion and World Politics,* edited by Peter Berger, 1–18. Washington, DC: Ethics and Public Policy Center; Grand Rapids, MI: Wm. B. Eerdmans, 1999.

Berger, Peter, Grace Davie, and Effie Fokas. *Religious America, Secular Europe?: A Theme and Variations.* Burlington, VT: Ashgate, 2008.

Blavatsky, H. P. *The Secret Doctrine.* Edited by Boris de Zirkoff. Wheaton, IL: Theosophical Society in America, 1978.

Blumenberg, Hans. *The Legitimacy of the Modern Age.* Edited by Robert M. Wallace. Cambridge, MA: MIT Press, 1985.

Bohm, David. *Wholeness and the Implicate Order.* New York: Routledge, 1980.

Boy, John D., and John Torpey. "Inventing the Axial Age: The Origins and Uses of a Historical Concept." *Theory and Society* 42, no. 3 (March 24, 2013): 241–59.

Bruce, Steve. *Fundamentalism.* Malden, MA: Polity, 2000.

———. *Secularization: In Defense of an Unfashionable Theory.* Oxford, UK: Oxford University Press, 2013.

Campbell, Joseph. *The Hero with a Thousand Faces.* Princeton, NJ: Princeton University Press, 1972.

Cannadine, David. "Review: 'The Transformation of the World,' by Jürgen Osterhammel." *Financial Times,* May 2, 2014. http://www.ft.com/intl/cms/s/2/5ea6d02e-cfc4–11e3-a2b7–00144feabdco.html#axzz32WOrXRQU.

Carlson, Thomas A. *Indiscretion: Finitude and the Naming of God.* Chicago, IL: University of Chicago Press, 1999.

Casanova, José. "Cosmopolitanism, the Clash of Civilizations and Multiple Modernities." *Current Sociology* 59, no. 2 (March 4, 2011): 252–67.

———. *Public Religions in the Modern World.* Chicago, IL: University of Chicago Press, 1994.

Collins, Randall. *The Sociology of Philosophies: A Global Theory of Intellectual Change.* Cambridge, MA: Belknap Press of Harvard University Press, 2000.

Comte, Auguste. *The Positive Philosophy of Auguste Comte.* Edited by Harriet Martineau. Cambridge, UK: Cambridge University Press, 2009.

Coomaraswamy, Ananda K. *The Essential Ananda K. Coomaraswamy.* Edited by Rama P. Coomaraswamy. Bloomington, IN: World Wisdom, 2004.

Dallal, Ahmad. *Islam, Science, and the Challenge of History.* New Haven, CT: Yale University Press, 2012.

Davie, Grace. "Religion in 21st-Century Europe: Framing the Debate." *Irish Theological Quarterly* 78, no. 3 (June 25, 2013): 279–93.

Dennett, Daniel C. *Breaking the Spell: Religion as a Natural Phenomenon.* New York: Penguin, 2006.

———. *Darwin's Dangerous Idea: Evolution and the Meaning of Life.* New York: Simon and Schuster, 1996.

Desmond, William. *Desire, Dialectic, and Otherness: An Essay on Origins.* New Haven, CT: Yale University Press, 1987.

——. *God and the Between.* Malden, MA: Wiley-Blackwell, 2008.

——. *Hegel's God: A Counterfeit Double?* Burlington, VT: Ashgate, 2003.

Dewey, John. *Art as Experience.* New York: Perigree Books, 2005.

——. *A Common Faith.* New Haven, CT: Yale University Press, 1991.

——. *Experience and Nature.* Mineola, NY: Dover, 1958.

——. *Liberalism and Social Action.* Amherst, NY: Prometheus, 1999.

——. *The Middle Works.* Volume 9, *1899–1924: Democracy and Education, 1916.* Edited by Jo Ann Boydston. Carbondale, IL: Southern Illinois University Press, 2008.

——. *The Quest for Certainty: A Study of the Relation of Knowledge and Action.* New York: Capricorn, 1929.

——. *Reconstruction in Philosophy.* Mineola, NY: Dover, 2004.

Di Cesare, Donatella. "Heidegger—'Jews Self-Destructed': New Black Notebooks Reveal Philosopher's Shocking Take on Shoah." Translated by Giles Watson. *Corriere Della Sera,* February 8, 2015. http://www.corriere.it/english/15_febbraio_09/heidegger-jews-self-destructed-47cd3930-b03b-11e4-8615-d0fd07eabd28.shtml.

Donald, Merlin. *A Mind So Rare: The Evolution of Human Consciousness.* New York: Norton, 2001.

——. *Origins of the Modern Mind: Three Stages in the Evolution of Culture and Cognition.* Cambridge, MA: Harvard University Press, 1993.

Dreyfus, Hubert, and Sean Dorrance Kelly. "Saving the Sacred from the Axial Revolution." *Inquiry* 54, no. 2 (March 25, 2011): 195–203.

Effendi, Shoghi, and Universal House of Justice. *Science and Technology.* Compiled by Research Department of the Universal House of Justice. Haifa, Israel, 1997. http://bahai-library.com/compilation_science_technology.html.

Eisenstadt, S. N. *Comparative Civilizations and Multiple Modernities.* Leiden, The Netherlands: Brill, 2003.

——. "Multiple Modernities." *Daedalus* 129, no. 1 (2000): 1–29.

——. "Multiple Modernities in an Age of Globalization." *Canadian Journal of Sociology* 24, no. 2 (1999): 283–95.

——, ed. *The Origins and Diversity of Axial Age Civilizations.* Albany, NY: SUNY Press, 1986.

——. "The Reconstruction of Religious Arenas in the Framework of 'Multiple Modernities.'" *Millennium—Journal of International Studies* 29, no. 3 (December 1, 2000): 591–611.

Eisenstein, Elizabeth L. *The Printing Revolution in Early Modern Europe.* New York: Cambridge University Press, 1983.

Eliade, Mircea. *The Myth of the Eternal Return: Cosmos and History.* Princeton, NJ: Princeton University Press, 2005.

Farmer, Tasmin Jones. *A Genealogy of Marion's Philosophy of Religion: Apparent Darkness.* Bloomington, IN: Indiana University Press, 2011.

Faye, Emmanuel. *Heidegger: The Introduction of Nazism into Philosophy in Light of the Unpublished Seminars of 1933–1935.* Edited by Michael B. Smith. New Haven, CT: Yale University Press, 2009.

Ferguson, Andrew. "The Heretic: Who Is Thomas Nagel and Why Are So Many of His Fellow Academics Condemning Him?" *Weekly Standard* (Washington, DC), March 2013. http://www.weeklystandard.com/articles/heretic_707692.html.

Feuerbach, Ludwig. *The Essence of Christianity.* Edited by George Eliot. Amherst, NY: Prometheus Books, 1989.

Finke, Roger, and Rodney Stark. *The Churching of America, 1776–2005.* New Brunswick, NJ: Rutgers University Press, 2005.

Flanagan, Owen. *The Bodhisattva's Brain: Buddhism Naturalized.* Cambridge, MA: MIT Press, 2011.

Fuller, Robert C. *Spiritual, but Not Religious: Understanding Unchurched America.* New York: Oxford University Press, 2001.

Gandhi, Mohandas K. *An Autobiography: The Story of My Experiments with Truth.* Mineola, NY: Dover, 1983.

Gauchet, Marcel. *The Disenchantment of the World.* Translated by Oscar Burge. Princeton, NJ: Princeton University Press, 1999.

Gaukroger, Stephen. *The Emergence of a Scientific Culture: Science and the Shaping of Modernity, 1210–1685.* New York: Oxford University Press, 2006.

Gorski, Philip S., David Kyuman Kim, John Torpey, and Jonathan VanAntwerpen. "The Post-Secular in Question." In *The Post-Secular in Question: Religion in Contemporary Society,* edited by Philip S. Gorski, David Kyuman Kim, John Torpey, and Jonathan VanAntwerpen, 1–22. New York: New York University Press, 2012.

Gould, Stephen Jay. *Rocks of Ages: Science and Religion in the Fullness of Life.* New York: Ballantine Books, 1999.

Gregory, Brad S. *The Unintended Reformation: How a Religious Revolution Secularized Society.* Cambridge, MA: Belknap Press of Harvard University Press, 2012.

Grim, Brian J., and Roger Finke. *The Price of Freedom Denied.* Cambridge, UK: Cambridge University Press, 2010.

Habermas, Jürgen. *An Awareness of What Is Missing: Faith and Reason in a Post-Secular Age.* Cambridge, UK: Polity, 2010.

——. "Secularism's Crisis of Faith: Notes on Post-Secular Society." *New Perspectives Quarterly* 25, no. 4 (2008): 17–29.

——. *The Structural Transformation of the Public Sphere: An Inquiry into a Category of Bourgeois Society.* Edited by Thomas Burger and Frederick Lawrence. Cambridge, MA: MIT Press, 1991.

Hagan, Steve. *Buddhism Plain and Simple.* Boston, MA: Broadway Books, 1997.

Harrison, Peter. *The Territories of Science and Religion.* Chicago, IL: University of Chicago Press, 2015.

Harvey, David. *A Brief History of Neoliberalism.* New York: Oxford University Press, 2005.

Hegel, G. W. F. *Lectures on the Philosophy of Religion.* Volume 3, *The Consummate Religion.* Edited and translated by Peter C. Hodgson. Berkeley, CA: University of California Press, 1986.

——. *Lectures on the Philosophy of Religion, One-Volume Edition: The Lectures of 1827.* Edited by Peter C. Hodgson. Translated by R. F. Brown, P. C. Hodgson, and J. M. Stewart. Oxford, UK: Oxford University Press, 2006.

Heidegger, Martin. *Phenomenological Interpretations of Kant's "Critique of Pure Reason."* Translated by Parvis Emad and Kenneth Maly. Bloomington, IN: Indiana University Press, 1997.

——. "Plato's Doctrine of Truth." In *Pathmarks*, edited and translated by William McNeill, 155–82. Cambridge, UK: Cambridge University Press, 1998.

——. *The Question Concerning Technology and Other Essays.* Translated by William Lovitt. New York: HarperCollins, 1982.

Hick, John. *An Interpretation of Religion: Human Responses to the Transcendent.* New Haven, CT: Yale University Press, 2005.

Hodgson, Peter C. "Editorial Introduction." In G. W. F. Hegel, *Lectures on the Philosophy of Religion, One-Volume Edition: The Lectures of 1827*, edited by Peter C. Hodgson, translated by R. F. Brown, P. C. Hodgson, and J. M. Stewart, 1–71. Oxford, UK: Oxford University Press, 2006.

——. *Hegel and Christian Theology: A Reading of the Lectures on the Philosophy of Religion.* New York: Oxford University Press, 2005.

Horkheimer, Max, and Theodor W. Adorno. *Dialectic of Enlightenment: Philosophical Fragments.* Edited by Gunzelin Schmid Noerr; translated by Edmund Jephcott. Stanford, CA: Stanford University Press, 2002.

Hunter, James Davison. *To Change the World: The Irony, Tragedy, and Possibility of Christianity in the Late Modern World.* New York: Oxford University Press, 2010.

Huxley, Aldous. *Brave New World.* New York: Harper Perennial Modern Classics, 2006.

——. *The Doors of Perception: And Heaven and Hell.* New York: Random House, 2004.

——. *Island.* New York: Harper and Row, 1962.

——. *The Perennial Philosophy: An Interpretation of the Great Mystics, East and West.* New York: Harper Perennial Modern Classics, 2009.

——. *Point Counter Point.* London: Chatto and Windus, 1928.

Ibn Khaldûn. *The Muqaddimah: An Introduction to History.* Edited and translated by N. J. Dawood and Franz Rosenthal. Princeton, NJ: Princeton University Press, 2004.

Iqbal, Muhammad. *The Reconstruction of Religious Thought in Islam.* Reprint. Stanford, CA: Stanford University Press, 2013.

——. *Thoughts and Reflections of Iqbal.* Edited by Siyyid Abdul Vahid. Lahore, Pakistan: Sh. Muhammad Ashraf, 1992.

Jaspers, Karl. *The Origin and Goal of History.* Translated by Michael Bullock. New Haven, CT: Yale University Press, 1953.

Joas, Hans. "The Axial Age Debate as Religious Discourse." In *The Axial Age and Its Consequences,* edited by Robert N. Bellah and Hans Joas. Cambridge, MA: Belknap Press of Harvard University Press, 2012.

Johnson, Richard L., ed. *Gandhi's Experiments with Truth: Essential Writings By and About Mahatma Gandhi.* Lanham, MD: Lexington Books, 2005.

Johnson, Todd M., and Brian J. Grim. *The World's Religions in Figures: An Introduction to International Religious Demography.* Malden, MA: Wiley-Blackwell, 2013.

Jonas, Hans. *The Gnostic Religion.* Boston, MA: Beacon Press, 1992.

——. *The Phenomenon of Life: Toward a Philosophical Biology.* Evanston, IL: Northwestern University Press, 2001.

Josephson, Jason A. *The Invention of Religion in Japan.* Chicago, IL: University of Chicago Press, 2012.

Karlberg, Michael. "Constructive Resilience: The Baha'i Response to Oppression." *Peace and Change* 35, no. 2 (April 2010): 222–57.

Karpov, Vyacheslav. "Desecularization: A Conceptual Framework." *Journal of Church and State* 52, no. 2 (2010): 232–70.

Kierkegaard, Søren. *The Concept of Anxiety: A Simple Psychologically Orienting Deliberation on the Dogmatic Issue of Hereditary Sin.* Translated by Reidar Thomte and Albert B. Anderson. Princeton, NJ: Princeton University Press, 1980.

King, Martin Luther, Jr. "I Have a Dream . . ." Washington, DC, 1963. http://www.archives.gov/press/exhibits/dream-speech.pdf.

Kingsnorth, Paul, and Dougald Hine. "Uncivilization: The Dark Mountain Manifesto." *The Dark Mountain Project,* 2014. http://dark-mountain.net/about/manifesto/.

Kirkbright, Suzanne. *Karl Jaspers, a Biography: Navigations in Truth.* New Haven, CT: Yale University Press, 2004.

Lakatos, Imre. *The Methodology of Scientific Research Programmes.* Volume 1, *Philosophical Papers.* Cambridge, UK: Cambridge University Press, 1980.

Lample, Paul. *Revelation and Social Reality: Learning to Translate What Is Written into Reality.* West Palm Beach, FL: Palabra, 2009.

Leiter, Brian, and Michael Weisberg. "Do You Only Have a Brain? On Thomas Nagel." *Nation* (New York), October 2012. http://www.the-nation.com/article/170334/do-you-only-have-brain-thomas-nagel.

Lewis, C. S. *Mere Christianity.* New York: HarperOne, 2009.

Lewis, Thomas A. *Religion, Modernity, and Politics in Hegel.* Oxford, UK: Oxford University Press, 2011.

——. *Why Philosophy Matters for the Study of Religion and Vice Versa.* Oxford, UK: Oxford University Press, 2016.

Lincoln, Abraham. "Second Inaugural Address of Abraham Lincoln," March 4, 1865. *The Avalon Project: Documents in Law, History and Diplomacy.* http://avalon.law.yale.edu/19th_century/lincoln2.asp.

Löwith, Karl. *Meaning in History: The Theological Implications of the Philosophy of History.* Chicago, IL: University of Chicago Press, 1949.

Lowney, Chris. *A Vanished World: Muslims, Christians, and Jews in Medieval Spain.* Oxford, UK: Oxford University Press, 2006.

MacIntyre, Alasdair. *After Virtue: A Study in Moral Theory.* Third edition. Notre Dame, IN: University of Notre Dame Press, 2007.

———. *Whose Justice? Which Rationality?* Notre Dame, IN: University of Notre Dame Press, 1989.

Madsen, Richard. "The Future of Transcendence: A Sociological Agenda." In *The Axial Age and Its Consequences*, edited by Robert N. Bellah and Hans Joas, 411–29. Cambridge, MA: Belknap Press of Harvard University Press, 2012.

Magee, Glenn Alexander. *Hegel and the Hermetic Tradition.* Ithaca, NY: Cornell University Press, 2001.

Majeed, Javeed. *Muhammad Iqbal: Islam, Aesthetics and Postcolonialism.* New Delhi, India: Routledge, 2009.

Marion, Jean-Luc. *Being Given: Toward a Phenomenology of Givenness.* Edited by Jeffrey Kosky. Stanford, CA: Stanford University Press, 2002.

May, Samantha, Erin K. Wilson, Claudia Baumgart-Ochse, and Faiz Sheikh. "The Religious as Political and the Political as Religious: Globalisation, Post-Secularism and the Shifting Boundaries of the Sacred." *Politics, Religion and Ideology* 15, no. 3 (2014): 331–46.

Mellor, Philip A., and Chris Shilling. *Sociology of the Sacred: Religion, Embodiment and Social Change.* Los Angeles, CA: Sage, 2014.

Menocal, Maria Rosa. *The Ornament of the World: How Muslims, Jews, and Christians Created a Culture of Tolerance in Medieval Spain.* New York: Back Bay Books, 2002.

Michalski, Krzysztof. *The Flame of Eternity: An Interpretation of Nietzsche's Thought.* Translated by Benjamin Paloff. Princeton, NJ: Princeton University Press, 2012.

Micklethwait, John, and Adrian Wooldridge. *God Is Back: How the Global Revival of Faith Is Changing the World.* New York: Penguin Books, 2009.

Midgley, Mary. *Evolution as a Religion: Strange Hopes and Stranger Fears.* Revised edition. London: Routledge, 2002.

Mir, Mustansir. *Iqbal.* London: I. B. Tauris, 2006.

Moser, Paul. *The Evidence for God: Religious Knowledge Reexamined.* Cambridge, UK: Cambridge University Press, 2010.

Munro, Thomas. "Meanings of 'Naturalism' in Philosophy and Aesthetics." *Journal of Aesthetics and Art Criticism* 19, no. 2 (1960): 133–37.

Nagel, Thomas. *The Last Word.* New York: Oxford University Press, 1997.

——. *Mind and Cosmos: Why the Materialist Neo-Darwinian Conception of Nature Is Almost Certainly False*. New York: Oxford University Press, 2012.

——. "A Philosopher Defends Religion." *New York Review of Books*, September 27, 2012.

——. *Secular Philosophy and the Religious Temperament: Essays 2002–2008*. Oxford, UK: Oxford University Press, 2009.

——. *The View from Nowhere*. Oxford, UK: Oxford University Press, 1986.

Neusner, Jacob, and Bruce Chilton, eds. *The Golden Rule: The Ethics of Reciprocity in World Religions*. New York: Bloomsbury, 2008.

Nietzsche, Friedrich. *The Gay Science: With a Prelude in German Rhymes and an Appendix of Songs*. Edited by Bernard Williams. Translated by Josefine Nauckhoff and Adrian del Caro. Cambridge, UK: Cambridge University Press, 2001.

——. *Thus Spoke Zarathustra*. Edited by Adrian Del Caro and Robert Pippin. Cambridge, UK: Cambridge University Press, 2006.

——. *The Will to Power*. Edited by Walter Kauffman. Translated by Walter Kauffman and R. J. Hollingdale. New York: Vintage, 1968.

Nikkel, David H. *Radical Embodiment*. Eugene, OR: Wipf and Stock, 2010.

Nongbri, Brent. *Before Religion: A History of a Modern Concept*. New Haven, CT: Yale University Press, 2012.

Norris, Pippa, and Ronald Inglehart. *Sacred and Secular: Religion and Politics Worldwide*. Second edition. New York: Cambridge University Press, 2011.

Nye, Malory. *Religion: The Basics*. New York: Routledge, 2008.

O'Regan, Cyril. *The Heterodox Hegel*. Albany, NY: SUNY Press, 1994.

Osterhammel, Jürgen. *The Transformation of the World: A Global History of the Nineteenth Century*. Translated by Patrick Camiller. Princeton, NJ: Princeton University Press, 2014.

Otto, Rudolf. *The Idea of the Holy*. Translated by John W. Harvey. New York: Oxford University Press, 1958.

Pals, Daniel L. *Nine Theories of Religion*. Oxford, UK: Oxford University Press, 2014.

Peat, F. David. *Infinite Potential: The Life and Times of David Bohm*. New York: Perseus Books, 1996.

Pew Research Center. "U.S. Public Becoming Less Religious: Modest Drop in Overall Rates of Belief and Practice, but Religiously Affiliated Americans Are as Observant as Before," November 3, 2015. http://www.pewforum. org/2015/11/03/u-s-public-becoming-less-religious/?beta=true&utm_ expid=53098246-2.Lly4CFSVQG2lphsg-KopIg.1&utm_referrer=http% 3A%2F%2Fwww.pewforum.org%2F.

Philpott, Daniel. "Has the Study of Global Politics Found Religion?" *Annual Review of Political Science* 12, no. 1 (June 2009): 183–202.

Pinkard, Terry. *Hegel's Naturalism: Mind, Nature, and the Final Ends of Life*. New York: Oxford University Press, 2012.

——. *Hegel's Phenomenology: The Sociality of Reason.* Cambridge, UK: Cambridge University Press, 1996.

Pippin, Robert B. *Hegel's Idealism: The Satisfactions of Self-Consciousness.* Cambridge, UK: Cambridge University Press, 1989.

Polkinghorne, John. *Belief in God in an Age of Science.* New Haven, CT: Yale University Press, 2003.

——. *Quantum Physics and Theology: An Unexpected Kinship.* New Haven, CT: Yale University Press, 2007.

——. *Science and Providence: God's Interaction with the World.* Philadelphia, PA: Templeton Press, 2005.

Popper, Karl. *The Open Society and Its Enemies.* Princeton, NJ: Princeton University Press, 2013.

Preston, Andrew. *Sword of the Spirit, Shield of Faith: Religion in American War and Diplomacy.* New York: Random House, 2012.

Proudfoot, Wayne. *Religious Experience.* Berkeley, CA: University of California Press, 1985.

Provan, Lain. *Convenient Myths: The Axial Age, Dark Green Religion, and the World That Never Was.* Waco, TX: Baylor University Press, 2013.

Putnam, Robert D., and David E. Campbell. *American Grace: How Religion Divides and Unites Us.* New York: Simon and Schuster, 2010.

Quinn, Frederick. *The Sum of All Heresies: The Image of Islam in Western Thought.* New York: Oxford University Press, 2008.

Rawls, John. *Political Liberalism.* New York: Columbia University Press, 2005.

Richardson, John. *Nietzsche's New Darwinism.* New York: Oxford University Press, 2004.

Rorty, Richard. *Essays on Heidegger and Others.* Volume 2 of *Philosophical Papers.* Cambridge, UK: Cambridge University Press, 1991.

Russell, Bertrand, and Alfred North Whitehead. *Principia Mathematica.* Cambridge, UK: Cambridge University Press, 1910–13.

Safranski, Rüdiger. *Martin Heidegger: Between Good and Evil.* Edited by Ewald Osers. Translated by Ewald Osers. Cambridge, MA: Harvard University Press, 1998.

Said, Edward W. *Orientalism.* New York: Vintage Books, 1979.

Saliba, George. *Islamic Science and the Making of the European Renaissance.* Cambridge, MA: MIT Press, 2007.

Salvatore, Armando. *The Public Sphere: Liberal Modernity, Catholicism, and Islam.* New York: Palgrave MacMillan, 2007.

Saunders, J. J. *The History of the Mongol Conquests.* London: Routledge and Kegan Paul, 1971.

Schilbrack, Kevin. *Philosophy and the Study of Religions: A Manifesto.* Malden, MA: Wiley-Blackwell, 2014.

Schimmel, Annemarie. *Gabriel's Wing: Study into the Religious Ideas of Sir Muhammad Iqbal.* Lahore, Pakistan: Iqbal Academy, 1989.

Schleiermacher, Friedrich. *On Religion: Speeches to Its Cultured Despisers.* Edited by Richard Crouter. Cambridge, UK: Cambridge University Press, 1996.

Schmitt, Charles B. "Perennial Philosophy: From Agostino Steuco to Leibniz." *Journal of the History of Ideas* 27 (1966): 503–32.

Schuon, Frithjof. *The Transcendent Unity of Religions.* Wheaton, IL: Quest Books, 1984.

Seligman, Rebecca. *Possessing Spirits and Healing Selves: Embodiment and Transformation in an Afro-Brazilian Religion.* New York: Palgrave MacMillan, 2014.

Sevea, Iqbal Singh. *The Political Philosophy of Muhammad Iqbal: Islam and Nationalism in Late Colonial India.* New York: Cambridge University Press, 2012.

Shariati, Ali, and Sayyid Ali Khamene'i. *Iqbal: Manifestation of the Islamic Spirit.* Translated by Mahliqa Qara'i and Laleh Bakhtiar. Albuquerque, NM: Abjab; Markham, Canada: Open Press, 1991.

Siderits, Mark, Evan Thompson, and Dan Zahavi, eds. *Self, No Self?: Perspectives from Analytical, Phenomenological, and Indian Traditions.* Oxford, UK: Oxford University Press, 2011.

Siedentop, Larry. *Inventing the Individual: The Origins of Western Liberalism.* Cambridge, MA: Belknap Press of Harvard University Press, 2014.

Skinner, B. F. "'Superstition' in the Pigeon." *Journal of Experimental Psychology* 38 (1948): 168–72.

Smith, Daniel. "It's the End of the World as We Know It...and He Feels Fine." *New York Times*, April 17, 2014. http://www.nytimes.com/2014/04/20/magazine/its-the-end-of-the-world-as-we-know-it-and-he-feels-fine.html?_r=0.

Smith, Huston. *Forgotten Truth: The Common Vision of the World's Religions.* New York: HarperOne, 1992.

———. *The World's Religions.* New York: HarperOne, 1991.

Sorkin, David. *The Religious Enlightenment: Protestants, Jews, and Catholics from London to Vienna.* Princeton, NJ: Princeton University Press, 2008.

Staddon, J. E. R., and V. L. Simmelhag. "The 'Superstition' Experiment: A Reexamination of Its Implications for the Principles of Adaptive Behavior." *Psychological Review* 78, no. 1 (1971): 3–43.

Stapp, Henry P. *Mind, Matter and Quantum Mechanics.* Third edition. New York: Springer, 2009.

———. *Mindful Universe: Quantum Mechanics and the Participating Observer.* New York: Springer, 2007.

Stark, Rodney. *Discovering God: The Origins of the Great Religions and the Evolution of Belief.* New York: HarperCollins, 2007.

———. *How the West Won: The Neglected Story of the Triumph of Modernity.* Wilmington, DE: Intercollegiate Studies Institute, 2014.

———. *The Triumph of Christianity: How the Jesus Movement Became the World's Largest Religion.* New York: HarperCollins, 2011.

Stark, Rodney, and William Bainbridge. *A Theory of Religion*. New Brunswick, NJ: Rutgers University Press, 1996.

Starr, S. Frederick. *Lost Enlightenment: Central Asia's Golden Age from the Arab Conquest to Tamerlane*. Princeton, NJ: Princeton University Press, 2013.

Stout, Jeffrey. *Blessed Are the Organized: Grassroots Democracy in America*. Princeton, NJ: Princeton University Press, 2010.

——. *Democracy and Tradition*. Princeton, NJ: Princeton University Press, 2004.

Stroumsa, Guy G. *A New Science: The Discovery of Religion in the Age of Reason*. Cambridge, MA: Harvard University Press, 2010.

Taylor, Charles. "A Catholic Modernity?" In *A Catholic Modernity: Charles Taylor's Marianist Award Lecture*, edited by James L. Heft, 13–38. Oxford, UK: Oxford University Press, 1999.

——. *The Ethics of Authenticity*. Cambridge, MA: Harvard University Press, 1992.

——. *A Secular Age*. Cambridge, MA: Belknap Press of Harvard University Press, 2007.

——. "What Was the Axial Revolution?" In *The Axial Age and Its Consequences*, edited by Robert Bellah and Hans Joas, 30–46. Cambridge, MA: Belknap Press of Harvard University Press, 2012.

Thomas, S. M. "Taking Religious and Cultural Pluralism Seriously: The Global Resurgence of Religion and the Transformation of International Society." *Millennium—Journal of International Studies* 29, no. 3 (December 1, 2000): 815–41.

Thomassen, B. "Anthropology, Multiple Modernities and the Axial Age Debate." *Anthropological Theory* 10, no. 4 (December 7, 2010): 321–42.

Thomasson, Amie. "Categories." *The Stanford Encyclopedia of Philosophy*. 2013. https://plato.stanford.edu/entries/categories/.

Thompson, Evan. *Mind in Life: Biology, Phenomenology, and the Sciences of Mind*. Cambridge, MA: Belknap Press of Harvard University Press, 2010.

Timberlake, William, and G. A. Lucas. "The Basis of Superstitious Behavior: Chance Contingency, Stimulus Substitution, or Appetitive Behavior?" *Journal of Animal Behavior* 44, no. 3 (1985): 279–99.

Toft, Monica Duffy, Daniel Philpott, and Timothy Samuel Shah. *God's Century: Resurgent Religion and Global Politics*. New York: Norton, 2011.

Toksvig, Signe. "Aldous Huxley's Prescriptions for Spiritual Myopia." *New York Times*, September 30, 1945.

Toynbee, Arnold. *A Study of History*. 2 vols. Edited by D. C. Somervell. Oxford, UK: Oxford University Press, 1987.

Trigger, Bruce G. *Understanding Early Civilizations: A Comparative Study*. Cambridge, UK: Cambridge University Press, 2003.

Universal House of Justice. *Turning Point: Selected Messages of the Universal House of Justice and Supplementary Material 1996–2006*. West Palm Beach, FL: Palabra, 2006.

van der Veer, Peter. *Imperial Encounters: Religion and Modernity in India and Britain*. Princeton, NJ: Princeton University Press, 2001.

———. *The Modern Spirit of Asia: The Spiritual and the Secular in China and India*. Princeton, NJ: Princeton University Press, 2013.

Varela, Francisco J., Evan Thompson, and Eleanor Rosch. *The Embodied Mind: Cognitive Science and Human Experience*. Cambridge, MA: MIT Press, 1993.

Voegelin, Eric. *Order and History*. Volume 4, *The Ecumenic Age*. Edited by Michael Franz. Columbia, MO: University of Missouri Press, 2000.

Ward, Keith. *More Than Matter?: What Humans Really Are*. Oxford, UK: Lion Hudson, 2010.

Wasserstrom, Steven M. "Islamicate History of Religions?" *History of Religions* 27, no. 4 (1988): 405–11.

Weatherford, Jack. *Genghis Khan and the Making of the Modern World*. New York: Broadway Books, 2004.

Weber, Max. *The Protestant Ethic and the Spirit of Capitalism*. Translated by Peter Baehr and Gordon C. Wells. New York: Penguin Books, 2002.

Whitehead, Alfred North. *Adventures of Ideas*. New York: Free Press, 1967.

———. *The Aims of Education and Other Essays*. New York: Free Press, 1967.

———. *The Axioms of Descriptive Geometry*. Cambridge, UK: Cambridge University Press, 1907.

———. *The Axioms of Projective Geometry*. Cambridge, UK: Cambridge University Press, 1906.

———. *The Concept of Nature: The Tarner Lectures Delivered at Trinity College*. Cambridge, UK: Cambridge University Press, 1920.

———. *An Enquiry Concerning the Principles of Natural Knowledge*. Cambridge, UK: Cambridge University Press, 1919.

———. *An Introduction to Mathematics*. London: Williams and Norgate, 1911.

———. *Modes of Thought*. New York: Free Press, 1968.

———. "On Mathematical Concepts of the Material World." *Philosophical Transactions, Royal Society of London* 205 (1906): 465–525.

———. *The Principle of Relativity, with Application to Physical Science*. Cambridge, UK: Cambridge University Press, 1922.

———. *Process and Reality*. Corrected edition. New York: Free Press, 1979.

———. *Religion in the Making*. Reissue edition. New York: Free Press, 1967.

———. *Science and the Modern World*. New York: Free Press, 1997.

———. *Symbolism: Its Meaning and Effect*. New York: MacMillan Company, 1927.

———. *A Treatise on Universal Algebra, with Applications*. Cambridge, UK: Cambridge University Press, 1898.

Wilson, Erin K., and Manfred B. Steger. "Religious Globalisms in the Post-Secular Age." *Globalizations* 10, no. 3 (June 2013): 481–95.

Wolin, Richard. "National Socialism, World Jewry, and the History of Being: Heidegger's Black Notebooks." *Jewish Review of Books*, Summer 2014.

http://jewishreviewofbooks.com/articles/993/national-socialism-world-jewry-and-the-history-of-being-heideggers-black-notebooks/.

Wrathall, Mark. *Heidegger and Unconcealment.* Cambridge, UK: Cambridge University Press, 2011.

Wrathall, Mark, and Morganna Lambeth. "Heidegger's Last God." *Inquiry* 54, no. 2 (March 25, 2011): 160–82.

Young, Julian. *Heidegger's Later Philosophy.* Cambridge, UK: Cambridge University Press, 2002.

———. *Nietzsche's Philosophy of Religion.* Cambridge, UK: Cambridge University Press, 2006.

Index